8.99

Engineers

The Welfare State Handbook

REVISED EDITION

Tony Coult is a playwright. His plays for young people and community audiences have been performed by, amongst others, Perspectives, Common Stock, and Combination Theatre companies, and Lancaster and Cockpit T.I.E. companies. He has been a regular contributor of short plays, dramatizations and set-text documentaries for BBC Radio Education, and has written for the Euston Films TV series *Shrinks*. His reviews and features have been published in *Time Out*, *Times Educational Supplement*, *Canadian Theatre Review*, *Englisch-Amerikanische Studien*, *SCYPT Journal*, and *Plays and Players*, and he is the author of the Methuen Theatrefile 'The Plays of Edward Bond'. He is married to the actress Tricia Kelly.

Baz Kershaw trained and worked as a design engineer before reading English and Philosophy at Manchester University. He has worked as a director and writer at the Drury Lane Arts Lab, staged large-scale environmental shows in Hawaii, directed for community theatre, initiated rural arts projects in several counties, and worked as an adviser to a wide range of alternative theatre companies. As co-director of Medium Fair Theatre Company, he founded the first mobile rural community arts group and the first reminiscence theatre company, Fair Old Times. He has published articles in *Theatre Quarterly*, *Dartington Theatre Papers*, *Platform*, *Theatre Ireland*, and *Performance Magazine*. He has taught in higher education for a number of years, and is currently Lecturer in Theatre Studies at Lancaster University.

Cover photos: St. Mungo. Celebration for Royal Institute of Scottish Architects' Conference May 1988 (photo: Steve Gibson).

Engineers
of the Imagination

The Welfare State Handbook

REVISED EDITION

EDITED BY
Tony Coult and Baz Kershaw

Graphic co-ordination by Tony Lewery

Methuen Drama

First published in 1983
as a Methuen Paperback original
by Methuen London Ltd.
Reprinted in this fully revised edition
in 1990 by Methuen Drama
an imprint of Reed Consumer Books Ltd.
Michelin House, 81 Fulham Road, London SW3 6RB
and Auckland, Melbourne, Singapore and Toronto

Distributed in the USA by
Heinemann, a division of Reed Elsevier Inc.,
361 Hanover St., Portsmouth, New Hampshire NH 03801 395

Reprinted 1993, 1995

ISBN 0–413–52800–6

A CIP catalogue record for this book
is available from the British Library.

Printed in Great Britain by
Redwood Books, Trowbridge, Wiltshire

On August 31st, 1989 Howard Steel died from cancer.
He had worked for Welfare State as the
company's chief administrator for over ten years.
He was crucial to the successful development
of the company. Without his good humour
and unflappable support, the First Edition of this book
would not have seen the light of day.
This Revised Edition is dedicated to Howard.

Contents

List of Illustrations

ACKNOWLEDGEMENTS

The Editors would like to express their special thanks to Tony Lewery, for his co-ordination of the graphic work of several hands, and to Sue Fox, for liaising so cheerfully and efficiently between ourselves and the company. Our thanks, too, to all the individual contributors who have made the book live.

This book was conceived and written during a time when Boris and Maggie Howarth were on sabbatical leave, and so their vast and continuing contribution to Welfare State may seem understated. No page of the book, however, does not bear in some part the mark of their work.

Special thanks to Dr Gill Hadley for her advice and assistance. And to students and staff of Lancaster University Department of Theatre Studies for support and stimulation in the preparation of the second edition.

DISCLAIMER

Preface to the Revised Edition

In the mid-eighties an apocryphal story was going the rounds of Welfare State artists. The then Minister for the Arts, Lord Gowrie, in a meeting with Margaret Thatcher, mentioned that the Arts Council was funding a particularly interesting and successful performance company based in Cumbria, called Welfare State. The Prime Minister replied that she was glad to hear that the company was doing well, though it was a pity about their name. Some versions of the story claim that she asked if it might be changed to something more appropriate to the times.

Of course, the eighties was the decade of Change, otherwise known as Reform. British society was subject to the most thoroughgoing 'overhaul' in post-war history. All the major institutions of the land, and much of its day-to-day living, were to be brought in line with the new imperatives of the international marketplace. Cultural practices of all kinds had to survive as best they could, bouncing about in the wake of economic revivalism.

Some theatre groups sank, more or less without trace. And some of them were from the same vigorous generation as Welfare State, the 'class' of '68. Joint Stock, Foco Novo, 7:84 (England), and too many others joined the big black-out in the sky. It was a bad decade for overtly political theatre, and for other types of radical performance. To survive as a radical in that climate meant the constant courting of fundamental contradictions, with the concomitant risk of incorporation into the neo-conservative circus. Always there was a heightening ideological tension between principle and practice, between ambition and reality.

The company featured in *Engineers of the Imagination* met the demands of the eighties with more than a modicum of canny creative manoeuvring. So this revised edition of the book celebrates the continuing evolution of an effective approach to the practice of radical performance. The edition differs from the first in a number of significant ways. It has a new final chapter that charts the company's progress into the eighties. It has new up-dated appendices which take into account changes in the legalities of staging outdoor performances, and which provide more information on the company's shows, suppliers, and documentation of its practices. It also includes statements outlining the company's most recent policy. Most of all, it provides an opportunity to re-issue a text that seems to have proved as practically useful as we had originally hoped it would – particularly in stimulating grass-roots creativity, hopefully for the common good.

So we are glad to report that the company concerned is still called Welfare State International, and that despite the turbulent eighties it is still doing well as we move into the nineties.

Preface to the First Edition

This handbook is edited by two long-time fans of Welfare State's work, who were asked by the company to make concrete an idea that had been floating for some years. Although we were employed by the company to edit the book, its structure and the individual contributions of the Editors are our responsibility alone.

This is only one of several Welfare State books that could have been written. At various times, histories, picture-books and poetic statements have been mooted, and this book owes something to all these. What we and our contributors have produced here, however, is a book we hope will be functional – an inspiration and a technical manual. It is itself a celebration of the work and the ideas it represents, but it is also part of the process of rebellion and reconstruction that it seeks to document and demonstrate. It is in no sense comprehensive. Rather it is one plateau on a journey, a point at which people concerned with the making of a living culture in a hostile environment can draw off ideas, inspiration, and techniques. We hope it will continue to spend at least as much time in kitchens and workshops as in studies and libraries.

T.C.
B.K.

I

One Foot on the Ground, One Foot Moving

An introduction to the work of Welfare State International

TONY COULT

Welfare State International, founded in 1968, is one of the most consistently exciting theatre companies born out of the cultural and political ferment of Britain in the late '6o's. Now, in the eighties, it has achieved international acclaim for its joyous blend of visual spectacle, popular theatre, and celebration. Its resources remain what they have been almost from the beginning – sculpture (using, as well as more conventional materials, elements such as ice or fire), puppetry, landscape, food, fireworks, music, technology, dance, performance and weather. These resources and skills, shared by a large and growing band of freelance artists rooted on a small core of permanent company members, have grown over the years in a context of both social and aesthetic experiment. This long-term process of research-and-practice seeks to re-establish, away from the conventional building-based middlebrow/middle-class theatre, the popular theatre traditions of the working class, such as Carnival, the Feast of Fools, the fairground, the mummers' plays, that vein of subversion-as-entertainment that runs through so much of folk theatre and song. Such a project is, of course, fraught with contradictions, and raises the spectres of fake-primitivism and rootless, academic revivalism. Welfare State tackle these problems head-on by creating new myths, new hybrid styles, and new celebrations on the matrix of the old, rather than simply reviving the old for its quaint or arcane qualities.

The essence of Welfare State's programme is stated by its founder, John Fox: 'Currently we live in a materialistic society; religious beliefs are declining and there is no structure of myth. We try to find archetypes that are universally shared, and present them in an idiom accessible to a broad audience.' This search for myth and its enactment, could become élite and introverted, and unrelated to the complex, messy culture that we live in. Welfare State, however, works from the assumption that myth and archetype are functional operations of human consciousness. It is not a word that would appeal to many of the company perhaps, but their use of myth is rational – not 'explainable' or 'reducible to a mechanical

Welfare State over almost a decade.
above: Requiem for Kirkgate Market, Bradford 1973.
below: Ulverston Carnival, Cumbria, 1980.

logic', but based in the reasonable needs of human beings to share and celebrate their humanity. The Greeks used myths to express truths about being human, and told stories about fallible deities who fought battles as winners and losers, who made love, and made mistakes. In doing so, they enacted on the public stage and in the inner mind the conflicts between Good and Evil, collective and individual, male and female, ruler and ruled, that were the daily material of everyday life.

Other societies have other myths, but common to most developed societies has been a battle for ownership of myths. Rulers have claimed their myths as justification for their own ruling, and the ruled in their turn, have clung to their interpretation of the myths as a defence against the rulers' oppressions. So it is that one mythological structure, such as Christian religion, can become a battleground of opposing interpretation. Divine Right of Kings, the State's system of law, the identification of State and Church, have all been sanctioned for Rulers, just as an opposing set of impulses such as the democratic ideal ('all men are equal in the sight of God') and the moral superiority of the poor ('it is easier for a camel to go through the eye of a needle than for a rich man to enter into the kingdom of God') can be claimed by the ruled as sources of strength, both personal and political. Working from an artistic base, in a mythological near-vacuum, Welfare State are setting about the reclaiming of myth and its theatrical enactment for the whole community. In a world where the shared culture of human beings is increasingly threatened by a largely imposed electronic culture, myths and archetype have to be discovered and re-made, not simply revived. To do this, Welfare State rummage eclectically through many different cultures (albeit with respect for them), in order to find new expressions of common archetypes. It is, indeed, policy to invite foreign artists as often as possible to broaden the pool of mythological reference.

Most of the theatre forms referred to so far have been public performances. Of equal weight in the company's policy is the work of making domestic ceremony – the Namings of children, Weddings and Betrothals, and (yet to be fully researched) Funerals. These moments of personal and social significance are usually marked by formalised celebration (or mourning) based on the prevailing culture. For most of us in Britain, that means the Church, although for most of us, the Church means little. To mark moments of ceremony in ways that would honour their importance, Welfare State began, in 1969, to devise for particular groups of people, new ceremonies, using the talents, personalities, images and ideas of the people for whom the ceremonies were made. These events have ritual elements, although they are not 'ritualistic' in the sense that some theatre people understand them, that is they are not about the inducing of trance-like states in which reflection, reason and awareness are suppressed or abandoned. On the contrary, these qualities are heightened. As Lois Lambert reports in Chapter V on the naming of

An image in stone and wood from the Garden of Contemplation, *Stillpoint*, in Cumbria.

her own child: 'We had confirmed and celebrated our shared humanity, making a public celebration of our love, our hopes for our children. There had been nothing strange or mystical about the day. We had not been seeking for a powerful magic in which to lose ourselves.'

If most Welfare State work swings between public performance and private ceremony, with the re-creation of myth as its pivot, there is a third, lesser-known, but in its own low-key way, equally important area of work. This could be described as Landscape Gardening, and is embodied most remarkably in a wood in the Cumbria hills, where Boris and Maggie Howarth have created a 'Garden of Contemplation' called Stillpoint. They have taken what is, in any case, a beautiful and intriguing site, and made a gentle enhancement of its every aspect. By adding small sculptural effects, most in the wood, stone and greenery that make up the wood itself, they have pointed up, with respect, humour and the occasional surprise, the natural characteristics of the site. The additions and modifications to the site never dominate, but sharpen the focus and quicken the appetite for what is already there. 'Stillpoint' at first glance seems far away from the aggressive, anarchic energies of the early Welfare State street theatre style. It may even seem to have little in common with an exploding, neon sign-bedecked Tower of Babel, around which, one November 5th, Bracknell's bikers circled like chariot-racers loose in a Fritz Lang film. Yet both the year-long 'event' in Cumbria of the changing wood, and the climax of several weeks work in Bracknell's 'Scarecrow Zoo', are characteristic Welfare State work. They are animated by a need to express in human terms, the mythical and the natural for a society which is becoming de-natured and de-humanised.

Welfare State's work has always been the creation of a collective of artists under the leadership (sometimes acknowledged, sometimes not) of its founder John Fox and its associate director Boris Howarth. Fox, as a librarian and lecturer at Bradford College of Art, and later, in 1971, as Senior Lecturer in the Fine Art department of Leeds Polytechnic, was able to draw on a pool of students and staff to collaborate on one-off events. These included 'St. Valentine's Firestorm' (1968) in which a public dance was interrupted by a re-creation of the Dresden bombing ('reducing the audience to a kind of hysteria in a way I wouldn't do now because it was a form of aesthetic fascism'), and 'The Tide is O.K. for the 30th', commissioned in 1968 by the Beaford Centre in Devon, and enacted on a nearby beach with Army DUKWs and fireworks. Like so much else that emerged from that Hydra-headed phenomenon, the so-called 'Alternative' culture, these events owed most to the Art Schools which had acted as a funnel into Britain for the Performance Art, Happenings and multi-media events then active abroad, particularly in America. 1968 also saw the take-over by students and staff of Hornsey Art College, an event which symbolised the irruption into political life of

Art School energies. The breaking down of barriers between previous
discrete art-forms was echoed in the active seeking by students c
involvement in social and political activity.

For many theatre groups looking to integrate art with ordinary lif
street theatre performance offered a natural form in which to work. A
the other end of the spectrum were the larger-scale, one-off events i
which jazz composer Mike Westbrook collaborated as musical directo
These were genuine multi-media events, involving image-makers, jaz
and rock musicians, writers, sound and light technicians, and circu
artists such as fire-eaters, sword-swallowers and wire-walkers.

Both the large-scale work and the street theatre, and all the one-o
events in between, were part of a ferment of energy and experiment tha
exploded from the late sixties. Much of that ferment drew its strengt
from a sense of being 'avant-garde', of pushing back musical, visual an
theatrical barriers that were previously rigid and orderly. Ye
paradoxically the essence of Welfare State's project was also conserva
tive, in that it was dedicated to the revitalising of traditional popula
theatre forms. Although they operated within the then current utopia
avant-gardism, they were also trying to uphold a tradition of popula
entertainment against much of the mind-blown, élitist experimentatio
of the time. Such a contradiction was bound to cause problems, and fc
John Fox, they were focused on a tour of 'The Sweet Misery of Lif
Show' in 1971: 'It was basically a satirical critique, an allegory of Britair
about a variety show that broke up and ended with a mock crucifixio
and a talent competition. The main aim of that show was to get as man
boos as possible. I think the climax came for me when we did
somewhere in South London, and we got all the trendies coming out t
see how well we performed, not listen to what we were saying. It becam
very much fringe people performing to fringe people. It wasn't achievin
anything at all. I think I shouted at people and swore at them. Actuall
we blew it because Oscar Lewinstein, from the Royal Court, was in to se
if he wanted to commission us, and we just stopped performing. So th
following week, in the same venue, we started the first of the Lancelc
Quail stories. We already had that kind of show in the bag, but it seeme
like overnight we just jumped from one show to the other. It became
positive thing, it wasn't aggressive, it was about making the audience fe
in some way better. And since then, the work's pursued a much mor
poetic pattern.'

The appearance of Lancelot Quail in the company's lists marked
definite development in the work. Embodied only by one performe
Jamie Proud, a pig-farmer turned performer and teacher, th
working-class hero, whose full name finally grew to Lancelot Icaru
Handyman Barrabas Quail, was an Everyman figure for the audience t
identify with as well as laugh at. He became a rough-hewn comic cent
around which extraordinary demons and spirits flew, tormenting hin

Lancelot Icarus Handyman Barrabas Quail, as seen in Burnley, in 1977.

inspiring him, and finally being defeated by his knotty human spirit. The 1972 tour 'The Travels of Lancelot Quail', in which the travels were enacted along a route from Glastonbury to Lands End using a circus tent to work in, has become almost an icon of its theatrical time, especially in Roger Perry's photographs. The tour culminated in the disappearance off the Cornish coast of the entire company in a submarine, H.M.S. Andrew, a bizarre instance of the military-artistic complex at work!

The company heads to its rendezvous with H.M. Submarine *Andrew* in 1972.

By 1972, Mid-Pennine Arts Association, in an act of exceptional imagination, had invited Welfare State to take up residence in Burnley as theatre fellow of the Association, and a new vein of work was opened up. This was based on skill-teaching, and research into the arts and the community. As well as consciously regenerating the popular theatre tradition, Fox had always wanted to work on the assumption that the company should teach people the skills necessary to make their own celebrations, skills fast disappearing in a mechanised and de-skilled society. In this he was helped by the man later to become Welfare State's co-director, Boris Howarth. Howarth had been involved in folk music, and in the pioneer community theatre work of John Arden and Margaretta D'Arcy, as well as staging concerts of music by John Cage ('So arty', remembers Fox, 'that I threatened to drive through the place with a dumper truck.') By the late Sixties, Howarth and his wife Maggie were running New Planet City, a community arts workshop in

Lancaster. From 1970, both were working on Welfare State events. Howarth has proved an effective foil to Fox over the years, bringing to the latter's quixotic creative personality a more measured, classical sensibility. In particular he and Maggie Howarth had developed at New Planet City a tradition of street theatre based on percussion bands playing Latin and African rhythms. Howarth was also knowledgeable about seasonal ceremonials, and was regularly creating special events around November 5th bonfires, for example. Together, they had begun to work with young people in Lancaster, many of whom were considered 'difficult' or 'delinquent'. With their joint energies, the Foxes and the Howarths had, by the early '70's, the essential elements which, refined over the years by a wide variety of talented associates, still form the basis of their work: a developed sculptural sense, a desire to revitalise popular theatre traditions, a commitment to drawing in local energies and leaving behind a residue of skills and confidence after the company's withdrawal, a set of musical techniques suited to the colour and energy of their street performance, and above all an ability to use eclectically styles, influences and techniques from almost any source.

While the Burnley residency gave Welfare State the opportunity to consolidate and develop its work, it wasn't a completely unalloyed time. They had assumed the role of 'Civic Magicians', spending about a third of the year in Burnley providing large-scale theatrical events such as the first 'Parliament in Flames' November 5th bonfire, as well as smaller sculptural pieces like Christmas cribs. The rest of the year was spent on tour, in Britain, and increasingly in Europe. There were, however, problems about relations with the community. One problem was partly Burnley itself. 'I think,' says Fox, 'it's a repressed working-class town, more so than many. I also think we looked like a bunch of freaks who lived on a rubbish tip.' (The Council had rented them a disused quarry for the burgeoning collection of trailers, lorries, land-rovers and caravans that now made up the Welfare State circus.) 'People thought we were hippies and our image and the kind of work we did was sometimes very alienating. We wore heavy make-up, we did very 'progressive' performances, we didn't actually go about it in the right way.' Given the continuing amount of exciting work produced by the company year by year, including a Burnley 'Parliament in Flames' that attracted close to ten thousand spectators, that self-criticism may be unduly harsh, but it highlights another event that was of crucial importance for the company's structure. In spite of a somewhat hippy-ish claim in an early manifesto that 'We fuse fine art, theatre and life-style', the life-style, or more properly the work-style, was in fact an uneasy coalition between the ideals of collectivity and the practice of a director/company model.

Fox had been the teacher of many of the early company members, and while he saw the teacher/student relationship being transformed into director/company, his students-turned-associates didn't. They wanted collective working on the company's products to be reflected in collective control of the company's processes. There were also fundamental disagreements from some members about the point of trying to work in the community as teachers. The consequent clash of principles and personalities resulted in the greater part of Welfare State leaving in 1976 to form I.O.U. (Independent Outlaw University) which has gone on to become one of the finest performance art companies in the country. From that split, Welfare State took the basic company structure that now obtains, of a two-man directorate, two full-time administrators and a technical director. All other workers are freelance associates who join the company for specific projects, often being invited back time after time. In the late Autumn of 1977, the company attempted a kind of synthesis of all the accumulated research and experience of the previous nine years, in 'The Loves, Lives and Murders of Lancelot Barrabas Quail'. On Fulledge Recreation Ground in Burnley, in a complex of tents around what looked like a medieval jousting space, the audience wandered amongst sideshows and giant puppets before entering a 'cinema' to see a film about Quail and his bizarre early life. After the film, there was opportunity to wander again, to buy tea and hot potatoes, to investigate the strange tableaux representing Quail's inner mind, to listen to the band's music, or just to keep warm by the glowing braziers. Finally the audience sat on either side of the open space for the play of 'Barrabas'. Giant puppet figures, and acting performances to match, called to the performance space an array of marvellous images to terrorise and torment Quail. As the performance drew to a close, two gross cooks distributed spicy, steaming-hot bread to the audience. 'Barrabas' was a summation of so many of the elements gathered under the Welfare State banner in preceding years. Its basic story-structure was bone-simple, a Birth, Death and Resurrection sequence happening to an Every-man figure. Its imagery was spectacular and beautiful precisely because its style was rich, quirky and obviously handmade. Its music was strongly-flavoured, and acoustic. Its references ranged from Buddhist metaphysics to TV soap opera. Most significantly for the company's development perhaps, the audience were invited in, literally, by an M.C. character, and figuratively in the attention paid to their comfort and pleasure in all aspects of the performance (given, of course, that it was late October and mostly open to the sky!)

With the company's departure from Burnley in 1978, a new phase began. John and Sue Fox, with their children, went on a sabbatical visit to Australia and Bali, and Boris Howarth took over as director of research. During this period, more local, intimate styles of work were developed. Events for seasonal occasions, such as Harvest and Christmas, were created in small communities with the active participation of local people, and the idea of the 'Feast' was elaborated. In this traditional form, food and drink are specially made for one place

The skeleton bearing Lancelot Quail is cut open—*Barrabas*, Burnley, 1977.

ind event, as at Digswell House, Welwyn Garden City in 1979 in 'When The Pie Was Opened'. Naming ceremonies, and the annual November 5th 'Parliament in Flames' became regular parts of the company's work, ind the basis was laid for one of the most successful and popular Welfare State creations, the Barn Dance. The working principle by now was to eek residencies in local communities or arts centres sympathetic to their open-door (and usually open-air) policy. Such residencies were duly indertaken in everything from the Cleveland village of Thorpe Thewles o the islands off Toronto Harbour in Canada. By 1981, the final ignificant piece of the present jigsaw was the use of a reconnaissance eam, lodged on site for weeks, or even months, before the main company's arrival. The respect for a community's life – inner and outer – pays off in two ways. It allows local people to adjust to an input which, however good, is these days out-of-the-ordinary and potentially disturbing, and it allows images from the landscape and from the stories ind experience of local people to filter back to the main architects of the project, who will be planning the basic structure of imagery and story.

Welfare State's work is never perfect or finished or without contradiction, which is to say that it is still vital, alive and in touch with he culture that feeds it. As the state's economic base crumbles, and as a genteel and philistine fascism threatens its people, it may seem incongruous to celebrate, and downright irresponsible to some to dance and create spectacular events, or quiet gardens of contemplation. The problem is not evaded by the company. As Fox says in one interview 'It's certainly the case in a lot of South American countries, where Carnival is used as a way of giving people a day of freedom so that they can be repressed the rest of the year. It's also literally used as a way of bumping people off . . . during the excesses of Carnival there are well-reported events where the police go round in plain clothes killing people. There will always be this argument. Basically you are saying 'Is this a time for art?'

If the answer for Welfare State is yes, there remains the thorny problem that the function of the shared beliefs and myths on which they build their work has generally been to reinforce the dominant politic and culture. Public ritual is usually thought of as essentially conservative, power-reinforcing activity, such as the crowning of monarch or a military funeral. In tribal societies, it is arguable that 'official' rituals gave an organic coherence to living that was essential to survival. In modern technocratic states, at war within themselves socially and morally, communal images and myths are highly likely to be empty relics of past organic culture, or state propaganda designed to subdue popular expression and action. The filling of that vacuum in human social needs is therefore left to artists, the 'unacknowledged legislators', and whether they fill that vacuum with more empty art or with something rooted in society's real needs often depends on their awareness of the political nature of art. By creating its new myths and rituals for limited spans and specific spaces, rather than making products for all time or posterity, Welfare State commit themselves to working in real world. Their work raises back into their proper places in the public culture, areas of experience that are under direct threat from the official culture – creativity, sensuality and communality. The company cannot of itself, change society, nor could a hundred Welfare States, but it can help to inform the inevitable large changes in society with kinds of feeling often neglected by conventional political art.

One of the (instinctive) ways that Welfare State avoid supporting reaction and the status quo is to work around the core concept of Change. The very recurrence of the archetypal Birth-Death-Rebirth cycle in the work implies the concepts of Change and Transformation. The idea permeates many levels, from the commissioning stage to the inner life of individual images. For example, ice and fire, both elements in the company's armoury are self-evident embodiers of change; the effect of giant puppets in the street forces an immediately pleasurable change of perception in spectators. Individual arts are continually changed and transformed. In music, for instance, you can catch the flavour of jazzband or folkband, which have a Fifties resonance, while drawing on popular music from the start of the century or earlier. It isn't long before hese are transformed – by a South American bayonne rhythm, by Celtic pipes, ska or South African Hi-Life textures, by reggae or by synthesiser. The new sounds do not replace the old ones, but colour them and move them on into new hybrid styles. Predictably, visual images are also subject to the processes of transformation. A black crow becomes a bomber, then a cross. A character is part Mad Angel, part B-movie test pilot, part Ariel and part clown. Tragedy and farce dance together, things die and new things are born. Even out of Death images, new images grow. The company's work pattern, too, embodies the idea of Change, with its shifting personnel show-to-show, working in different venues, effecting transformations and encouraging them to occur after departure. There is little that is predictable in the work, for the overall vision mapped out by the two directors is subject to transformations wrought upon it by the collective of artists employed for each project, and once started, the making process on site tends to have a life of its own. Thus, while Change in the work process might be unpredictable, it is not in fact random or arbitrary but based on past experience and shaped to satisfy present needs.

The future, we must accept, is fraught for both the theatre and society in general. Britain, to say nothing of the wider world, is turbulent with the crumbling of old structures, and the struggles of new ones to come into being. To describe yourselves, as Welfare State do, as 'Pathological Optimists' might seem like empty idealism, were it not for the vein of sharp irony that runs through so much of the work, and colours that slogan – 'You have to be mad to be an optimist!' There is also, I suspect, an act of will implied in it, echoing one of Brecht's favourite phrases 'Pessimism of the Intellect, Optimism of the Will!' Also emblazoned on the side of the company's Leyland truck is 'Engineers of the Imagination', a label that succinctly reflects the combination of technology, craft and art that the company deals in. It is the Imagination, above all, that powers all the processes of rational and creative action that make up social living, and the transforming power of the imagination that makes change possible. Without it, there can be no learning and no morality. Welfare State recognise that the creative imagination is the enemy of the fragmenting and the dehumanised. In modern society, a great deal of effort goes into keeping the lid on creative energy, using everything from outright oppression to the subtler ideological machineries of the education and communications systems. That is why it is vital to mount, alongside a theatre of analysis and rationality, what one company associate calls 'The Imagination Recovery Service', not as a diversion from, or substitute for, the active changing of the world, but as a vital partner and precondition of Change.

In India, there is a word, 'parampara', whose rough translation is 'tradition'. It means literally 'one foot on the ground, one foot moving', and it suggests something of the spirit of Welfare State's work. The

The image of Dancing—Ulverston Carnival 1980.

image describes a tension between opposites, between the still and the moving, between the fixed past and the changeable future. It makes of tradition, not a static millstone around the neck, but a dynamic process which can be created as well as observed. Above all, it is an image of pleasure, for 'one foot on the ground, one foot moving' is an image of Dancing.

2

Commissions and Audiences

*How Welfare State's events are commissioned,
conceived and carried out*

JOHN FOX

Welfare State shows have always existed in the spaces between form
theatre and ordinary life. These spaces are both geographical – the sho
usually occur in public, communal space – and conceptual – the sho
have elements of formal theatre as well as elements of everyday life li
eating, standing on a street and looking, celebrating a birthday. In th
chapter, the editors talk to John Fox about the relationship between t
company's work and its audience.

JF: The basic movement over the last 15 years has been to move aw
from pure product performance. In our street theatre, we used
get out of the back of a truck, put out a circle of oildrums and dra
people into the circle. Then we'd pass the hat round at the en
Sometimes we would do more elaborate shows with electron
music in dance halls or whatever, but we still turned up wi
products. As we got more interested in what you might c
anthropology, we began to do more residencies, where we
actually stay for two or three weeks and build up a show. Over t
last two or three years, the orientation has been increasingly to ta
much longer residencies, where we have people who specifica
focus the energy within a community. We act more as a catalys
and although there is product in that, it's part of a total envelop

Eds: *Has there been a gradual evolution into this pattern?*

JF: Yes, there has. We have grown organically but plan instinctive
about five years ahead. Although there are reactions a
counter-reactions to immediate situations (like the swing of t
pendulum) with hindsight we realise there has been steady grow
between a series of rising plateaux. Very simply we have mov
from parody and self-contained repeatable products and one nig
stands to long residencies in communities of up to three months
where the process can mature over a long period eventua
culminating in a short lived climax.

It took, I suppose, 2 or 3 years to become self-conscious enough about what we were doing. We started street theatre because it was fun to do and it was a quick way to work. You just get up, get in a lorry, go into the street and do it. Eventually of course, the more you do, the more self-conscious you become, then you start to project ahead, project patterns which you didn't have the luxury to do before. The work's generally more open now. It's grown in the sense that it's become more secure. That's partly through reputation, partly through money, and having the ability to take more risks. It's interesting how, at certain times in our course when there were difficulties within the company, we seemed to put a wall round ourselves and become rather isolated, including a facial wall of extreme make-up. We started to drop that more and more and become more open. I suppose now that at least 50% of the show is what drops into the net when we go to a place, whereas earlier on, we didn't have either the time or the awareness to let that happen. We were performing at people rather than letting the show grow around a node of energy that we were part of.

Eds: *Who commissions you now?*

Festivals in Britain and abroad, The British Council, Arts Associations, Art Centres and private individuals for namings and weddings. Most work comes through word of mouth and personal recommendation. We are offered much more work than we can handle ourselves but are always interested in new challenges. The spectrum extends from the very local to the very prestigious. Often we want to develop a particular line of research and have to find an interested host. Usually there is a happy marriage of both but often the difficulty is that potential bookers have inadequate knowledge, and base their expectations on old copies of Theatre Quarterly (1972). Only *after* the experience do most bookers understand our philosophy. The worst demand is for psychedelic elastoplast where we are expected to patch up all the social ills in their neighbourhood and provide massive turn-on entertainment more likely to benefit an administrator's career than the community itself.

Eds: *Would you say 'No', if you got a demand for 'elastoplast'?*

F: It would depend on how bad the wound was (and how poor we were). Normally we are wary of guilt money, adventure playgrounds and institutionalised community art. But we react to each particular demand and don't have rigid rules. We have for instance worked a couple of times at the Crawford Centre in Liverpool which is really an elaborate youth club; mainly because we knew personally a few dedicated, overworked and underpaid people whom we liked. We have also worked twice for the Neighbourhood Open Workshop in Belfast where they are working against enormous odds. At first they wanted us to do a show only but eventually we convinced them that it was better for them if we left skills behind through doing workshops with their own staff. Often it's more productive to teach the teachers and we frequently back this up with an invitation for people to come on our annual Summer School.

Eds: *Do you ever make approaches to organisations, as opposed to them contacting you?*

JF: Yes, occasionally when we have specific ideas (especially for our gardens) but we also do regular mail-outs to potential bookers, so that contacts are maintained and built up over the years. Sadly in Britain now there are really very few bodies who have the money, the organisation and the commitment for our kind of work. We are trying to extend our range to cover recreation departments, trade unions and industry as so much of our current patronage is totally dependent on The Arts Council of Great Britain – directly or indirectly.

Eds: *Once someone is interested in commissioning, and you have agreed what happens?*

JF: We do a reconnaissance. We spend a good part of the budget hunting out, divining, finding what is around. We take slides and films and publicity to the potential bookers to give them confidence and evidence that we can do the job. We warn them we might fail and can't *guarantee* success, but we promise to do the best we can. We have to find out from the management what they actually do want. And then tailor-make it accordingly, or lead them gently to a point where we give them something they perhaps didn't know at first they did want, or didn't even know existed. It's like the overture to the whole thing. The style of the publicity is the opening of the curtain. One problem with reconnaissance is you've got to guess what you'll be wanting to do a long way ahead. I was writing an initial brief for example for the 1982 November 5th gig for Bracknell just a few weeks after November 1981. In the case of Tempest in Canada, that took two years, with a number of meetings in London and Canada, showing of slides, chatting to people, building up a trust. But most important is the visit. We always visit in advance because most of the ideas come from the space. Whether it is in Japan, a Pennine village, or Barrow-in-Furness. From then on, it's a combination of the ideas in our head, the space we find, the season of the year, the occasion, the local need and the money.

Increasingly I've less and less faith in quick turn-ons, although there can be value in the once-off. For instance, when Mike Westbrook was young, his dad took him to see Humphrey Lyttleton at the local palais, and after that he decided he wanted to run a jazz band. And now he's a world famous jazz composer, so I'm not saying you can't do turn-ons. There's always a case for doing performances well. It's just that we are doing that *plus* something else, and so we have to do long recces beforehand – find what's ideal for the situation, then follow it through later. The kind of information that we need before a commission's accepted is first why do people want us, then technical information like widths of entrances, where the water and electricity supply is, but first always, what is the basic reason for being there. Sometimes things go wrong, when the recce hasn't been done properly or we have been misinformed. In Birmingham, we were booked to do the Doomsday Colouring Book shows over and over again in a field in the middle of tenement blocks. We would have have been ripped apart! The first thought was that we would have to cancel, but we knew someone there who had helped us on an earlier show, and he would have been very badly let down if we had pulled out. So at short notice we came up with a show, 'Hockley Port Non-Stop Honkey Tonk Technicolour Knees Up' which was very suited to the situation. What we should have done ideally was a carnival with local people, but that would have taken at least four months to do well and we had a fortnight. One of the problems in working class areas like that is that very often there isn't the organisation. First of all you've got to help people to organise, to build up a consciousness because middle-class people are used to (a) reading, (b) going to Arts Centres and (c) holding meetings. You learn all these skills in the 'A' stream but often there's no local community organisation at all. You need a long time to build up trust for anything really, never mind theatre.

Ids: *Does this mean that there are no problems with middle class venues, like arts centres?*

F: No! People who run arts centres, who are often sensitive and generally aware in many ways, have often been reared on a certain notion of what Art is and how it's good for you. They've got a big building with a big staff and big overheads and a set of consumable products. They've got to pack the building with people and fill the shop window. Bums on seats. They have to sell art. Those places are often very well meaning and well used. But when you start to talk about re-focusing a mainstream tradition of guizers, carnival and subversive folk art which was the heritage of the working class, actually using the art centre as a tool, a resource centre where

people can work together in studios making big carnival floats and
so on, they don't know what the hell you're talking about. Not
because they're baddies but because they've been brought up with
a certain narrow, academic and middle class history of art. So
(having shown you know your Art and even having degrees in it!)
you then try to show there are other ways. Then we have to excite
them with a bumper bundle of stunning pictures of past carnival
work, people evidently enjoying themselves, and so convince them
that you can pack the art centre with happy folk. Very often people
need showing a way, or given a bit of confidence. I'm not saying
that everyone we meet doesn't understand. A lot of people do
understand, but have never known how it might be possible to
change anything. When we offer a small trigger they jump at the
chance. They're ready and willing to be steered.

Eds: *So you've got the commission, you've set up the recce, what then?*

JF: There are three main aspects – The organisation; The people; and
the Dreaming.

I have a notion of a molecular core so that all events, big and
small have a similar underlying structure. An event might be made
up with one candle, a drum, a false nose and a pair of webbed feet
and be performed on a grass verge. Another event could contain
one thousand pounds worth of fireworks, an orchestra, a company
of twenty with red masks, a flotilla of frogmen and a prairie.* The
first event might last three minutes and the second three hours (or
three months) but in each case the pattern is the same.
Considerations of time (the wait, the performance, the climax, the
wind-down), geography (space and place), symbols (death,
resurrection, transcendence) and context all have to be examined
and ideally, even for a tiny work, there should be a reconnaissance.

However, having said that, the organisational problems are
obviously entirely different for a solo piece from the back of a bike
to a symphonic statement at a major festival. In a tiny celebration
the planning might take three minutes and in a big one three years.
The main thing that changes is that on a big scale piece there have
to be more organisers (director, production manager, stage
manager etcetera). The responsibility and complexity demands a
bureaucracy and a hierarchy. The difficulty is to balance flexibility
and efficiency with a full creative involvement of everyone. We are
wary of over specialisation and the false separation of artists and
enablers: we try to make (ideally) a social microcosm of a 'better

*Ken Feit, the late American nomadic Holy Fool story teller once told me that he
did celebratory *im*plosions with a spoon, a drop of olive oil, a candle flame and one
piece of pop-corn – whereas we did *ex*plosions.

society but it's not easy. Some people prefer to be key dreamers – or are actually better at it than others. I believe you have to give access to that central role to as many people as possible and train people into it by allowing the inexperienced to rise to the occasion. We prefer to give one person the 'gaffer's baton', and they take primary artistic (and other) responsibility. The buck stops at them. Everyone should have access to that role if they want it. I.O.U. – generally a much smaller group than us – do produce wonderful work by, to the outsider, a seemingly perfect collective structure. That's very special.

In our case roles change from gig to gig to an extent: there is little spare training time but we do build a percentage of 'apprentices' and volunteers and 'sabbaticals' into every event and every year to allow for change. We try not to give people only those tasks we know they are good at.

ds: *Is it the case that you and Boris Howarth are the Artistic Directors in all senses? Do the artistic visions all start with you and him?*

F: In Welfare State's case most events are devised by Boris Howarth or myself – either separately or together. Currently about 10% of the work is devised by others (from the regular company associates) but this should increase. Finding the key Dreamers, the initiators – is not easy. There is always the question of how much I am prepared to delegate, how much I am temperamentally capable of it, and indeed how much the company wants me to. It varies.

I find I am increasingly out of joint with the 19th century concept of the romantic specialist super-creator. I would like to believe this is only a historic hiccup – that in an ideal culture the 'artist' merely serves (not leads) the community in a functional capacity and that necessary images and archetypes naturally and inevitably reveal themselves. It is only because we allow so few people to Dream profoundly in our society that we set up the specialist ARTIST. Hopefully this will change but for the meantime we have to live with it.

Boris and I certainly are the primary creators. We write the scenarios. But this needs qualifying. We pick a team that can work together and that is ideal for the gig – but we often write the work round the needs of the people we choose. It's like a good band. We provide the tunes but the soloists explore harmonies and we love to write work to incorporate imaginative engineers, or wonderful sculptors, people we can enjoy creating with. Then in practice we all learn from each other through observation and consultation and helping each other. As the work grows, in practice, on the best occasions it feels like being inside a great rolling planet of creative fission.

Eds: *What do you mean by Dreaming?*

JF: You have to get a foot in the door as it were, find an angle tha
seems to be the right one. If you're working for Hallowe'en an
November 5th, as we were at Bracknell, then we've got our ow
track record of bonfires (12 in all). There is some literature abou
traditional customs. So we've got a pattern of the way things hav
been done in certain traditions to draw upon. The reading we stor
in our heads, then we visit the place and just by talking to people i
pubs, and reading local papers, looking at the place, you find wha
the local preoccupations are. For instance, we found at Brackne
that the local electronics industry is important. Then you think
it's Hallowe'en, you've got scarecrows – you pick scarecrow
because it's a simple image that anyone could get hold of, an
anyone could make. You start to talk about black crows and yo
think perhaps the black crows should be missiles, because Ferran
and others make missile control gear. And you say 'How do w
update Hallowe'en, do we update it at all, or do we chuck it out c
the window?' But if it still means something about externalised fea
and getting rid of demons that are going to terrify you over the lon
winter, then why aren't the demons of today black missiles up th
road at Greenham Common, where the women are clamberin
over bulldozers trying to act out everyone else's soul by sayin
'Let's stop this, these are the black crows of modern technologica
society.' So that gets mixed up with traditional imagery, but yo
have to be wary . . . if you make it too agitprop, you only preach t
the converted, or you alienate. If you make it too sweet, all yo
come up with is a jolly spectacle which probably makes thing
worse in the long run by stopping people thinking. So you've go
your own traditions, you've got the country's traditions, you've go
the specific preoccupations of the place, like the electronics; you'v
also got the pattern of the season and the specific geography of th
place you're in. They all start to go together in a sort of cauldron –
cauldron in my head, and hopefully in company members' heads
and then it starts to simmer and distil, and you start to conjure
few key images in the steam.*

Eds: *What would then determine the order of the images, the events?*

JF: If you're dealing with theatre at any level, you're dealing wit
things like beginnings, middles and ends. You know that you'r
going to have 800 people who're going to look on a space an
they've got to be first of all drawn into the spell. They have to g

*The form of the communication becomes part of the problem. Didactic and litera
illustration can be counter to a more poetic, intuitive and sensual approach. Fals
polarisations can be induced by the method of simply demonstrating.

through the decompression chamber. Then you have to somehow change time to the point where the audience become absorbed in the place, having its own rhythm. I like to call it a Dream Time, which is a link between my imagination and their imagination and the imagination of one's ancestors. And that usually has to come to some kind of fruition or conclusion. Then you play around with it. It's like playing around with a sculpture, and feeling the height of things, and wondering whether they work, trying things out. You either do that from experience, in which case you probably don't need a lot of rehearsal, or, ideally, you block things out in the space to get a sense of how it's going to work on the ground. I usually draw a grid in fact. I write down something like Scene/ Mood/Music/Time/Technical/Miscellaneous, with people's names written into it, with specific words which might say atmosphere: 'storm' or atmosphere: 'lyrical' or 'comic/melancholy'. You find little key phrases that people could follow. And all the company would have them.

ds: *Is making the grid part of the Dreaming process, or does it come after?*

F: No, it's more after. It's a clarification, it's like a sieve of the Dreaming. It's making the images from the Dreaming concrete.

ds: *Dreaming can be a very obscure, private process, can't it?*

F: For me the process *is* personal and private – like water divining. But the discoveries, the images I find should be clear and common archetypes. I think at some point, whether you use Jungian phraseology or not, at some point you're looking down into the Collective Unconscious through your own subconscious. Like a glass-bottomed boat, and the artist is floating around letting people see down into the images. The job of the artist is to have antennae to pick it up and reveal it, articulate it for other people to read. It is to objectify his subjective experience in a form that's accessible to the majority. Our job, or the job of any artist, I would submit, who works publicly, is to find the images that are the pegs a lot of other people connect with. A good example of the way this imagery grows and changes was at Haverhill. I was thinking about rats, which was a spillover from an earlier gig for scientists at Babraham where they were all cutting up rats. I was going to create an event which I thought was relevant because everybody had been moved out from the GLC to this town which was, at that time, nowhere. I wanted a piece called The Great Rat Race. I knew there were a lot of punks and motorbike boys, and I wanted to have people riding round the streets as packs of rats, with all these psychedelic jesters trying to catch them. It would actually be the Rat Race, but it would also be the Pied Piper comes to town. Then Kevin West, who was our recce man on the ground, rang and said whatever you do, *don't* do the rat race.★ So I said give me another idea then. So he said 'Windmills'. Now the Ministry of Defence blew up the last windmill there in the war, because it was supposed to help German bombers to navigate. And everyone resented it because it was apparently one of the best working windmills left in the country. So this image happened to be, for whatever reason, at the back of people's heads. People could identify with it. They love making windmills. I'd no idea about doing windmills, but having done windmills, you naturally think of Don Quixote and start to invent character called Donald Quixotty, a development of a kind of lunatic angel Andy Burton's been developing for years. And he went into the Bracknell gig too, left over from Haverhill. There were some bike boys in the bar at Bracknell who told me about seeing the Peter O'Toole Don Quixote film, and they immediately knew the story. Half the time your stories might be culled from 'Tradition', but they may also come from a James Bond movie. It's what people know about, and what dreams they themselves put into these images. If you have, as we did, a procession of bike boys with Donald Quixotty, you're dealing with young men with dreams, but you're also dealing with all the films that've been around, be it 'Easy Rider' or 'Mad Max II'. It doesn't matter, so long as you can use the imagery in a positive way to release energy for good.

Eds: *When the recce's done, and the Dreaming, and the company starts to assemble for the gig, on site, presumably the imagery then starts to come from the space?*

JF: Yes, that, and the time of year. You collage stuff together really. Someone might be playing a piece of music, because it seems to fit with the season – wet and cold, the Autumn bit, and the trees going brown. So I hear it and say great, let's use that and we play it at slightly different speed as part of a procession. By the fact that you're making in the place, the moods drop in. If you've got group of people who are sensitive to change and you have the time to actually let the space get into you, it's inevitable that it will change the way things are made. In quite obvious ways, like the colours that you use, or the fact that it's getting dark at night, so you've got to use stuff that's black and white so you can read it at night, or it's very muddy, so you make a procession where you stamp heavily because of the mud on the ground.

  The working outside is important to us – increasingly in sophisticated economies we've lost touch with the planet, and this

★It was too close to the truth for comfort. The inhabitants felt they were victims of the Rat Race – being moved out of London at the behest of politicians.

is quite dangerous. Most of us in the company have lived in caravans and tents for quite a long time, and you pick up certain rhythms, a certain attunement to the space, which you don't normally do living in the city. I'm convinced that the best things just drop in. You put out antennae, and things just find you.

Eds: *What about materials? Do you always choose certain materials, like bamboo?*

JF: We do now, but that's a luxury since we've had a waggon to carry the stuff in. We carry really a great palette of both information and materials which you can draw on. We carry string, we carry glue, paint, cloth, bamboo, resin cloth, nuts, bolts, nails, stuff we can take off the shelf. And more specialised things like costumes, masks, fireworks, sound gear, and, obviously, musical instruments. We then scrounge whatever we can locally (although it's getting expensive – to get free wood for a bonfire might cost you £200 in fuel). But we try to cannibalise, to re-use stuff that's around the site, whether it's mud and straw when you're making a sculpture, or computer paper in Bracknell for making papier mâché, or newspapers.

Eds: *In particular gigs, have there been materials unique to one place?*

F: The best one I can think of was some clay we used in Rotterdam. The city was being totally changed in some areas. They were making very deep pile foundations and some mud came up that by the smell of it was obviously from the Middle Ages. We incorporated that into an altar-piece about the life of Rotterdam. I made a little Dutch model organ, and the different textures of black and grey were really quite a beautiful thing. Vegetation's important too, particularly straws or grasses.

Eds: *Size and scale are important aspects of your work. Is that for the audience's sake?*

F: Objects or images in the street need to be seen, need to be above people's heads. So if you're talking about a puppet, you're talking about something at least ten or twelve feet high for a start. Once you start to make that, all the other scale tends to follow. I think we also do *enjoy* the spectacle. We're a bit wary of the spectacle being purely an opium, though. But if it can also release the image, then the power of it, the scale of it, is all right. I think Breton's right about the poet of the future making dreams concrete. People have seen our Houses of Parliament structure and actually thought that a building had gone up in the town. They couldn't believe that it had gone up virtually overnight. There's something about the power of that. It's there in front of you, you can't deny it, which affects everybody. If nothing else, it affects policemen and politicians to know you won't go away.

Eds: *At the other extreme, there are the flimsiest of objects like lanterns.*

JF: Yes. The fragility of it, the transience of it, is very important. The fact that you've got to make it there and then. It's perfectly clear the lanterns are made on site because they wouldn't stand being carted round in a lorry. It's fun, because you don't quite know what you're going to make, then suddenly you see it in front of you. It's exciting for us, and I think the excitement communicates itself to the audience as well. The immediacy, the handmade, the transience are useful counters to phoney propaganda which tries to pretend that LIFE is fixed and permanent and that if you are insured Death will go away.

Eds: *Are there styles that are special to this company?*

JF: We've talked about archetypes, and about the quality of making, which is, if you like, home-made; we demystify the process so opening up possibilities for others. The other obvious things are carnival style and fairground style. Like the Circus, Punch & Judy and the guizers it's a very brightly coloured and quite crude style, with a rather garish and immediate quality. It's to do with a painterly way of looking at things. That's a fairly specialised term. It means really, the feeling for the texture of the whole set of images, including the space. We made a giant lantern for the Hallowe'en celebrations. That lantern is both a lantern, like the romantic image you see on a Christmas card, but it's also the centre of a roundabout. And could it be the roundabout of the Cosmos . . . ? I suppose people who are into theatre often aren't too happy with aspects of the roughness. If I don't stop myself, half the time I'm just seeing patterns of colours and shapes. What I'm aware of in a shopping precinct is an overall greyness. Then a big slab of yellow, which are our Firemen with their ridiculous hats on, and then a big slab of black and yellow which are the scarecrows. And they're making a frame of colour around a big lantern in the middle. So the whole thing is composed, even though it's crudely put together in the street. It's actually composed from a painterly sense. It's probably what gives our better things a kind of sensual, overall unity. That is something to do with the common language people speak, because a lot of people have been trained as makers, or painters, rather than as performers and writers.

Eds: *Do you ever exercise 'quality control' on things that are built?*

JF: Ideally 'quality' should be self-evident; within the company it usually is. We expect of each other that things are well made and they usually are. You have to believe that everyone wants to do their best. If something is badly produced it usually means a shortage of time, a lack of resources (a lack of belief in what you are doing – either because you are doing the wrong thing or someone's ripping you off) or a lack of experience and practice. I believe if you set up the right situation there's no problem. People are open with each other, they can take honest criticism from each other and quality is *self*-controlling. Having said that I do believe that it is foolish to pretend that everyone is good at everything and because art should be accessible everyone should immediately be able to do it. A lot of people can in Bali (but even there, there *are* experts). However, we are not sentimental. The public has a right to expect professional work. I would believe that everybody's potentially an artist, but it needs experience, just as it needs experience to learn to take an engine to bits. It's patronising, and counter-productive, to actually believe that because somebody's made something it must therefore be good. It doesn't actually help them in the end because the quality and excellence of things is important. Life is improved by cooking a good meal or making a fabulous puppet, by hearing somebody else who can play the cello marvellously, and I love that difference.

So very occasionally I have stopped something because it's bad – not I hope because it's different from my taste – but because it gives a totally wrong sense to the overall imagery. (It could be an immature, a gratuitously violent piece of cruel imagery for instance, or it could be something that is just very badly made.) Basically I reserve the right to veto an object or a performance but I think it's only happened a dozen times in fifteen years. If there is constant and trusted communication between experienced artists working in a team, there is very rarely in my experience any unresolvable disagreement.

.ds: *Does the fact that the training of most people in the company is in making or painting, rather than acting, lead to a different perform-ance style?*

F: I think it *is* different. The simple answer is that we started off learning by the fact that we worked in the street and if we didn't get an audience, we hadn't the money for the fuel home, and therefore we had to learn tricks to keep an audience. And also to stop people throwing rubbish at you, or shouting abuse. So we learnt just as much as a salesman in a market learns – devices for holding audiences, for projecting our voices, for making an image in the street. We made our own internal proscenium. This has meant that we've learnt some skills you probably wouldn't pick up in a drama school. Often, colleges, whether they be for art or acting, condition

people to the point where they can actually reduce talent an
ability.

I think we can do a lot more than we do. I would like th
company to be able to sing much more in the street, to be able
project much more with their voices. And there are acting ski
now we think we might need, like the skills for dialogue an
relationships. I think these help you tell a story bette
communicate with an audience better. We have recently broug
in more people with acting training to help us, who will perform
actors and some directors and writers. We've never worked wit
actors as such before. One of them trained at RADA. So we teac
her making skills, and she teaches us acting skills as we go along.
think all our work develops in context. We work as clowns, v
work in relationship to what the audience does when we look
them and when it's not working we change it. Nevertheless,
would quite value having, say, six months to go away and lea
more skills. We know the skills we want to learn, quite obvio
skills that are under-developed in the company – like singin
dancing, acrobatics.

Eds: *Do the same things apply to music?*

JF: There we're giving access to people who are not necessarily ve
skilled musicians, but who can actually play one or two notes, an
play them in time. As and when people can play more, then the
get more offered. We now know the style of music to go for, whic
is to do with music that works in the street, and is not military, b
has a certain kind of funky openness. An openness in exactly th
same way one is looking for openness in the image. It's got spa
within it. It's not imperialist. It allows space for the beat and
allows space for the audience. It's also theatre music, and n
thought of separately from the image. Not everyone can wri
theatre music, and not everyone wants to. It's a particular sk
which I think is neglected. As 'music' music, it has its limitation
but again, you see, it's about breaking categories. We don't thir
of ourselves as a theatre company or whatever. We think
ourselves as a group of artists who use whatever we need to mak
the poetry.

Eds: *That kind of openness makes the relationship with the audience speci
in ways that are probably unique to Welfare State.*

JF: They shouldn't be. They should be common to all theatre, ideall
because you're waiting for the energy of your audience. If you s
up theatre so you're just taking a wall off a room, then you'
already set up tableaux which you're separate from. It's th
difference between a circle and a square, really. If you're one end

a square, it's quite hard to relate to the other end, but if you're in a circle, you can run round the edges and you're all together. That's why in terms of audience spectacle, we often use a circle. The audience puts in 50% of the energy. In terms of its psychology, it's probably more Female than Male. (Nothing to do with men or women here.) But fundamentally we show a reality not an illusion.*

Eds: *At each moment of the show, there's a kind of invitation to the audience. Not exactly to get up and do something, but they are participating in a way they wouldn't in other types of theatre.*

JF: And the meeting with the audience is very important. That initial contact. What kind of atmosphere they make, and how far they feel they can go from their world into your world. We are, ideally, trusted dream-weavers. In the old tribe, it would have been the shaman, who is given the right to take his audience on a trip and to earth them again, once you've taken them away on a trip. It's a contract, a deal you make with them. The audience surrenders a certain right to you, which you have not to abuse. The audience is a guest, and you take them on a magic carpet, and you bring them back again. It's terribly important to bring them down again, in the sense of placing them back with their feet on the soil.

Eds: *Isn't that what all good theatre should do?*

JF: Yes, I wouldn't want to make exclusive claims for it. I think it's a comment on a lot of modern theatre that because of the very buildings . . .

Eds: *Is it the buildings themselves, or the assumptions that the buildings support, and the way the audience is trained to see theatre, and work with theatre?*

JF: They are closed systems. Our research is into nascent ritual (*using* theatre) as part of a way of living rather than a repeated dramatic production, where theatre is an end in itself.

Eds: *But there have been, in history, extremely dynamic relationships between audiences and an end-on stage. It's not the building so much as the culture that creates the audiences and the people who run the places.*

F: I'd agree with that. I think that in some peculiar way, we've actually gone through the history of theatre. We've worked through street theatre, Carnival Theatre, and we've moved around ritual, and what we set out to do at Bracknell, mad as it seemed, was to build an eight hundred seater theatre! We found we needed

*But in the jargon of Castenada 'a non-ordinary reality' – that some would call magic.

a focused space for 800 people, which is exactly the problem they've solved at the National, or Leeds Playhouse. Of course, we can use fire and fireworks, which they can't. The problem with most theatre is the cultural ambience that goes with it, a social ambience that slightly nauseates me, I suppose. It tends to reinforce values I don't agree with.

It may be that the time is not right now to work in theatres. It' like having to go through the whole business of breeding the badgers to grow the hair to make the brushes to paint the canvas. Then you've got to grow the jute as well . . . In a way it's tedious but it's culturally necessary. It's all about the thing that happen between us and the audience really. Really, we don't make theatre we use theatre to make magic. I would measure the success of a show according to whether the magic works. It can happen that you play out of tune, you can fall over, but the magic will work. It can also be pouring with rain, or perhaps *because* it's pouring with rain, it's particularly magical. But what happens is some kind o release of energy, that is special. There's a heightened awareness and there's a communication between audience and makers and performers which is unusual, and it's something that's a lot bigger than everybody. When it all comes together – the image, the sound, the flow of the energy, the weather and the sense of well-being afterwards, that you've made something very special - that's very rare. It probably happens about 2 or 3 times a year.

I think most magicians would agree that they are using commonly agreed devices. The shaman is not a manipulator Commonly agreed codes or devices are practised, in some sense to change perception. And it's the change of consciousness which is crucial, rather than the producing of the fine product. The product can be very fine, but if it doesn't have a reasonably profound effect on the changing of consciousness, then it's a waste of time.

*For ritualising to occur the surroundings must expose a vulnerable side (vulnerable equals wound). Whether the vulnerability stems from a human or divine face does not seem to be definite but that some aspect of the Cosmos appears to be responsive to present a face, is necessary for ritualising to gestate. The more deeply an enactment is received the more deeply an audience becomes a congregation and the more a performance becomes ritualised. 'SACRED' is the name we give to the deepest forms of receptivity in our experience.

RON GRIMES published in *Defining Nascent Ritual*

3

Street and Outdoor Performance and Music

(i) *Street and outdoor performance*

SUE FOX

Welfare State learnt some of its craft on the streets. Getting out there, banging a drum, drawing a crowd and performing for them.

From the earliest attempts in 1968 to more skilled and sophisticated recent work, certain things never change. With street theatre you are as good as the moment and no more. You have no reputation in the places you will normally work. Yours is not a theatre audience. They have never heard of you, and usually they were not intending to see a show. They have chanced upon you while they were out, as a rule, and if they don't like the show they can walk away. But if they love it, they forget the shopping, they are late back to work after lunch. They get lost in your dreams and share them for a few moments. There's an honesty in the contract between street theatre performer and audience. That's why it is a trade to work at and to be proud of. As performers you KNOW when it is working – you never get a bored, indulgent audience.

Street theatre has been used as a powerful vehicle by several leading radical companies: San Francisco Mime Troupe gave birth to guerilla theatre and were well known for their anti-Vietnam war platform, Teatro Campesino raised consciousness among the Californian grape-pickers in their political struggle, Bread and Puppet developed their holy theatre and Odin Teatret from Denmark continue to present the same truly spectacular street pieces, sometimes for five or six years.

The content does not have to be agit-prop. At first sight any English audience assumes it is students protesting about 'the cuts' and they turn off. Hectoring people with statistics does a disservice to theatre and to your cause. The form can certainly show struggle and violence, but also the emotional world with hope and longing, humour and celebration, and most of all dreams, presented in a sensual way with dance, music, energy and colour.

Street theatre is NOT taking the walls and roof off your regular theatre show. It is a different beast altogether, with its own terms and conditions. In a conventional theatre the performer has all the advantage of a stage with dramatic lighting, and a seated audience in a quiet room.

Early Welfare State street theatre in 1973. 'Getting out there, banging a drum, drawing a crowd and performing for them.'

The architecture serves to provide the focus for the audience. The audience has a real investment. They have bought tickets, and there is a recognised and shared social tradition surrounding a visit to the theatre.

Working in the street is NOT an apology. It is NOT done because you're not yet good enough to get into a real theatre. You are not hoping to get spotted and move up into the REAL (?) world of television or rep. Street theatre companies have CHOSEN it for political (and philosophical) reasons. They want to be there, have devised work that is appropriate to the street, and are proud to show it.

A good street theatre piece will be primarily visual, not verbal. Small interchanges and witty dialogue alone are hopeless. The piece must dance and move, making its statements through clear images. There can be jokes, oratory, dialogue, song, rhetoric if necessary. Rhythm and posture, colour and texture speak volumes when employed with care and imagination.

It should be possible to conceive of a street theatre piece as a series of sculptural pictures, to draw the key frames as a strip cartoon. Put yourself in the position of someone on the top of a passing bus, glimpsing your show for a moment – at any moment. They should be able to make something out of what they see . . . .

   . . . . a jet bomber menaces a cardboard city . . . .
   . . . . a sailor is hypnotised and dreams of a ghost ship . . . .
   . . . . the death of a gluttonous fatman . . . .
   . . . . the holy fool hunts for a nest . . . .

Although your script should be clear and simple – take a basic story to start with – it should not be simplistic. It still can, and should, work subtly, and on many levels. Later, certain devices are discussed to make this possible. A short piece, under half an hour in length, can move through many moods. It may open with up-front knockabout comedy, turn through sinister hunting and stalking to a dramatic fight, followed by a slow and tender lament. Maybe a joyous re-birth or resurrection completes the cycle.

First you need a story. Twenty minutes is a good length for a street piece. You can always extend it with music before and after, and that length gives you the possibility of repeating it a few times on the same day to fresh audiences.

> 'the object is to work at a presentation that talks to a community of people and that expresses what you (as a community) all know, but what no-one is saying: thoughts, images, observations and discoveries that are not printed in newspapers or made into movies: truth that may be shocking and honesty that is vulgar to the aesthete.'
>
> R. G. DAVIS
> *The San Francisco Mime Troupe: The First 10 Years*

Don't get into complex sub-plots that take up time to communicate. If you find you are wrestling with that problem, it is probably because your script is three shows rolled into one. Step back, re-look and think again. Tackle one show at a time. It's good to have a couple of pieces in the repertoire, but not essential. Decide that you intend to do one piece over and over again. You will learn fastest that way. Notice the point where you start to lose the audience, change it, rework it, try again.

Working completely in the round is very difficult in the street, unless the show is extremely minimal. We prefer to work to an audience that makes up two-thirds of a circle. The other sector can be made up of musicians, screens, flags, banners, or a vehicle. It is good, almost essential, to perform with your backs to something.

Start with an area at least ten paces wide by five paces deep. That is your performance area. Mark it out – we have used traffic cones painted up. Small painted oil drums will do. Behind the performance area you

The audience making up two-thirds of a circle— *The Eye of the Peacock*,
Brewery Arts Centre, Kendal, 1980.

need MORE space – roughly as much again, depending on the size o:
your props, where you can get ready, make quick costume changes, anc
store your stuff. It is useful to have the possibility of going out of sight
Park your van, if you have one, or wheelbarrow, or cart, put up a line o:
banners or a cloth screen as backdrop. You also have the possibility of a
box, a pair of steps at the back, or the roof of the van for height, which
helps with certain images tremendously, as you can frame the action, o»
comment upon it simultaneously. At the end of one story about property
and greed, during the singing of a curse, a burning city (cardboard inside
chicken wire, doused in paraffin) appeared high up at the back.

On the street, the performer must take power and charge the space, so
that no matter how many trucks drive past, or jets fly over, the audience's
attention is seized. That does not necessarily mean belting it out to
drown the surrounding din (although good lungs are a first require-
ment). It can mean a performance so totally still, controlled anc
concentrated that no-one can walk away from it.

Never forget to perform to the sides as well as the centre. The audience
is almost all round you. Showing a surprise object, for example, may
require a brisk tour along the entire front of the audience, holding it up
high. This takes longer than you think. Music helps, of course, to keep
the flow, and other characters on stage are wisest to freeze so as not to
distract. Signal clearly to the audience what you are going to do, then do
it purposefully. REACTION: This is the biggest whale I have ever seen
and I am going to harpoon it. Or REALIZATION: I have been too late

Taking power and charging the space to seize the audience's attention—*The Eye of the Peacock*, 1980.

rescuing these infants from the burning house but I shall hand them to their grieving parents.

Eye contact is vital – sharing with the audience. It is a vibrant communication. They can, after all, reach out and touch you if they want to. You are there – it is not the telly – it is really happening live before them. It may go wrong, it may be marvellous. The tensions are real, and that bond is what the performer works with, and must be awake to. After all, when I perform, what am I? I am just this 43 year old woman standing there on her two feet, singing to them, calling to them, speaking for them. I speak on behalf of any woman in that audience. Totally visible and vulnerable – not faked by any tricks of sound-mix, camera angles or lighting filters. I am no more or less than what they can see. But at the same time, I have to come over as larger than life, because this is performance. I have to hold the focus.

Always rehearse in a space of the proper size, and outdoors. It useless to work in a room. You have to learn to sing in the wind and be heard, to operate giant puppets in the rain and not slip over. The use of large puppets, masks or sculptural costumes changes the dynamic of the performance. Three masked madmen in a conspiratorial huddle would be positioned a few feet apart. They would never actually touch. The inclination of the head and body suggests the relationship. Circling, advancing, bowing with large puppets needs long and tiring rehearsal. The operators must be comfortable, secure and in full control, and have visual markers to know precisely where they are in the arena and what patterns they are making. Getting irrelevant characters off and out of the way is important. Clutter is confusing. Frame the scene with a tableau, then break it and move the story on. A bell, and/or placard can frame the scene: 'the man and woman quarrel' – but that device can get tedious over-used.

When two characters are having a dialogue, it is not usually necessary for them to look at each other, even to face each other. Each should address the audience, but it will be perfectly clear that they are having conversation. Gestures between them need to be large and clear. This sounds simple but is unbelievably difficult for beginners. This stylist device is least like any other 'acting' anyone will have done before. It may feel odd, but it does not look it. Make it appropriate to the scale you are working on. Get plenty of people to watch you in rehearsal, and position them all around the arena. They will soon tell you which bits were not clear, what they missed, and by employing this style you will feel that you are projecting to them. Remember in the street to make gestures twice as big, and if you're moving slowly, move *twice* as slowly.

One principal rule to adhere to is that it is the job of every performer and musician ALL THE TIME to concentrate completely on the action, particularly when it does not include them. The piece is strengthened by 100% attention.

Where you place musicians is most important. They must have an uninterrupted view of the action at all times, but the demands of the range of instruments may fix them to one spot. Performers who have time between their scenes can join the band, but only if this is possible without fuss. We generally place the band at one side of the action, near the back of the performance area, allowing room for an entrance between

Gestural acting, making shapes with bodies and costumes—*Summer Stories*, Milton Keynes, 1976.

them and any screen or vehicle serving as a backdrop. This way they are also near part of the audience. People enjoy watching music played almost as much as hearing it. Many people in England have never seen music played live and simply want to touch the saxophone or the percussion. We meet people who have never seen live performance either, and that is why sometimes they overstep the bounds and prod and bait you with sharp instruments (one performer was even set on fire!). It's all so exciting that they go over the top, and I suspect they have not really acknowledged that you are just a real person like them.

Assuming that all props and costumes are made, working hard all day will yield 3–5 minutes of performance ready to take out. So cut your scripts according to the time available. It is far better to take out a tight ten minute piece with all cues and movements well practised, than a sloppy half hour epic. With street theatre you often have ample opportunity to repeat your show two or three times. But, do allow yourself enough time to reset properly, repair things and draw a crowd. A simple sign, 'Next show here at 3 o'clock' builds anticipation, while you snatch a cup of tea.

When planning a street theatre tour, we always work by invitation and are paid a fee for a week's appearances, or more. Choosing where and when to perform is an art in itself. We prefer to slot into an existing framework of shows, fairs, carnivals, rather than do the tour of suburban shopping precincts that art administrators so readily wish to arrange. Playing to six bemused mums and a dog assuages the guilt of the administrator. They collect points via crosses on the map of their patch where they have injected product, meanwhile the poor street theatre company can so easily get demoralised. Aim to play where it is happening, rather than where it isn't. The show will be better. The English are reserved and will not easily venture out of their front doors on impulse, however dynamic the parade might be that's passing. Also it is a common fallacy that if it's on the street, it must be for the children. As we have little viable street life in this cold damp corner of northern Europe (we prefer to scuttle inside and shut the door) we do not have the outdoor performance traditions of the Mediterranean countries where much social life happens on the street.

The section in this book on processions, and the appendix on legal and safety aspects give useful advice also for staging a street theatre show. One particular point always to look into is suitable access to the playing area. Get someone to measure the width of the gates, if you hope to take in a vehicle, and also the width of the road you will be turning from. Some pedestrian precincts, which are wonderful street theatre venues, have their own problems. Sometimes the elevated ones, if you can ever find the service entrance to approach them, have a weight restriction covering vehicles allowed to drive on. They also get upset if the van leaves a patch of oil on their new paving – and quite rightly. You can always take precautions against this with an old sack or polythene sheet. We have always found the authorities co-operative in putting out parking cones for us the night before, to ensure enough parking space in the right area when we are due to perform in a public place next day.

When considering devices to enrich your performance, bear in mind that their function should not be to complicate the show, but to simplify and help the audience's understanding. Never be afraid to tell the same story in different ways in the same piece. We did a piece about landowners hunting stags. Although it certainly was more expansive than a street theatre show, some description will serve to indicate how we use scale change, and tell a story over and over again. This show was staged in the grounds of a stately home.

Ten stags were seen flitting from one copse to another, at a distance of five hundred yards. These were masked children holding antlers above their heads. Let's call them the stags. One broke away, came 'downstage' and became the victim of a savage hunt and disembowelling. This was a woman with back-pack puppet, giving a height of about eight feet, with good mobility. Let's call her the super stag. Things went from bad to worse and later in the show a giant tortoise crept into the arena, bearing model of the stately home on its back. This flipped over, and out came hand puppets which were miniatures of the land owners. Up came puppet stag, no more than fifteen inches high, and killed them. This was a premonition of their death, which we were about to see. Powerful, although it was a mini-stag. The focus then shifted and from the deep distance we saw two megastags. These were giant constructions, running on a triangular welded metal frame with car wheels, pushed by operators hidden inside, and standing nearly fifteen feet high. They dwarfed the land owners and eventually ran them down and into the ground. The essential point here is consistency of design, colour, modelling features, etc., so that it is unquestionable that one puppet is a miniature of another, or of a performer (a device we frequently use).

We mix puppets with live actors; sometimes giant puppets, sometimes rod puppets showing above a backdrop – never marionettes. An evolutionary procession of dinosaurs may be nothing more complex than large two dimensional cut-outs on sticks, painted white (beware cardboard in the rain – varnish it if you can). This use of puppets can be simultaneous with the action, commenting upon it, framing it, not simply illustrating it. This way you can expand the scale and escape from the mundane. A puppet can be seen to make a journey to another planet, which later is revealed as no planet at all, just the tip of a grinning skull!

Transformations are exciting. The audience enjoys and admires seeing something amazing happen before their eyes. At its simplest, the Fairy Godmother's head-dress might become a disturbing insect mask, as she sings; or a greedy old woman's cloak is drawn out to become a motorway. Escalation in a story can be graphically portrayed via objects, or by costume changes. The old woman in question acquires bigger and more monstrous hats as her greed grows. Characters can get fatter and fatter, or a large monster can totter and crash down, only to reveal a performer coming out from inside wearing something quite different. To avoid too much unnecessary walking to and fro, which is uninteresting, a stagehand can walk on and formally remove one hat and replace it with a bigger one.

Hats feature a lot – this is because height is important. Never have important action happening on the ground. Only the first couple of rows can see, because your audience is often standing. Toss things, have them up on poles, wave them in the air. We use windsocks a lot. A black one can be the definitive funereal touch to a death, several brightly painted ones dancing in the air can be a celebration all on their own. We often release large helium balloons, to carry aloft an image or a seed of the performance. You will learn by trial and error about gas spanners, reserve balloons in case of accident, wind direction, high buildings. A useful rule of thumb: you may need at least three 4 foot balloons tied together to bear the weight of even an origami paper bird.

How many performers? Six good people is usually enough. You can do a good show with less. More is not necessarily helpful, as each of your six can take several roles, with careful planning. Problems can arrive if you

'Above all, enjoying it ... that communicates most of all'—*The Eye of the Peacock*, 1980.

want a procession to come through – be it black submarines or carnival animals. The temptation is to grab volunteers. Do rehearse them; it is a learnt technique to know how fast to move, what space to leave behind the one in front, and most important, how to give life and energy to a puppet. There is a legendary company that trains for five years to wave a banner! Also, have a bag of black trousers always. Nothing diminishes an image more than the universal tired blue jeans revealed at the bottom.

Our attitude to make-up is changing. We stopped using severe and extreme make-up in the street after a few years. We found it was alienating to the audience. We do use lots of disgusting false noses.

As you go along you will learn about the audience. Why the three-year olds cry, when the one's and two's don't, why the dog on a piece of string dragged behind the children on the front row is a nightmare, and why so many people choose to watch you at work back-stage rather than watch your show. Above all, enjoy it, be proud of your performance and open up to the audience – that communicates most of all.

(ii) Music

LUK MISHALLE, with amendments from BORIS HOWARTH and PETER MOSER

From the beginning, Welfare State has used music to make theatre. It has always aimed to be a functional music, neither a decoration of the theatre, nor music in its own right. It joins words, images, movement and environment to make up the total performance. In most cases, it will be played by the performers in the show, who will also have been the makers of costumes, and of the sculptural images which play a major part in Welfare State work.

There are seldom Welfare State musicians as such. Most company members play an instrument at some usable level of skill. This often results in an unpredictable combination of sounds, and the overall sound of a Welfare State band will certainly be fresh and eclectic. The conscious use of a wide range of source material, and the different inputs of specialist, highly-skilled musical directors, have together contributed over the years to make the distinctive Welfare State band sound. It is a sound based on popular forms from around the world and back in history, the quirky, rich, humane sound of players enjoying themselves.

In many ways, the basic reasons for the company's style have not changed from the company's beginnings. Early shows were rough and physical, and sharp enough to ride over and cut through traffic noise, as

'Strong, energetic, acoustic sound'—Welfare State's Blood-stained Colonial Band on the street in Burnley, 1976.

well as being able to attract audiences who might be some streets away. Music was used in the overture procession to attract the audience with a strong, energetic, acoustic sound, rather than the smooth, pre-recorded music they would be used to. In performance, music gives atmosphere and punctuates the performers' every move. Words are often difficult to project outside and so music takes over and gives life and emotion to images and performance. This 'silent film' style relies on simplicity and allows anybody to be a 'musician' if they summon the right theatrical energy. This was, and remains, the basis of Welfare State's outdoor style.

The Professionals

Most cultures produce the specialist musicians whose technique and understanding of the complexity of musical form are essential for the continuation and richness of pure music. Theatre music and musicians work in an entirely different art form, with new parameters governed by the servicing of word and image. Rarely is music the sole focus.

Initially with Welfare State there were no teachers and the beginnings were an instinctive 'catch as catch can'. 'No musos around? Never mind. Just bang this drum when I say so!' When professional musicians of the calibre of Mike Westbrook, Lol Coxhill and Greg Stephens were engaged, their virtuosity called into question the validity of this hybrid theatre music that ordinary jack-of-all-trades theatre musicians could produce. The beauty and technique of the professional is hard to resist, but, convictions apart, sheer economics won the day and laid the firm foundations of a musical style that is still evolving.

Software – *Musical Sources and Models*

Where skills are limited, and a wide variety of textures required, the Musical Director becomes a musical collator as much as a composer in his own right. Each M.D. used by Welfare State would bring his own style, his own amalgam of sources, and this would merge with the pool of knowledge acquired from previous shows. A proportion of this input only lasted for one show, perhaps because it was unique to one player and lost with him, perhaps because it required too much skill or too precise instrumentation, perhaps because it was too esoteric for audiences to enjoy. A large proportion, however, was incorporated into an ever-widening source-pool which became base-material for the next show. Welfare State's music is the sum of it's history, in which new influences are constantly being woven into an ever-growing patchwork. 'Mad Song', composed by Westbrook, with Fox lyrics, is an example of an old piece often revived in new circumstances. It was written in the early seventies* and has been used again and again, but recently became the Falcon tune and song in 'Bellevue' in the Doomsday Colouring Book tour of 1982.

As well as writing fresh music, contributing new sources or a particular style, each musical director also helps to equip the company to play that type of music. They also help to stack up and maintain the musical bank of the company.

Hardware – *Instruments*

What follows are suggestions that have grown out of the practical experience of Welfare State's music-making. While we don't claim to have said the last word on street music, these reports from the front-line

Recorded on Welfare State Songs, 1978.

will certainly give less experienced theatre musicians a basis from which to make successful music.

Percussion
Everyone who dances, claps or taps their feet has a sense of rhythm. Given the right situation everyone can 'keep time'. However, playing percussion effectively requires discipline, concentration and as much practice as any other instrument. Many percussion instruments are technically simple but putting a drumming piece together with five people can take hours of practice.

There are some percussive instruments which are very useful played solo in theatre work, because they provide particular atmosphere with little means. A bass drum for building tension, underlining action, death; a cymbal for expectation, creation; a gong for sudden change of atmosphere or announcement; a bell for a distant procession . . . It is easy to experiment with these.

The bass drum played with a large headed stick is the basis on which most of our drumming rests. Three main sounds can be made.

♩   Hitting the open skin

♩   Damping with the other hand

♩   Hitting the dampened skin

Using these three sounds, a typical Latin riff would be:

Waltz time would be:

Add to this a snare drum, shakers, cowbell and cymbal and you have the basis of a drumming band.

Stick and hand drums (congas, tom-toms, bongos) are technically more difficult to play and should not be handed out freely. They can be boring and confusing when not played clearly. The drumming techniques in W.S.I. seem to be passed on aurally. There are plenty of book tutors, teaching records, but finding a teacher is more satisfactory.

Skin and hand drums carry a long way, but are difficult to handle on processions.

W.S.I. uses an enormous amount of small percussion: here is a list with brief suggestions:

Tambourine	can give an enormous lift played well. Leave spaces though. This avoids the common pit-fall of slowing down.
Cowbell	mainly used as a good loud time-keeper, and for adding top 'free' layers.
Shakers	have incredible drive. Mobile replacements for hi-hat cymbal. Choose the right one for the job. Very easy to make.
Maraccas	good rhythm instrument. Difficult to keep precise. Better used indoors.
Guiro (fish)	scraped with a stick. Important in salsa-based music.
Cymbals	proper marching cymbals are very expensive; cheaper (Chinese) ones tend to crack. Possible to use an old hi-hat pair. Can be played open, or damped against the chest.
Vibraslap	a good extra marker, with an idiosynchratic (and humorous!) sound.
Triangle	useful in dance music, especially cajun. Can be played open or damped.
Agogo	double cowbell tuned in fifths. Good solo instrument.
Cuiché	can replace guiro and/or maraccas. Very penetrating sound inside and out. Needs some skill or it can sound messy.
Claves	carry a long way; give typically Latin sound. Better used indoors.
Gongs, Cymbals, Temple blocks	good atmosphere instruments.

It is possible to make equivalents of some of these instruments; experiment with this. The 'real' thing often costs a lot of money.

Brass

Trumpets/ Cornets	very useful outdoors for their cutting tone, but require experienced players. Invariably stand out as main melody instrument. In the rain, wet lips can be a problem.
Tenor Horn	sweet sounding (like Flugel horn). Reads in Eb.
Trombone	provides a rich body to the sound and can stand in for a bass instrument.
Euphonium	easier to learn than the above. Very useful bass

instrument in a small band, especially if you don't fancy carrying a sousaphone around!

Baritone Horn	has the same range as euphonium, but a differen bore, and sounds less sweet in the top register.

Note to brass arrangers: check out which clefs and keys the players rea in and also their comfortable range. All except trombone and tenor hor players usually read in Bb. Horn players with brass band training wi usually read Bb treble clef, but otherwise C bass clef.

Reeds

Saxophones are ideal outdoor instruments. However, they must b cleaned and oiled regularly, or rusty springs and stiff keys will incu expensive overhaul costs.

Soprano sax	good solo instrument for creating a wide variety of moods. Can be difficult to tune.
Baritone sax	delivers an excellent bass tone. Reads in Eb.
Tenor sax	gives body, like a trombone. Outstanding solo instrument, capable of sounding either sweet or bluesy.
Alto sax	a good range for melody lines, and parallel harmonies with trumpet or tenor. Reads in Eb.
Clarinets	are a little fragile for playing outside and are difficult to keep in tune with the brass. Susceptible to rain and sun, and to temperature changes, so have to be used carefully outdoors. Clarinets have very distinctive sounds in their different registers. In a big band, are excellent used in the top registers.
Alto and bass clarinet	expensive and rare, but useful for indoor theatr music.
Double reeds (oboes, bassoons)	a very rich sound used on the Winter Satellite show for carolling at the end of 1982 was oboe, flugelhorn and trombone. A bassoon was used for a reggae bass line in 'Camel March' on Starship Vesuvius tour, early 1982. Fragile, and not really suited for walking with. W.S.I. tend to substitute double reed folk instruments such as:
Bombardes	French instrument, often used with bagpipes and drums. Can be difficult to keep in tune, bu does have a very direct sound which carries well.

agpipes	create an enormous full sound; immediate audience response.
accordion, melodeon and oncertina	can also be classed as reed instruments. They give tune and harmony, and can move! Melodeons are exceptional in giving drive and lift to dance music. Accordion gives a smaller band a rich texture, but can sound over-sweet to some. Both, when accompanied by a lead solo instrument, provide a good busking band sound. However, they all suffer in the rain. Can be played under a plastic cape.

Baritone Sax and Bagpipes at *Parliament in Flames*, Milton Keynes, 1978.

histles and Flutes

in whistle	probably the toughest instruments you can buy cheaply, and not too hard to learn. Very good outdoors, and for dance music. They're usually slightly sharp, and so stick out more than you would expect them to. Very good atmospheric theatre sound.

Concert flutes	can be helpful doubling a clarinet part. Tend t‹ be too soft to use in combination with brass an‹ reeds. The 'rough' quality of W.S.I.'s music means that they are not used much.
Piccolo	carries a long way, but otherwise of limited us‹

Strings

Stringed instruments will usually need amplification in outdoor wor‹ and are not particularly mobile. (Although good processions have be‹‹ done using a violin amplified by a battery-powered 'Pignose' amp.) Ca‹ must be taken to keep the rain off them.

Banjos	work well in acoustic bands, but audiences tend to thi‹ you are a Dixieland jazz band!
Violins	have been used extensively in Barn-Dance music, and
Guitars,	accompany individual songs.
Mandolins	

Electrical

From time to time W.S.I. has used amplified sound for particul‹ purposes. This ranges from general use of a P.A. system to, mo‹ recently, the use of electric piano, bass and guitar to create ‹ contemporary rock sound. We rarely use a drum kit, therefore it ‹ possible to do with a minimal P.A. system, although this will also deper‹ on the size of the space and audience.

Do not underestimate the problems of using a P.A. system. Practi‹ with mikes, make sure you can hear yourself AND EACH OTHER. Be su‹ the mixer knows the sound you want, and can be relied on.

Synthesisers, taped sound and effects have all been used for particul‹ shows. 'Starship Vesuvius' tour had a 'spacey' feel and the use ‹ electronic sound enhanced this, and ranged from background atmc‹ pheres to an over-the-top electronic version of a folk dance tune 'Winst‹ Gallop'. For the last large-scale bonfire shows 'Parliament in Flames' ‹ Tamworth and Catford, all of these sounds have been used to accompa‹ the large images.

Buying Instruments

It is usually better to buy a good second-hand instrument than a che‹ new one. Cheap ones aren't usually strongly built, and street music ‹ hard on them. Well-used, cheap instruments have poor second-ha‹ value. It is a good thing when buying instruments to take along ‹ experienced musician to spot faults and potential trouble areas. Anoth‹ way to gain access to a good instrument is to join a brass band; some w‹ provide you with an instrument, and teaching is free! A theatre gro‹ might want to invest in a basic percussion set. One way of doing this is ‹

cannibalise from an old drumkit, taking the bass, snare and cymbals especially, and either make or buy the odd bits of small percussion. Small percussion instruments for latin-style music can be expensive, and should be bought only when you have a good idea how to use them to best advantage.

In Performance – *Three situations*

1. Processions

From its beginnings, Welfare State has used processional music as self-contained mobile theatre, sometimes to advertise another event, sometimes to take people to a new space for more focused theatre or music performances.

No matter what instrumentation is used, it is vital to play music that is easy enough for all players to feel confident with. Confidence and discipline go together, and only when you have the two together is it possible to start moving and dancing as you play so that your pleasure in the music starts to communicate. This is particularly important when you work 'cold', arriving unannounced in a shopping street, for instance, where the individual people have no 'audience' expectations. Uncertainty and aggression will both alienate, whereas confidence and pleasure coming from the performers will generate the same in the audience. Choosing a simple basis for the music also opens up possibilities for local musicians to join the band, and ensures that things don't stop because one player is absent, or has had to drop out of the band temporarily.

The organisation and line-up of a marching band is very important. W.S.I. tends to put the percussion at the back, then, moving forward through tenor saxes, altos and trumpets and clarinets. Often the trombones would be at the front, however, to give them room for their slides. It is important that a strong player is in the middle rows to give signals and hold the band together. Brass instruments are uni-directional so often the percussionists cannot hear the front-line melody players. From tune to tune, melody players can move and turn round for sections, to help overcome this. There must be an acknowledged band leader, from whom musical cues are taken. A separate job is pacing the band, keeping them tight and looking out for traffic or obstacles. This person can either be a confident player in the front with sufficient experience of marching bands, or a non-musician out front (ours often carry and twirl a huge parasol) who will liaise with the band leader.

So, the band has formed up, knows where it is processing, who is giving it cues, and is confident in what it is playing. From now on, it is important to remember that the band is to be looked at as well as heard. It is a visual spectacle, wearing visually exciting costume, and existing as a single visual image. Moving and playing, then, is not just walking but more like dancing, which can get out of control, and so it is important to

A Welfare State band processing through Ackworth, West Yorkshire, for *The Plague and the Cowman*, 1979.

stay close enough to the other players to hear what they are playing. the open air, the whole sound your band is making may well be uncle It is essential to play physically and to communicate visually, bu especially with less experienced players, the constraints of listenin playing and remaining disciplined mean that it is useful to have geometrical reference point, to bear in mind the overall shape the ba makes as it moves along.

Once a Welfare State procession band has moved off, we try not stop. After all, in most processions, the audience changes all the time, there's no need to change the music for them! If, for the players' sake change is required, we try to do it where hundreds of people are watching. Energy will sag in both performers and audience otherwise. there is to be a change of mood or rhythm, it should be known abo before, by other members of the procession. Dancing performer especially those with giant puppets, will be thrown by unexpect changes, and the confusion will look sloppy.

It is important to organise how the band will form up when you sto Whether you form a semi-circle, for instance, or remain in marchi order will be decided by dramatic factors related to the performan piece, as a rule. If it is possible, on your route, try to go through a cover precinct; the band will always sound good and it boosts confidence

The following two pieces were used throughout the Doomsday
·louring Book tour in 1982, and have excellent street music qualities.
ovious beginnings and endings are vital for giving confidence to the
ayers and a good impression to the audience.

DESPEDIDA

This is a Peruvian tune that was used in various arrangements. At its
nplest it was played in unison by a band of up to fourteen wind players
th a three person percussion accompaniment.

A simple accompanying part was added and for more focused
uations a middle section and more complex parts came in. It was
ened by a simple solo trumpet fanfare that gave the beat and called the
nd to order and concentration.

'Despedida' and the following piece 'Boogie' were both learnt aurally,
ən though this took some time to teach some players. Reading music
ile processing puts a barrier up to the giving of right energy.

BOOGIE

oven Jan Buiten Western Boogie

In contrast to Despedida this piece was started by the bass drum:

The riff repeats three times, then moves straight into the first bar of the piece. After maybe three repeats of the 'tune' the brass dissolves into total chaos and free improvisation for a short break, the bass drum breaking in with the riff above just once to start the piece again. The ending comes out of the chaos in the same way, ending on the brass chord with no movements into the piece again. A simple but effective piece.

Both Despedida and Boogie are up tempo numbers and suit the feel of a carnival procession. Slower pieces are also strong, but be careful. It is hard to walk briskly and play slowly!

2. Theatre Music

Welfare State's theatre performances can be indoors or out, static or moving, and music to accompany performance has to be able to embrace all that variety. At one extreme, for instance, was the many-houred vigil kept by Lol Coxhill, Lou Glandfield and Colin Wood at the Memorial for the First Astronaut, a static sculptured space in the Lancashire countryside. The first requirements of *that* situation were stamina and strong lips! Most Welfare State music reflects the tastes and inclinations of particular musical directors and is either 'mood' music to support images and words, or settings of songs. The common factors in most of our music have been its unusual instrumentation and its eclectic use of styles. There are few hard-and-fast rules in the company about theatre music other than the obligation to express in sound what is being expressed in words and images. Music is present as an element in the total theatre experience to heighten its intensity, and to lend coherence to sometimes disparate and contradictory images.

Outdoors, where the scale must be larger, instrumentation must be geared to the need for volume, and the need to be weatherproof, so we are usually back to the procession instrumentation. Where it is possible, however, we will use electrical amplification both for instruments and synthesisers, and for pre-recorded sound tapes. When music accompanies large outdoor events, such as the 1982 'Scarecrow Zoo' at Bracknell Arts Centre, which had a centre-piece based around fire, it is important to be flexible enough to cope with unpredictability. In these situations we use 'process' music – music with no defined beginning or end – which can be 'faded' in or out as it is needed. For more precise moods we use a repertoire of pieces with particular feelings to them. You can usually rely on certain archetypal actions appearing in a Welfare State show; after the

WELFARE STATE INTERNATIONAL

present

A NEW ALBUM

OF

SONGS

Curses   Carols   Rants   Lullabies

Calypso   Ballad   Reggae   Invocation

THE BEST OF THE DECADE:

Ten years of rich, diverse & unparalleled creativity
brought together on one album of

EXQUISITE BEAUTY & BACCHANALIAN JOLLITY

With a Remarkable Collection of Unusual Instruments

CELEBRATE THE SEASON WITH MAGIC

welcome, birth, death, entry of good or evil, a dance between opposi
forces, a farewell . . . and there are obvious, but effective, musical mea
to accompany them. Good creations, for instance, have a cymb
crescendo, bad ones a bass drum roll. 'Rasa Sayang', a tradition
Malaysian tune has been one of our favourite farewell tunes of late. (S
appendix.)

Within any one show a wide range of musical effects may be used. .
the following music script for 'Wasteland and the Wagtail (Japan, 198:
demonstrates.

Setting – a mountain side, half an hour before dusk. The audien
       assembles at the bottom, climbs steeply to the mummers spac
       After holocaust, descends scene by scene to the bottom for
       celebratory dance.
Overture – whistle players situated in bushes and trees as audien
       ascends the slope.
Mummers play – accompanied by congas and small percussion.
Wasteland Dinner Party into Holocaust – tape, live synthesis
       explosives and firework noise. Ending in silence and solo voi
       song.
Procession down with Giant Puppet – mad brass band playi.
       Despedida (in the dark down the rocky slope).
Shadow Play – violin, Northumbrian pipe, gongs and percussion.
Short 'mystical' procession – two Highland Bagpipes.
Lighting of lantern images and fireworks – Flugelhorn joins bagpipe
Procession to Dance – Drumband – (Bayonne).
Dance – stage band with small P.A.
Farewell – Bagpipes 'Auld Lang Syne'.

All of these dovetailed into each other and created a continuous mus
pattern. Silence was used for effect only once.

3. Dance Music
W.S.I. found it was also easy to make social dancing possible
semi-private situations, such as a party after a naming ceremony or
wedding. In public performance, however, there were difficulties
getting our audiences to dance in an unselfconscious, relaxed way. V
had been experimenting with different styles of ethnic dance, includi
Ghanaian-based styles, but we could seldom make it shift in
'participatory' dance. Then in 1980, we started to experiment with t
traditional 'barn dance' format. We advertised the shows as 'Ba
Dances', and people came, and they danced, especially in the North
England, where social dancing of this kind still has some meanin
Interestingly, within this format we were able to put some hard theat
pieces. Slowly we built up a fairly straightforward repertoire of mus

ased on the English folk music tradition. Next, we began to
xperiment, using a rhythm box, or reggae and latin-based percussion
ombined with traditional square dances. Finally, we simply used our
wn intuition as to which different elements from which traditions
ould fuse together, a principle much like that employed by the makers
the company. That principle has its dangers. For a time we tended to
eggaefie' everything; after a while it reduced to a crude formula: two

A Barn Dance Band, Ulverston, 1980.

ts on the cowbell on the offbeat. Now we try to exercise more care –
orrowing from all styles and cultures, but borrowing with respect both
r the style and for the music in general.

Some situations won't need, or can't take, set dances. When there is
ready a shared intimacy in the audience, set dances can impose a false
llity. More often, a *few* set dances are needed to relax people who are
lative strangers to one another, before opening out into more 'free'
nces. Welfare State has a repertoire of waltzes, rock 'n' role, reggae,
nk etc., and over the summer of 1982, when we performed 'The
oomsday Colouring Book' shows, we greatly increased the 'dance
otential' of our music by adding electric guitar, piano and bass to our
ormal' brass, reed and string ensemble.

Learning and Playing Together

It was suggested above that joining a brass band would be a useful way o
learning an instrument. There are also recognised schools, and teacher
of music, which it is as well to use in order not to build up bad habits. A
for individual practice, the old adage 'little and often' applies. Te
minutes a day is worth more than two hours on end on Sunday afternoon
As important for theatre music like ours is to play with other people, i
order to learn about harmonies and ensemble sounds in practice.
group of inexperienced musicians playing together can still learn fror
each other, but they will also learn far quicker by together employing
teacher, whose fee they can split amongst themselves. It is important t
distinguish between performance and practice. We never allow peopl
casually to join in a performance. 'Jamming' in a performance situatio
usually boils down to the lowest common denominator ('Oh, When th
Saints . . .') and only people who share a common musical languag
should risk exploring. Above all, avoid practising publicly, i
performance. Better to feel confident in something simple an
well-rehearsed than nervous in something over-ambitious.

Our workshop techniques take five broad forms.

1. A given arrangement, rehearsed as written, with some r
   arrangement according to capabilities.
2. Workshop arrangements, in which the arrangement is develope
   experimentally.
3. Parameter Improvisation. We define certain areas of operation f
   each instrument such as following one particular character,
   defining a mood to accompany an action.
4. Ethnic Skills. Learning by rote traditional patterns, such as Africa
   and Latin percussion, that are later used out of their tradition
   context.
5. Dances. Musicians learn to do the dances they are to accompany (e.
   in the Barn Dances) so that they know which cross-rhythms they c
   and can't use.

Finale and Looking to the Future

At present, Welfare State is consolidating its peculiar, home-mad
eclectic house-style. All musical members of the company contribu
material to a greater or lesser extent, drawing freely from mainly ethn
roots, but with some influences from the classical traditions of East a
West. The overall multi-skill ethic of the company extends to musi
expertise, and that results in music rich in tone-colour (because of t
unusual combinations of instruments) and 'amateur' in execution (th
is, energetic, committed, and disciplined without sounding slick). T
company works on two levels at once, for it has a full-time professio
commitment to the excellence of its product musically, and a full-ti

multiplicity of roles creating popular accessibility and possible amateur models. Within this dichotomy could be the seeds of destruction, were there not a constant re-assessment of standards. We aim not to lower our standards but to broaden them by creating the theatrical equivalent of the Decathlon. We seek a diversity which is itself professional, but which allows each separate activity to be amateur, in the best sense. Ultimately, we are looking for a new Primitivism, where the shaman gets his ticket by vision, rather than by simply professional expertise. Welfare State's music is central to the establishment of that vision.

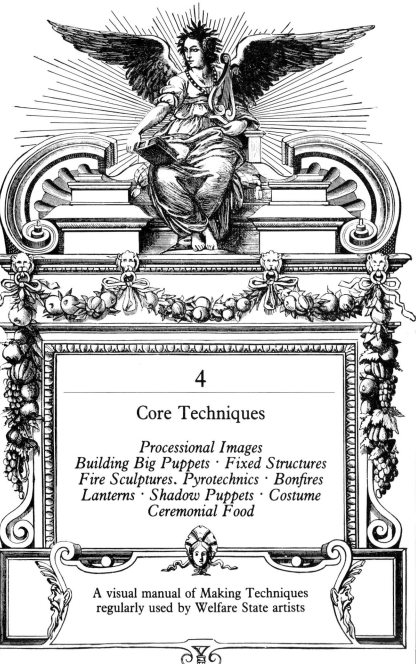

4

Core Techniques

Processional Images
Building Big Puppets · Fixed Structures
Fire Sculptures. Pyrotechnics · Bonfires
Lanterns · Shadow Puppets · Costume
Ceremonial Food

A visual manual of Making Techniques
regularly used by Welfare State artists

PROCESSIONAL IMAGES

- TONY LEWERY -

WINDSOCKS CAN BE MADE FROM
ANY LIGHT CLOTH — (MUSLIN OR FINE COTTON IS BEST)   MAKE THE SOCK
SHAPE FAIRLY SIMPLE — A TAPERING TUBE WHICH IS LARGER AT THE FIXED END THAN AT THE TAIL, OR
THE WIND WILL NOT FILL IT PROPERLY. KEEP THE MOUTH OPEN WITH A HOOP OF WILLOW WITHIE SEWN C
STUCK INTO THE TUBE. ATTACH AT LEAST THREE STRINGS TO THE LOOP OR IT WILL TRY TO SQUEEZE
CLOSED OR BREAK. KEEPING THEM ALL THE SAME LENGTH, TIE THEM TO THE POLE. (FOR PERFECTION
FIX TO A FISHING LINE SWIVEL FIRST) USE DYES OR INKS FOR COLOURING, AS PAINT WILL STIFFEN THE
MATERIAL AND SPOIL THE FLOW AND RIPPLE OF THE CLOTH.

ANY BAND NEEDS A BANDLEADER BOTH VISUALLY AND
PRACTICALLY — SOMEONE WHOSE MAIN CONCERN IS THE
OPERATION OF THE BAND AS A UNIT — CONTROLLING
THEIR MARCHING SPEED, KEEPING THEM TOGETHER AND
ON THE RIGHT ROUTE WHILE THEY CONCENTRATE ON
THE MUSIC. AN IMPORTANT JOB NEEDING A GOOD
PERFORMER.

S, BANNERS AND ALMOST ANYTHING CARRIED ON
F POLES ARE VALUABLE PROCESSIONAL IMAGES.
HT IS IMPORTANT — CLEARLY SEEN ABOVE THE
S OF THE CROWD — DEFINING AND PUNCTUATING
PACE OCCUPIED BY THE PROCESSION. A SIMPLE
IS A GOOD PERFORMANCE TOOL — ALSO GIVES
ARRIER VISIBLE AUTHORITY, MAKING HIM OR HER
FUL LEADER AND STEWARD.

A PROCESSION IS A CROSS BETWEEN A PIECE OF SCULPTURE AND A DANCE — EACH INGREDIENT NEEDS FRAMING
BY ITS NEIGHBOUR, SEPARATE ENOUGH TO BE SEEN AS AN IMAGE BUT CLOSE ENOUGH TO BE AN OBVIOUS LINK IN
A PROCESSIONAL CHAIN. IT NEEDS TO MAKE AN IMMEDIATE AND COHERENT IMPACT, PROJECTING A BLEND OF
SOUND, IMAGERY AND ENERGY WITHIN A FEW SECONDS.

BAND IS LIKELY TO BE THE BIGGEST SINGLE IMAGE — THEIR
ARANCE NEEDS CAREFUL CONSIDERATION — MAYBE ALL DRESSED
ACK AND WHITE, OR STRIPES OR WITH PART OF THE BODY BAND—
— A BLOCK OF COLOUR AND TEXTURE THAT RELATES TO THE
LE IMAGE AND STYLE OF THE REST OF THE PROCESSION.

INFLATED RUBBER GLOVES.

THATCHING STRAW

RED REAR REFLECTOR

BAMBOO FRAMEWORK→

EX-INDUSTRIAL ROADSWEEPER BRUSHES.

HESSIAN COVERING STRING

PAPIER MACHÉ TEETH OVER WIRE FRAME

CRUSHED PAPER 'SCALES' ON WIRE NETTING

COLOURED RAG STRIPS.

ROLLED CARDBOARD CHIMNEYS GLUED INTO A BLOCK OF POLYSTYRENE

SMOKE PELLETS BURN INSIDE ONE TIN-CAN FITTED INSIDE ANOTHER WITH ALUMINIUM FOIL INSULATION BETWEEN THEM.

SUPERSTUCTURE HAS WHITE PAINTED DESIGN ON TRANSPARENT SHEET, WITH SIX BATTERY-LIT BULBS MOUNTED INSIDE

HULL AND CABIN MA OF SHEET FIBREGL WIRED AND NAILED TO WOODEN DOWELL FRAMEWC GLUED TOGETHER

BOW, STERN, AND ENDS OF CROSS STRENGTHENED WITH FIBREGLASS RESIN

SEPARATE LOWER FRAME MADE WITH BAMBOO AND SPLIT BAMBOO WITH JOINTS BOUND WITH RESIN CLOTH; BLACK FLOOR-LENGTH SKIRT STUCK TO OUTER BAR, WHITE TASSEL CLOTH OVERLAPPING TO INNER BA

CARDBOARD CONSTRUCTION

CUT OUT SHAPES WITH SCALPEL OR
SHARP KNIFE — WORK FAST, BY TRIAL
AND ERROR — EXPECT AND ACCEPT
SOME WASTAGE

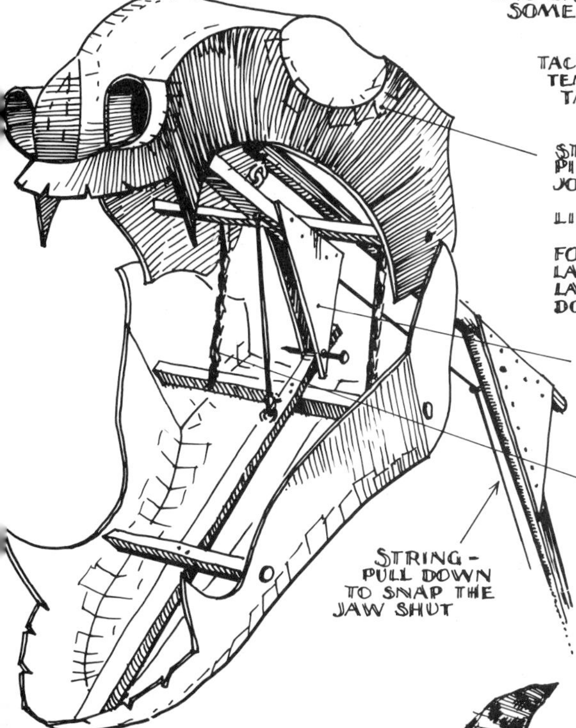

TACK CORNERS TOGETHER
TEMPORARILY WITH MASKING
TAPE

FOR FINISHED
STRENGTH, PASTE OVERLAPPING
PIECES OF PAPER ALONG THE
JOINT

USE A STRONG GLUE
LIKE P.V.A. WOOD GLUE

FOR MASSIVE STRENGTH
LAMINATE ON A SECOND
LAYER OF CARDBOARD AND
DOUBLE THE JOINTS.

LIGHT WOODEN FRAMEWORK
WITH LOOSE JOINT TO
ENSURE EASE OF
MOVEMENT OF
LOWER JAW

SHOCKCORD, OR STRIP OF
CAR INNER TUBE, JUST
SUPPORTING WEIGHT
OF LOWER JAW

STRING —
PULL DOWN
TO SNAP THE
JAW SHUT

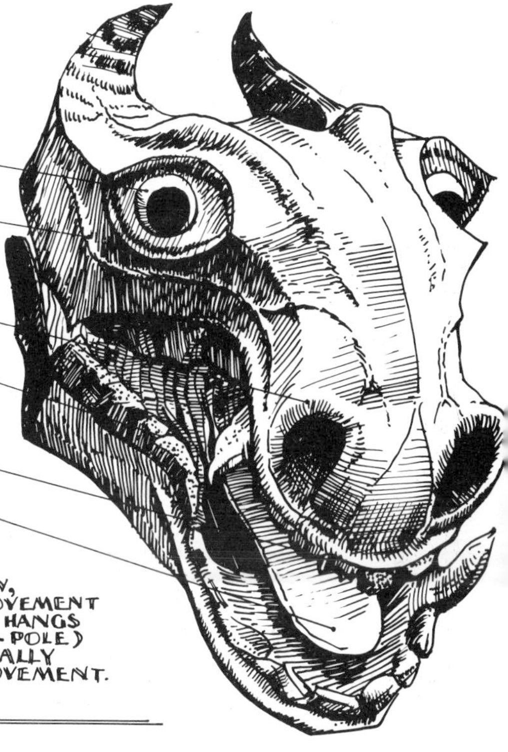

HALF A TENNIS BALL USED
FOR THE EYEBALL

BALER TWINE GLUED ON
AS VEINS

EXTRA BUILT-UP SHAPE
AND MODELLING WITH
PAPIER-MACHE

BACK TEETH CUT OUT OF
BLOCK OF FOAM RUBBER
STAPLED IN POSITION

PAINTED WITH EMULSION
PAINTS THEN VARNISHED
FOR EXTRA WEATHERPROOFING

FRONT TEETH THICKENED
WITH SHEET FOAM RUBBER

TONGUE MADE FROM SPRINGY
SHEET PLASTIC, COVERED WITH
SILKY CLOTH

BECAUSE OF THE ELASTICATED JAW,
QUIVERY TONGUE, AND LOOSE MOVEMENT
OF THE HEAD (ALL THE WEIGHT HANGS
FROM ONE POINT ON THE NECK-POLE)
THE WHOLE IMAGE IS AUTOMATICALLY
ANIMATED BY THE SLIGHTEST MOVEMENT.

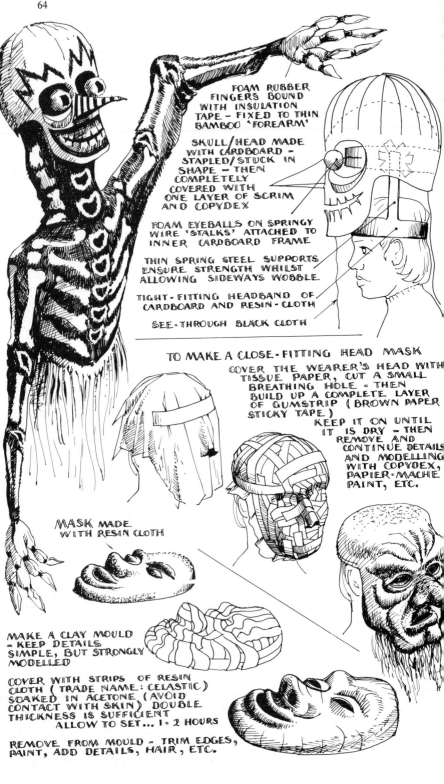

FOAM RUBBER FINGERS BOUND WITH INSULATION TAPE - FIXED TO THIN BAMBOO 'FOREARM'

SKULL/HEAD MADE WITH CARDBOARD - STAPLED/STUCK IN SHAPE - THEN COMPLETELY COVERED WITH ONE LAYER OF SCRIM AND COPYDEX

FOAM EYEBALLS ON SPRINGY WIRE 'STALKS' ATTACHED TO INNER CARDBOARD FRAME

THIN SPRING STEEL SUPPORTS ENSURE STRENGTH WHILST ALLOWING SIDEWAYS WOBBLE

TIGHT-FITTING HEADBAND OF CARDBOARD AND RESIN-CLOTH

SEE-THROUGH BLACK CLOTH

TO MAKE A CLOSE-FITTING HEAD MASK

COVER THE WEARER'S HEAD WITH TISSUE PAPER, CUT A SMALL BREATHING HOLE = THEN BUILD UP A COMPLETE LAYER OF GUMSTRIP (BROWN PAPER STICKY TAPE.)

KEEP IT ON UNTIL IT IS DRY - THEN REMOVE AND CONTINUE DETAILS AND MODELLING WITH COPYDEX, PAPIER-MACHIE PAINT, ETC.

MASK MADE WITH RESIN CLOTH

MAKE A CLAY MOULD - KEEP DETAILS SIMPLE, BUT STRONGLY MODELLED

COVER WITH STRIPS OF RESIN CLOTH (TRADE NAME: CELASTIC) SOAKED IN ACETONE (AVOID CONTACT WITH SKIN) DOUBLE THICKNESS IS SUFFICIENT ALLOW TO SET... 1 = 2 HOURS

REMOVE FROM MOULD - TRIM EDGES, PAINT, ADD DETAILS, HAIR, ETC.

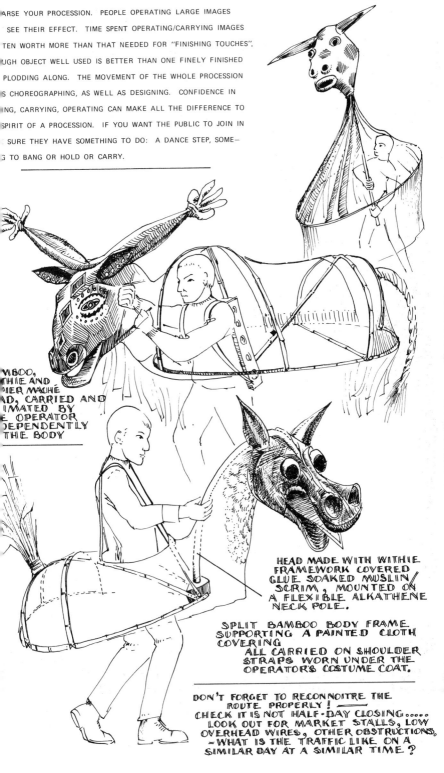

ARSE YOUR PROCESSION. PEOPLE OPERATING LARGE IMAGES
 SEE THEIR EFFECT. TIME SPENT OPERATING/CARRYING IMAGES
TEN WORTH MORE THAN THAT NEEDED FOR "FINISHING TOUCHES".
UGH OBJECT WELL USED IS BETTER THAN ONE FINELY FINISHED
 PLODDING ALONG. THE MOVEMENT OF THE WHOLE PROCESSION
S CHOREOGRAPHING, AS WELL AS DESIGNING. CONFIDENCE IN
ING, CARRYING, OPERATING CAN MAKE ALL THE DIFFERENCE TO
SPIRIT OF A PROCESSION. IF YOU WANT THE PUBLIC TO JOIN IN
 SURE THEY HAVE SOMETHING TO DO: A DANCE STEP, SOME—
G TO BANG OR HOLD OR CARRY.

MBOO,
THIE AND
PIER MACHE
AD, CARRIED AND
IMATED BY
E OPERATOR
DEPENDENTLY
THE BODY

HEAD MADE WITH WITHIE
FRAMEWORK COVERED
GLUE SOAKED MUSLIN/
SCRIM, MOUNTED ON
A FLEXIBLE ALKATHENE
NECK POLE.

SPLIT BAMBOO BODY FRAME
SUPPORTING A PAINTED CLOTH
COVERING
    ALL CARRIED ON SHOULDER
STRAPS WORN UNDER THE
OPERATOR'S COSTUME COAT.

DON'T FORGET TO RECONNOITRE THE
      ROUTE PROPERLY !
CHECK IT IS NOT HALF-DAY CLOSING.....
LOOK OUT FOR MARKET STALLS, LOW
OVERHEAD WIRES, OTHER OBSTRUCTIONS.
– WHAT IS THE TRAFFIC LIKE ON A
SIMILAR DAY AT A SIMILAR TIME ?

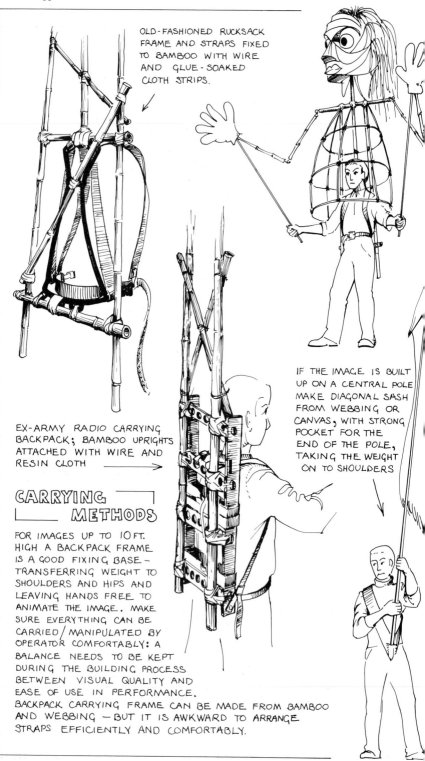

OLD-FASHIONED RUCKSACK FRAME AND STRAPS FIXED TO BAMBOO WITH WIRE AND GLUE-SOAKED CLOTH STRIPS.

EX-ARMY RADIO CARRYING BACKPACK; BAMBOO UPRIGHTS ATTACHED WITH WIRE AND RESIN CLOTH ⟶

CARRYING METHODS

FOR IMAGES UP TO 10 FT. HIGH A BACKPACK FRAME IS A GOOD FIXING BASE – TRANSFERRING WEIGHT TO SHOULDERS AND HIPS AND LEAVING HANDS FREE TO ANIMATE THE IMAGE. MAKE SURE EVERYTHING CAN BE CARRIED / MANIPULATED BY OPERATOR COMFORTABLY: A BALANCE NEEDS TO BE KEPT DURING THE BUILDING PROCESS BETWEEN VISUAL QUALITY AND EASE OF USE IN PERFORMANCE.

BACKPACK CARRYING FRAME CAN BE MADE FROM BAMBOO AND WEBBING – BUT IT IS AWKWARD TO ARRANGE STRAPS EFFICIENTLY AND COMFORTABLY.

IF THE IMAGE IS BUILT UP ON A CENTRAL POLE MAKE DIAGONAL SASH FROM WEBBING OR CANVAS, WITH STRONG POCKET FOR THE END OF THE POLE, TAKING THE WEIGHT ON TO SHOULDERS

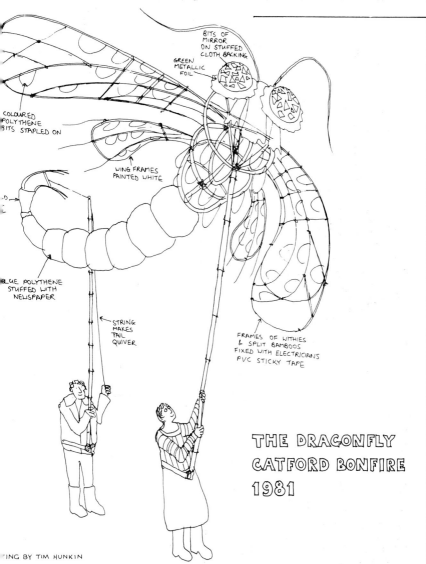

BITS OF MIRROR ON STUFFED CLOTH BACKING

GREEN METALLIC FOIL

COLOURED POLYTHENE BITS STAPLED ON

WING FRAMES PAINTED WHITE

-D →

BLUE POLYTHENE STUFFED WITH NEWSPAPER

← STRING MAKES TAIL QUIVER

FRAMES OF WITHIES & SPLIT BAMBOOS FIXED WITH ELECTRICIANS PVC STICKY TAPE

THE DRAGONFLY
CATFORD BONFIRE
1981

'ING BY TIM HUNKIN

WINDAGE. DON'T MAKE A SAIL: CUT CRESCENTS, SMALL SLITS IN SOLID SURFACES; OR USE STRIPS OF MATERIAL/ROPE/STRING TO "DRAW" THE IMAGE IN THE AIR; OR OVERLAP SHAPES LIKE TILES TO GIVE AN IMPRESSION OF SOLIDITY WHILE LETTING WIND PRESSURE ESCAPE; RAG STRIPS CAN BE STIFFENED WITH PAINT OR GLUE — TIGHT CLOTH VIBRATING IN THE WIND CAN LOOK GOOD. IF SOMETHING BIG MUST BE SOLID USE GUY ROPES TO HOLD IT STEADY AGAINST LEVERAGE OF WIND.

<u>Above</u>: Mrs. Thatcher
   Catford Bonfire '81
<u>Above right</u>: Stags
   Lyme Park Festival '81

<u>Right</u>: Uncle Sam Eagle
   Bracknell '82
<u>Below</u>: The Spaceman
   Toronto '81

BUILDING BIG PUPPETS

ALISON WOOD

IS A BIG ELEMENT IN WELFARE STATE WORK; THE 'BEST' WAY OF MAKING
ETHING OFTEN MEANS THE QUICKEST. WORKING QUICKLY YOU OFTEN FIND
T THE SIMPLEST SOLUTIONS TO PROBLEMS ARE THE MOST EFFECTIVE, AND IT
MPTS YOU TO WORK FOR A BIG STRONG IMAGE INSTEAD OF A COLLECTION OF
AILS. THE FOLLOWING IS BASED ON A FAIRLY BIG PUPPET MADE FOR A SOUTH
ARTS CENTRE PROJECT IN 1982: AN AMERICAN EAGLE, UNCLE SAM.

le sam was to be ugly fat
decrepit grotesque. His movement
to be comic. He had to be seen
rly by an audience of 800, some
yards away from the action.
gh Image — with large
e building it is very
rtant to have a clear
of the structure and image
 the beginning, as
nges at a later stage
difficult and laborious.
ugh sketch is essential
l stages of the building
eter to for scale and
spective. As well as
character and overall
t of the puppet you
to consider how long it
be seen for, what kind
ocus and attention will
ceive.
nember that the way
uppet is moved or
mated can totally transform it.

EAGLE BASE - STRONG STRUCTURES

BASE - TOP VIEW

The structure is made from 12-15 ft Bamboo - about 2" diameter. Ideal as it is light and strong - and a little flexible - so it will bend rather than break.

All the joints must be strong and must not slip preferably use wire and resin cloth

FRONT. WIDE enough for 2 people's shoulders

Back pack - leaves operator arms free

Padded for shoulders

temporary string triangul (as the rest of the structure is buil will become unnecessary)

The eagle was to be carried so it had to be made as light as possible

The base - carrying frame was very simple - big enough for three or four people to carry.

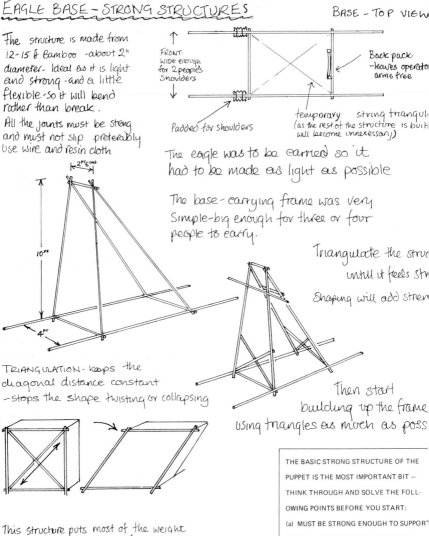

Triangulate the struc until it feels str

Shaping will add strem

2ft 6ins

10ft

4ft

TRIANGULATION. keeps the diagonal distance constant - stops the shape twisting or collapsing

Then start building up the frame using triangles as much as poss

This structure puts most of the weight to the front of the base (enabling the person at the back to operate the head)

to spread the weight more evenly you would build a structure like this

THE BASIC STRONG STRUCTURE OF THE PUPPET IS THE MOST IMPORTANT BIT — THINK THROUGH AND SOLVE THE FOLL-OWING POINTS BEFORE YOU START:

(a) MUST BE STRONG ENOUGH TO SUPPOR ITSELF — AND SKELETAL STRUCTURE DETERMINES FINISHED SHAPE OR IMAGE.

(b) MUST HAVE GOOD BASE FOR CARRY-ING COMFORTABLY — LEAVING OPERAT-ORS FREE TO ANIMATE IMAGE.

(c) STRUCTURES MUST REACH TO SUPPOR MOVING PARTS, APPENDAGES, ANIMATION

(d) WEIGHT MUST BE BALANCED AND LOW DOWN — WATCH FOR TOP HEAVINESS.

STRONG FIXED JOINTS FOR BASIC STRUCTURES

I usually work with Gaffa tape (sticky cloth tape) till I'm sure about the framework – then strengthen with wire or resin cloth.
Nails usually split bamboo.

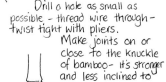

Drill a hole as small as possible – thread wire through – twist tight with pliers.

Make joints on or close to the knuckle of bamboo – it's stronger and less inclined to split

Bind around both bamboos, both ways tightly – to stop splitting

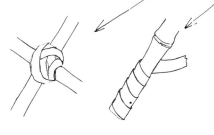

BINDING THE JOINT WITH RESIN CLOTH WILL HOLD THE ANGLE FIRMLY – IT CAN SAVE USING TRIANGULATION. CUT RESIN CLOTH IN STRIPS 1" – 2" WIDE, 2' LONG. SOAK IN ACETONE FOR A FEW SECONDS, BIND VERY TIGHTLY ALL WAYS ROUND JOINT, MAKING A SOLID LUMP. (REMOVE GAFFA TAPE BEFOREHAND) LEAVE IT STILL TILL IT'S HARDENED – 4 - 5 HOURS, DEPENDING ON ATMOSPHERE.

ALSO USE RESIN CLOTH AS A BANDAGE TO STRENGTHEN LENGTHS THAT MUST TAKE PARTICULAR STRAIN, i.e. SUPPORTS FOR PIVOTS, MOVING PARTS.

(ACETONE IS BAD FOR YOUR SKIN AND EYES – BE CAREFUL AND WEAR RUBBER GLOVES IF POSSIBLE)

BINDING WITH STRIPS OF COTTON SOAKED IN COPYDEX WILL SERVE A SIMILAR PURPOSE – IT IS CHEAPER BUT NOT AS RIGID AS RESIN CLOTH.

MOVING JOINTS
– lots of different ways – invent to suit your purpose – really depends on strength required.

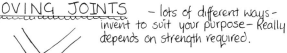

Scissors movement – Eagle wing joints – heavy wire threaded, and bent at both ends

For a stronger version use a bolt, or nail. (Drill the hole first)

Plywood wired to Bamboo – stronger because you don't have to drill any holes into the bamboo.

Bolt

Catapult elastic – or strips of car inner tube (free from tyre fitters)

Poly alkathene tubing – will bend all ways – (water piping) It comes in various thicknesses + is strong, hollow bendy whippy.

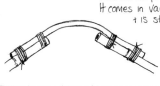

Strong joint – it moves all ways. – not so easy to control.

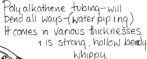

Strong baler twine or rope.

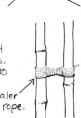

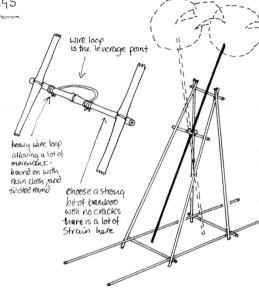

wire loop
is the leverage point

heavy wire loop
allowing a lot of
movement -
bound on with
resin cloth, and
twisted round

choose a strong
bit of bamboo
with no cracks
there is a lot of
strain here

THE HEAD WAS FIXED ON A LONG BAMBOO
POLE WHICH PASSED THROUGH A WIRE
LOOP, SO THAT IT COULD MOVE UP AND
DOWN, BACKWARDS AND FORWARDS, AND
TWIST FROM SIDE TO SIDE.

WHEN CARRIED AT SHOULDER HEIGHT
THIS PUPPET WAS ABOUT 20' HIGH — A
STRUCTURE ANY BIGGER THAN THIS
WOULD HAVE TO BE CARRIED BY MORE
PEOPLE ON A LARGER BASE — OR ON A
WHEELED BASE.

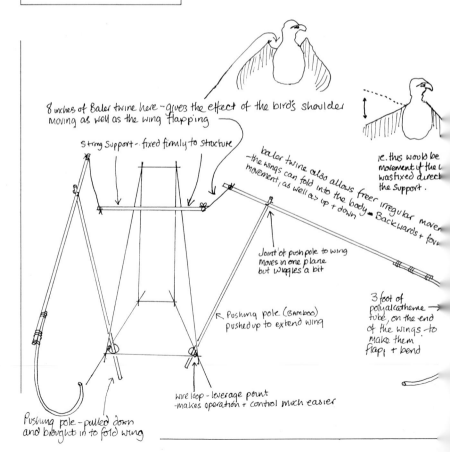

8 inches of Baler twine here — gives the effect of the bird's shoulder
moving as well as the wing flapping

Strong support - fixed firmly to structure

baler twine also allows freer irregular movement
- the wings can fold into the body - Backwards + forwards
movement, as well as up + down

Joint of push pole to wing
moves in one plane
but wiggles a bit

ie. this would be
movement if the wing
was fixed direct to
the support.

3 foot of
polyalcathene
tube, on the end
of the wings, to
make them
flap + bend

← Pushing pole (Bamboo)
pushed up to extend wing

Wire loop - leverage point
- makes operation + control much easier

Pushing pole - pulled down
and brought in to fold wing

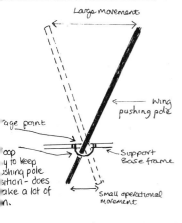

Large movement

wing pushing pole

...rage point

...oop ...y to keep ...shing pole ...sition - does ...ake a lot of ...n.

Support Base frame

Small operational movement

BOTH THESE MOVING PARTS GREATLY AFFECTED THE BALANCE AND THEREFORE THE WEIGHT OF THE PUPPET WHEN IT WAS BEING CARRIED — ANY WEIGHT WHICH IS HIGH UP, AND MOVES AWAY FROM THE CENTRE OF GRAVITY, WILL PULL MUCH MORE THAN ITS ACTUAL WEIGHT. (AND PUT A LOT OF STRAIN ON ITS SUPPORTS, WHICH MUST BE STRONG.) I WANTED THIS PUPPET TO HAVE A LOT OF MOVEMENT, SO THE TOPHEAVINESS OF THE HEAD, AND THE IMBALANCE CAUSED BY THE WINGS MOVING, WERE CALCULATED TO BE JUST MANAGEABLE — THE WIND COULD HAVE DISASTEROUS EFFECT IF NOT TAKEN INTO ACCOUNT. YOU OFTEN HAVE TO GUESS ABOUT THE WIND BUT DON'T UNDERESTIMATE IT.

...ause of their size, both the head and the wings were operated

...ough leverage points

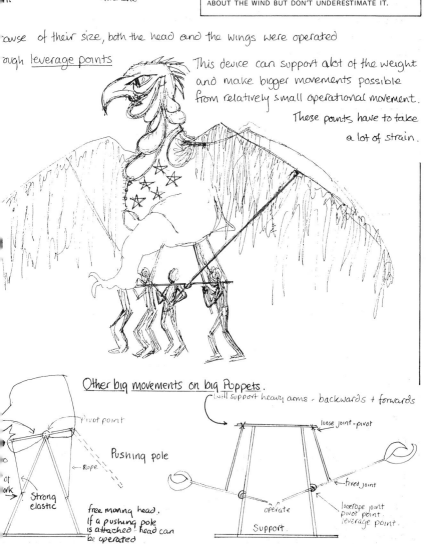

This device can support alot of the weight and make bigger movements possible from relatively small operational movement.

These points have to take a lot of strain.

Other big movements on big Puppets.

Will support heavy arms - backwards + forwards

Pivot point

Pushing pole

← Rope

...o ...of ...ork

Strong elastic

free moving head. If a pushing pole is attached head can be operated

loose joint - pivot

operate

fixed joint

loose rope joint pivot point. leverage point.

Support.

STRENGTHENING & SHAPING

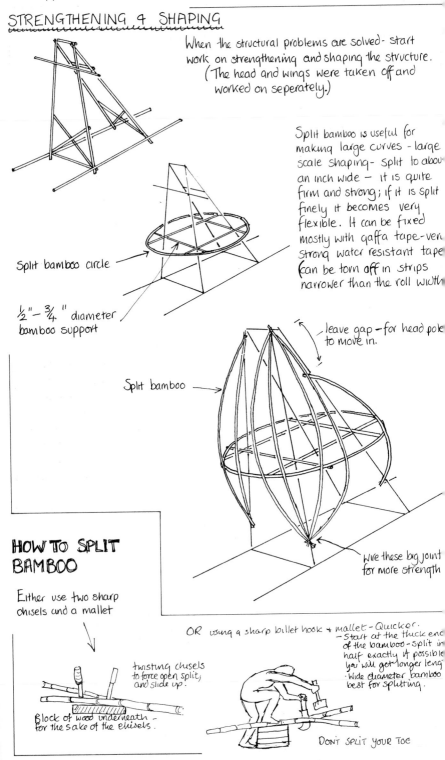

When the structural problems are solved - start work on strengthening and shaping the structure. (The head and wings were taken off and worked on seperately.)

Split bamboo is useful for making large curves - large scale shaping- split to about an inch wide — it is quite firm and strong; if it is split finely it becomes very flexible. It can be fixed mostly with gaffa tape- very strong water resistant tape can be torn off in strips narrower than the roll width.

Split bamboo circle

½" — ¾" diameter bamboo support

leave gap - for head pole to move in.

Split bamboo

Wire these big joints for more strength

HOW TO SPLIT BAMBOO

Either use two sharp chisels and a mallet

twisting chisels to force open split, and slide up.

Block of wood underneath - for the sake of the chisels.

OR using a sharp billet hook + mallet - Quicker.
- Start at the thick end of the bamboo - split in half exactly if possible you will get longer length
· Wide diameter bamboo best for splitting.

DON'T SPLIT YOUR TOE

ut the shape with damp
ies (thin lengths of
w used in basket making)

thies are soaked for a
c they become very flexible—
will keep their shape when dry.

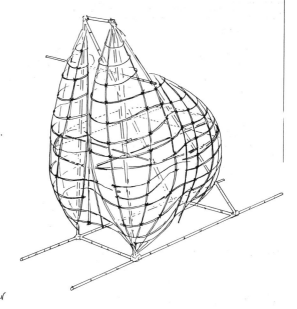

head was made with
ies, fixing as many
possible to the neck pole.
st two or three withies together
stronger bits.

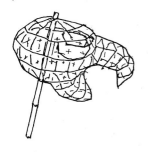

THROUGHOUT WORKING OFTEN WALK BACK FROM THE
THING TO SEE IT FROM A DISTANCE, COMPARING IT TO
THE ROUGH SKETCH — SEE THE BIT YOU'RE WORKING
ON IN RELATION TO THE WHOLE THING.
ALSO THINK ABOUT THE SHAPING IN RELATION TO THE
COVERING — i.e. IF YOU WANT TO USE COPYDEX AND
NEWSPAPER MAKE SURE THAT THE GAPS BETWEEN THE
WITHIES ARE SMALLER THAN YOUR AVERAGE SHEET OF
NEWSPAPER AND IF YOU WANT TO USE FABRIC MAKE
SURE THERE IS SOMETHING TO STAPLE/GLUE ROUND
OR TO.

HER LIGHT MATERIALS

NE — WHICH IS NOT HOLLOW AND IS MORE FLEXIBLE
AN BAMBOO — GOOD STUFF — CAN BE COAXED INTO
APE BY LIGHTLY TOASTING WITH A BLOW LAMP.

HITE WITHIES — LONGER THICKER AND STRONGER
AN WITHIES — CAN BE SOAKED AND SHAPED —

ATTAN — VERY THIN AND FLEXIBLE — NOT AS STIFF
 WITHIES — COMES IN LONGER LENGTHS — MAKES A
RE REGULAR CIRCLE THAN WITHIES.

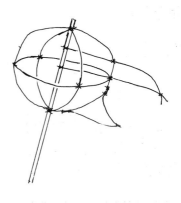

CLADDING

COPYDEX OR INDUSTRIAL LATEX — GLUE THAT DRIES AS A THIN LAYER OF RUBBER — MAKES VERY GOOD
PAPIER-MACHE. IT DRIES QUICKLY SO YOU CAN WORK QUICKLY WITH QUITE LARGE SHEETS OF PAPER. ONLY
ONE LAYER WAS USED ON THE EAGLE HEAD FOR THE SAKE OF LIGHTNESS AND BECAUSE IT ONLY HAD TO LAST
THROUGH ONE PERFORMANCE. THREE OR FOUR LAYERS WILL MAKE A GOOD STRONG SKIN, BUT IT IS
RELATIVELY HEAVY. TO MAKE A STRONG BUT LIGHT CLADDING USE ONE LAYER OF NEWSPAPER/COPYDEX AND
ONE LAYER OF THIN COTTON FABRIC (OR GAUZE OR SCRIM) WITH COPYDEX. COPYDEX STICKS MOST NATURAL
FIBRES, BUT IS NOT MUCH GOOD WITH MAN-MADE FIBRES. IT MAKES A GOOD BASE TO PAINT ON.

HEAD AND NECK. THE EAGLE'S HEAD WAS COVERED WITH A SINGLE LAYER OF NEWSPAPER WHICH HAD BEEN
SOAKED IN, OR PAINTED WITH, COPYDEX: YOU STICK THE PAPER TO THE FRAME WHILE THE COPYDEX IS STILL
WET. WHEN THE PAPER HAD DRIED IT WAS 'PAINTED' WITH ANOTHER COAT OF COPYDEX TO MAKE IT MORE
WATERPROOF.

THE EAGLE HAD A NECK WHICH WAS A COTTON FABRIC TUBE, GATHERED AND BUNCHED UP WITH STAPLES AND
COPYDEX: FOAM RUBBER STRIPS AND WITHIES WERE STAPLED IN SO IT HUNG IN BAGS AND WRINKLES. IT
WORKED LIKE A CONCERTINA WHEN THE HEAD WENT UP AND DOWN.

PAINTING. THE EAGLE HEAD WAS PAINTED BY
SHADING AND SMUDGING, EMPHASISING THE CONTOURS
OF THE SHAPE. THE NECK WRINKLES WERE PAINTED
WITH THE SAME COLOURS SO THAT FROM A DISTANCE
IT LOOKED UNIFORM.

LARGE SCALE PAINTING IS IDEALLY DONE FROM THE
DISTANCE IT WILL BE SEEN FROM! IMPOSSIBLE —
SO KEEP STEPPING BACK AND LOOKING AT THE
WHOLE THING. REMEMBER THE AUDIENCE PROBABLY
WON'T SEE SMALL DETAILS, BUT THE MAIN LINES
WILL SHOW UP.

A SIMPLE COLOUR SCHEME IS OFTEN THE MOST
EFFECTIVE. USE OIL BASED PAINTS OR GOOD
QUALITY EMULSIONS TO INCREASE WATERPROOFING.
COAT WITH CLEAR VARNISH TO WATERPROOF
STILL MORE.

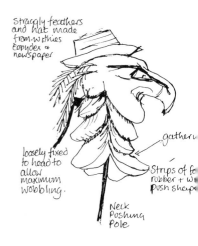

Straggly feathers and hat made from withies Copydex & newspaper

loosely fixed to head to allow maximum wobbling.

gather

Strips of foam rubber + withies push shape

Neck Pushing Pole

THE BODY. WITH LARGE PUPPETS PEOPLE ARE FIRST STRUCK WITH THE OVERALL IMAGE, BUT THERE ARE
ALWAYS FOCUS POINTS — LIKE THE HEAD — WHICH NEED TO BE MORE DETAILED IN FINISH. FOR LARGE AREAS
OF THE IMAGE, THOUGH, CLADDING CAN BE QUITE TATTY.

THE EAGLE'S BODY WAS COVERED WITH TATTERS OF FABRIC AND POLYTHENE, USING STAPLES AND COPYDEX TO
STICK THEM TO THE FRAME. A HEAVY DUTY STAPLE GUN WILL WORK ON BAMBOO, IF THE BAMBOO IS
SUPPORTED FROM BEHIND WITH SOMETHING SOLID. THE TATTERS GAVE A STRONG IMPRESSION OF MOVEMENT
AND GAVE THE WINGS VERY LITTLE WIND RESISTANCE.

...LYTHENE IS GOOD FOR ITS SHINYNESS AND
...IGHTNESS, AND IT WON'T ABSORB WATER IF IT RAINS.
...T IT IS DIFFICULT TO FIX — COPYDEX WON'T STICK
...D EVOSTICK MELTS IT. IT CAN BE STAPLED IF IT
...THICK ENOUGH NOT TO TEAR, OTHERWISE STICK A
...RIP OF GAFFA TAPE OVER IT AND STAPLE THROUGH
...AT. OR TIE IT ON WITH STRING, ETC.

Gaffa tape
Bamboo
polythene

... TAKE CARE. POLYTHENE IS A PARTICULAR
...E HAZARD. WHEN ALIGHT IT DRIPS LIQUID PLASTIC
... GIVES OFF TOXIC FUMES. BE EXTRA CAREFUL
...N USING IT WHERE ACCIDENTAL FIRES COULD
...RT.

...YSTYRENE IS ALSO A FIRE RISK. BUT IT IS VERY
...T, CAN BE THREADED ON WIRE OR BAMBOO, AND
...OD FOR MAKING APPENDAGES.

MELLINEX OR MIRRORED CELLOPHANE IS VERY GOOD
FOR REFLECTING LIGHT. STRONGER AND LIGHTER
THAN TINFOIL.

BROKEN MIRRORS CAN BE STUCK ONTO CLADDING
WITH EVOSTICK - SO CAN BITS OF TIN, FEATHERS,
STRAW, WHAT-HAVE-YOU.

FOAM RUBBER AND DACRON HAVE USEFUL WOBBLING
OR STUFFING QUALITIES. IT IS POSSIBLE TO BUY
FOAM RUBBER GLUE TO MAKE BIG OR DIFFICULT
SHAPES FROM SMALL PIECES. BUT REMEMBER FOAM
RUBBER, AND UNWATERPROOFED FABRIC, BECOMES
MUCH HEAVIER IN THE RAIN!

Flimsy withie framework to give some form.

Stapled on.

tatters

tatters of red and silver— tied in to catch the light.

...guessed the shape of
...waistcoat - stapled on
...stars and stripes— before fixing
...o the structure.

CHOOSE CLADDING TO SUIT THE FINISHED EFFECT FROM
THE AUDIENCE'S POINT OF VIEW. FOR HOW LONG, AT
WHAT DISTANCE, AND IN WHAT KIND OF LIGHT — SPOT-
LIGHT, MOONLIGHT, DAYLIGHT, FIRELIGHT — WILL IT
BE SEEN? i.e. FOR NIGHTIME WORK PICK OUT BLACK
IMAGES WITH LINES OF SILVER OR WHITE. CONSIDER AS
WELL THE BACKGROUND THE IMAGE WILL APPEAR
AGAINST. KEEP STANDING BACK AND LOOKING AT THE
TOTALITY.

LEVERS

MOVING EYEBALLS

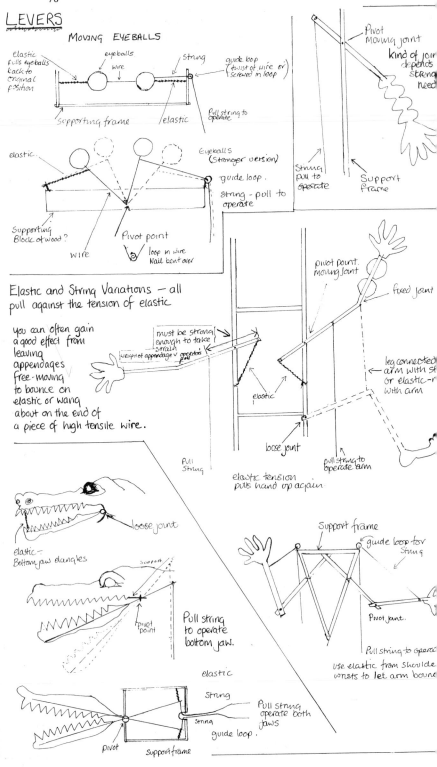

elastic pulls eyeballs back to original position

eyeballs

wire

string

guide loop (twist of wire or screwed in loop)

Pivot Moving joint

kind of joint depends strength need

Supporting frame

elastic

Pull string to operate

elastic

Eyeballs (stronger version)

guide loop.

string - pull to operate

String pull to operate

Support frame

Supporting Block of wood?

wire

Pivot point

loop in wire Nail bent over

Elastic and String Variations — all pull against the tension of elastic

you can often gain a good effect from leaving appendages free-moving to bounce on elastic or wang about on the end of a piece of high tensile wire.

must be strong enough to take strain

weight of appendage v operators pull

elastic

pivot point. moving joint

fixed joint

leg connected arm with st or elastic-r with arm

loose joint

Pull String

elastic tension pulls hand up again

pull string to operate arm

loose joint

elastic — Bottom jaw dangles

Pull string to operate bottom jaw.

support

pivot point

elastic

Support frame

guide loop for string

Pivot joint.

Pull string to operate

use elastic from shoulder wrists to let arm bounce

string

Pull string operate both jaws

string

guide loop.

pivot

support frame

ANIMATIONS

Movement from wheels

link spins around sprocket.

Sprocket fixed solid to wheel

link pieces can be made with thin bamboo slices, or castors.

Varied movement of animation.

Support frame.

wheel moves along ground.

For a heavy and large thing to spin smoothly

Spindle turns in hole in bottom disc

Spindle fixed to top disc

Support

Spindle - wind to operate

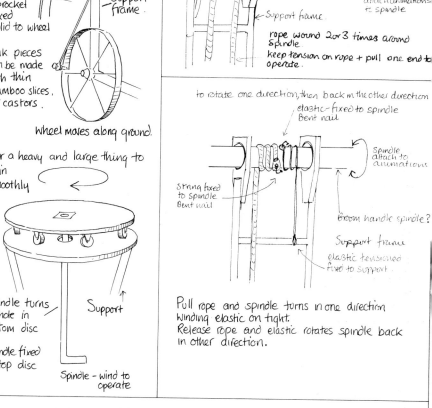

to make something spin continually in the same direction

Bamboo spindle - surfaced to stop slipping with fabric + copydex / rope binding / resin cloth.

Spindle rotates in plywood support.

to make plywood supports use electric drill + large drill bit - enlarge with jigsaw if necessary

attach animations to spindle

Support frame.

rope wound 2 or 3 times around spindle.

keep tension on rope + pull one end to operate.

to rotate one direction, then back in the other direction

elastic - fixed to spindle Bent nail

Spindle attach to animations

String fixed to spindle Bent nail

Broom handle spindle?

Support frame

elastic tensioned fixed to support.

Pull rope and spindle turns in one direction Winding elastic on tight.
Release rope and elastic rotates spindle back in other direction.

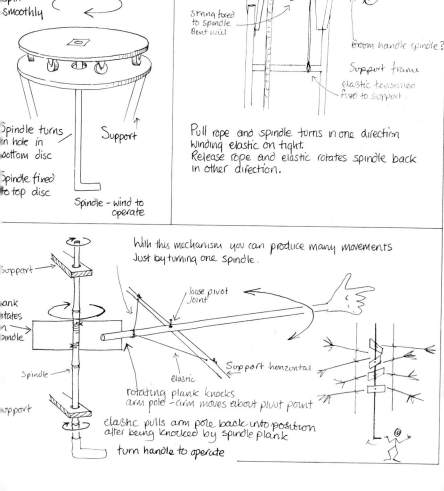

With this mechanism you can produce many movements Just by turning one spindle.

Support

Crank rotates on spindle

Spindle

Support

loose pivot joint

Support horizontal

elastic

rotating plank knocks arm pole - arm moves about pivot point

elastic pulls arm pole back into position after being knocked by spindle plank

turn handle to operate

MOVING LARGE IMAGES

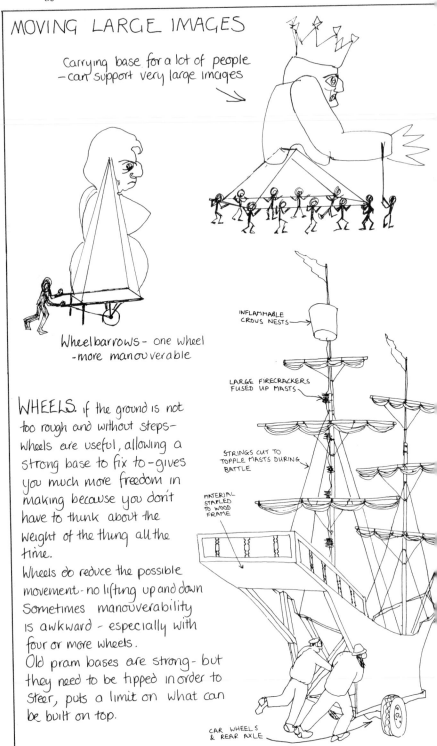

Carrying base for a lot of people
— can support very large images

Wheelbarrows — one wheel
— more manouverable

WHEELS. If the ground is not
too rough and without steps —
wheels are useful, allowing a
strong base to fix to — gives
you much more freedom in
making because you don't
have to think about the
weight of the thing all the
time.

Wheels do reduce the possible
movement — no lifting up and down
Sometimes manouverability
is awkward — especially with
four or more wheels.

Old pram bases are strong — but
they need to be tipped in order to
steer, puts a limit on what can
be built on top.

INFLAMMABLE
CROWS NESTS

LARGE FIRECRACKERS
FUSED UP MASTS

STRINGS CUT TO
TOPPLE MASTS DURING
BATTLE

MATERIAL
STAPLED
TO WOOD
FRAME

CAR WHEELS
& REAR AXLE

CAR AXLES/CARS

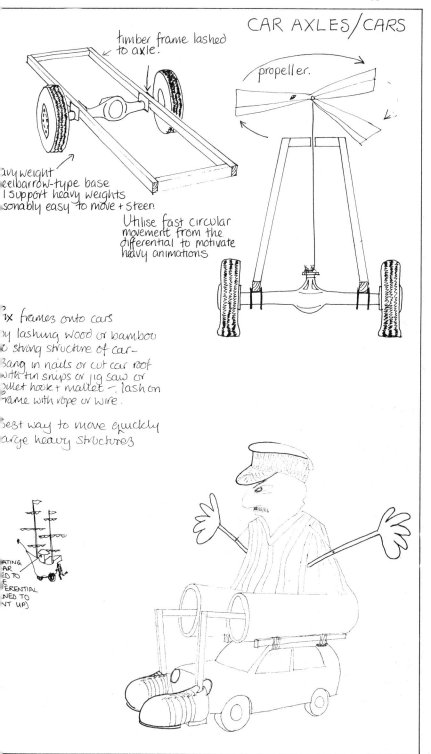

timber frame lashed to axle.

propeller.

~avy weight
~eelbarrow-type base
~l support heavy weights
~sonably easy to move + steer.

Utilise fast circular movement from the differential to motivate heavy animations

~ix frames onto cars
~y lashing wood or bamboo
~o strong structure of car—
~Bang in nails or cut car roof
~with tin snips or jig saw or
~ullet hook + mallet —. lash on
~rame with rope or wire.

~est way to move quickly
~arge heavy structures

~ATING
~AR
~ED TO
~E
~FERENTIAL
~NED TO
~NT UP)

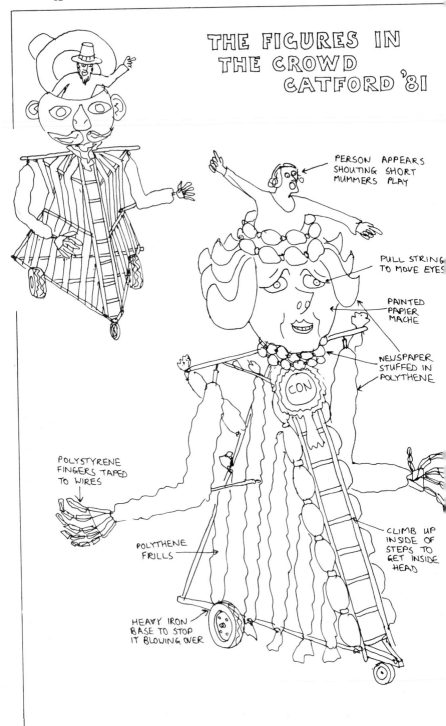

THE FIGURES IN THE CROWD CATFORD '81

PERSON APPEARS SHOUTING SHORT MUMMERS PLAY

PULL STRING TO MOVE EYES

PAINTED PAPIER MACHE

NEWSPAPER STUFFED IN POLYTHENE

CON

POLYSTYRENE FINGERS TAPED TO WIRES

POLYTHENE FRILLS

CLIMB UP INSIDE OF STEPS TO GET INSIDE HEAD

HEAVY IRON BASE TO STOP IT BLOWING OVER

DRAWINGS ON THIS PAGE AND FACING PAGE BY TIM HUNKIN.

THE STORK

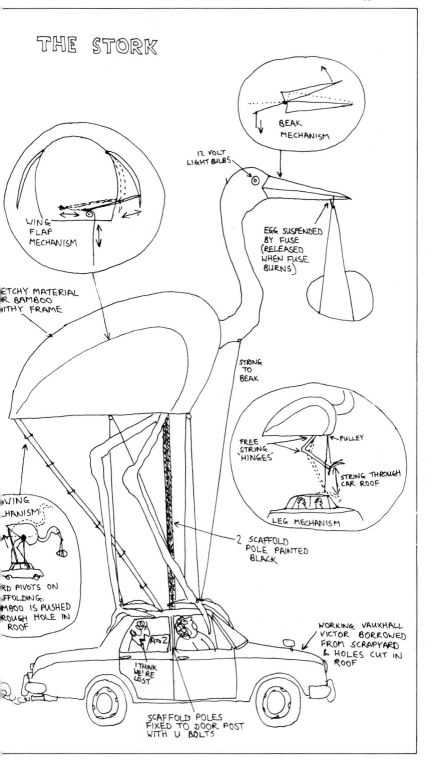

BEAK MECHANISM

12 VOLT LIGHT BULBS

WING FLAP MECHANISM

...ETCHY MATERIAL
...R BAMBOO
...ITHY FRAME

EGG SUSPENDED BY FUSE (RELEASED WHEN FUSE BURNS)

STRING TO BEAK

FREE STRING 'HINGES'

PULLEY

STRING THROUGH CAR ROOF

LEG MECHANISM

...WING
...HANISM

...RD PIVOTS ON
...FFOLDING.
...MBOO IS PUSHED
...ROUGH HOLE IN
ROOF

2 SCAFFOLD POLE PAINTED BLACK

WORKING VAUXHALL VICTOR BORROWED FROM SCRAPYARD & HOLES CUT IN ROOF

A to Z

I THINK WE'RE LOST

SCAFFOLD POLES FIXED TO DOOR POST WITH U BOLTS

FLAGPOLES HAVE AN IMPACT OUT OF ALL PROPORTION TO THEIR SIZE OR COMPLEXITY PARTLY BECAUSE OF THE MOVEMENT AT THE TOP EVEN IN THE SLIGHTEST BREEZE, AND PARTLY BECAUSE OF THE ANGLE AT WHICH THEY ARE SEEN AGAINST THE UN—CLUTTERED BACKGROUND OF THE SKY. ALMOST ANYTHING STRUNG UP ON THE TOP OF A POLE HAS A STRONG PRESENCE AND VISUAL IMPACT, A BUNCH OF RAGS, A BOUQUET OF FLOWERS, OR SCARECROWS. SKULLS AND COSTUMES.

FIXED STRUCTURE

TONY LEWE

FLAGPOLES

ANY OLD BIT OF WOOD WILL DO, BUT THE STRAIGHT POLE IS, THE EASIER IT WILL BE TO FIT UP RELATIV WEIGHT. THE HIGHER THE GUY ROPES ARE ATTACH MORE EFFECTIVE THEY ARE AND THE THINNER THE CAN BE. THE LOWER DOWN THE POLE THEY ARE TH GREATER IS THE LEVERAGE OF THE WIND AT THE T TENDING TO KICK THE BASE AWAY IN THE OPPOSITE TION TO COUNTERACT THIS, SET THE BASE A F INCHES INTO THE GROUND, OR BANG A STA AND LASH THE POLE TO IT. IF THE PE TOO CLOSE TO THE BASE THE GUY ARE USING MOST OF THEIR TEN TRYING TO PUSH THE POLE I THE GROUND WHILE SIM TANEOUSLY PULLING PEGS OUT.

SILLY.

FLAGS CAN BE MADE IN A VARIETY OF WAYS, TORN, SEWN, PAINTED OR APPLIQUED. THE TRADITIONAL FLAG LOOKS A BIT WEAK IF THERE IS NO WIND. SO THE 'MEDIEVAL' BANNER STYLE IS PROBABLY MORE USEFUL, WITH THE CLOTH HANGING DOWN FROM A HORIZONTAL BAR. TO PRODUCE A NUMBER OF SIMILAR ONES AT SPEED USE A SIMPLE STENCIL, CUT OUT OF CARDBOARD, OR VINYL FLOOR COVERING. LAY THE CLOTH FLAT ON A TABLE WITH THE STENCIL ON TOP AND STAB THE PAINT THROUGH WITH A SHORT BRUSH.

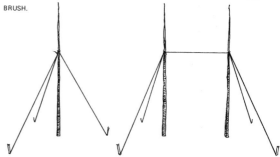

ALTHOUGH ONE FLAGPOLE NEEDS A MINIMUM OF THREE GUY-ROPES TO KEEP IT UP, TWO POLES ROPED TOGETHER NEED ONLY FOUR GUYS, AND THREE WILL STAY UP WITH ONLY THREE. A LARGE NUMBER OF POLES GUYED TOGETHER AT A HIGH LEVEL NEED ONLY THE OUTERMOST ONES PEGGED DOWN TO THE GROUND. THIS LEAVES MORE USABLE SPACE ON THE GROUND AND AN INTERESTING CONSTRUCTION OF LINES AND VERTICALS OVERHEAD. THIS CAN BE DESIGNED TO BE A STRUCTURE IN ITS OWN RIGHT, OUTLINING AND DEFINING A SPACE, OR AS SKELETAL ARCHITECTURE.

USE STRIPS OF WHITE RAG FOR MAXIMUM IMPACT AT NIGHT.

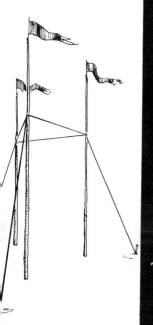

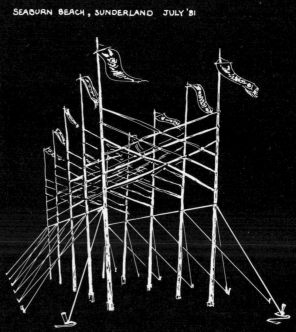

SEABURN BEACH, SUNDERLAND JULY '81

LARGE LANTERNS FOR INTERIOR OR EXTERIOR USE CAN BE SIMPLY
MADE WITH A TUBE OF WHITE CLOTH — CALICO OR COTTON — PAINTED
WITH INTENSE DYE COLOURS. ATTACH HOOPS OF HEAVY GAUGE
WIRE, EITHER BY SEWING OR STICKING THEM IN PLACE WITH COPYDEX
AND ANOTHER STRIP OF CLOTH, OR BY INSERTING THEM INTO
PREPARED POCKETS BEFORE STICKING THE TUBE TOGETHER. TIE
STRING ROUND BETWEEN HOOPS TO PULL IN THE WAISTS. THEY LOOK
BETTER IS THE BULB HAS ITS OWN WHITE LAMPSHADE TO DIFFUSE
THE LIGHT ONTO THE CLOTH.

SEVERAL VARIATIONS OF SHAPE ARE POSSIBLE; ALL ARE EASY TO
PACK AND TRANSPORT AS THEY COLLAPSE
FLAT CONCERTINA STYLE.

TORONTO, MAY '81

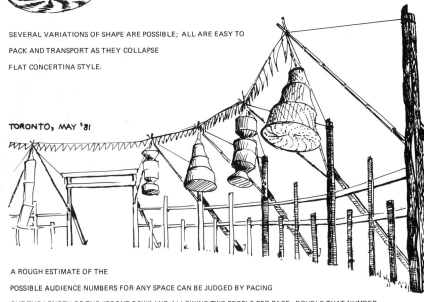

A ROUGH ESTIMATE OF THE
POSSIBLE AUDIENCE NUMBERS FOR ANY SPACE CAN BE JUDGED BY PACING
OUT THE LENGTH OF THE "FRONT ROW" AND ALLOWING TWO PEOPLE PER PACE. DOUBLE THAT NUMBER
AND YOU HAVE THE SIZE OF A STANDING AUDIENCE WITH A REASONABLE VIEW. RAISE THE NEXT TWO
ROWS OF PEOPLE BY ONLY NINE INCHES AND YOU WILL DOUBLE THE AUDIENCE — SIT TWO MORE DOWN
IN FRONT AND IT IS TREBLED.

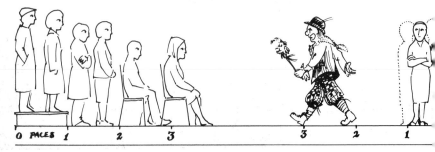

0 PACES   1   2   3   3   2   1

CAFFOLDING IS CHEAP TO HIRE, ESPECIALLY FOR LONG PERIODS AS THE
DADING AND DELIVERY CHARGES ARE A GOOD PROPORTION OF THE
RICE. THE BASIC PRINCIPLES OF ORDINARY SCAFFOLDING ARE FAIRLY
FRAIGHTFORWARD TO ANYONE OF A CONSTRUCTIVE MIND, WITH THE
DDED ADVICE THAT, IF IN DOUBT, BOLT ON ANOTHER DIAGONAL BRACE
D STIFFEN IT. BOARDS SHOULD BE SUPPORTED EVERY 1.5m, AND
DRIZONTAL LOAD-BEARING POLES EVERY 2.5m. MODERN 'H' FRAME
ND 'ZIP-UP' SCAFFOLD TOWERS ARE SIMPLE AND SUPER, AND IDEAL FOR
OST LIGHTING AND SOUND EQUIPMENT NEEDS, ALTHOUGH RIGGING AN
DEQUATE ROOF CAN BE AWKWARD. (RIGGING ADEQUATE ROOFS OVER
GHTING IS ALWAYS AWKWARD ANYWAY ....)

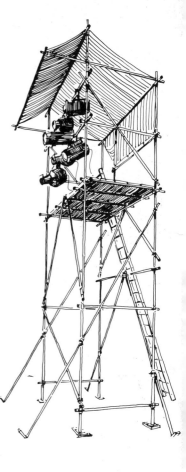

AFETY FIRST! NOBODY SHOULD BE UNDERNEATH DURING THE ERECTION
R DISMANTLING — A POLE OR CLIP FALLING A VERY FEW FEET CAN KILL,
ND SAFETY HELMETS SHOULD BE WORN BY THE CONSTRUCTION TEAM AT
LL TIMES. BEWARE NOT TO CREATE 'TRAPENDS' WHERE SCAFFOLD PLANKS
XTEND MORE THAN 150 mm BEYOND THEIR SUPPORT, CREATING A TRAP
DOR EFFECT IF SOMEONE STANDS ON IT. ANYONE WORKING UP IN THE AIR
N SCAFFOLDING MUST BE ABLE TO TRUST THE PLANKING UNDERFOOT WITH-
UT HAVING TO CHECK EVERY STEP. SAFETY-FIRST — AND SAFETY RAILS
LL ROUND ALL PLATFORMS.

CAFFOLDING TAKES TIME AND A LOT OF PHYSICAL EFFORT TO ERECT,
SPECIALLY FOR THE NOVICE. IF YOU HAVE A BIG JOB TO DO, GET THE
ROFESSIONALS IN, ESPECIALLY WHERE PUBLIC SAFETY IS CONCERNED. FOR
OMPLICATED STRUCTURES TAKE TIME TO DO A SCALE DRAWING FIRST,
ND WORK OUT REQUIREMENTS FROM THAT. YOU CAN ORDER PRECISE
UMBERS OF CERTAIN LENGTHS, BUT REMEMBER THEY WILL VARY BY
VERAL INCHES. INCREASE YOUR CALCULATED ORDER BY A GENEROUS
MOUNT TO COUNTERACT THE MURPHY LAW WHICH STATES THAT THERE
ILL NEVER BE QUITE ENOUGH OF THE RIGHT SORT OF POLES OR CLIPS
D FINISH THE JOB PROPERLY.

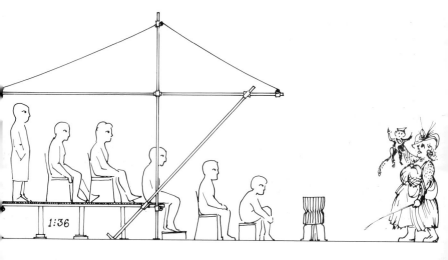

1:36

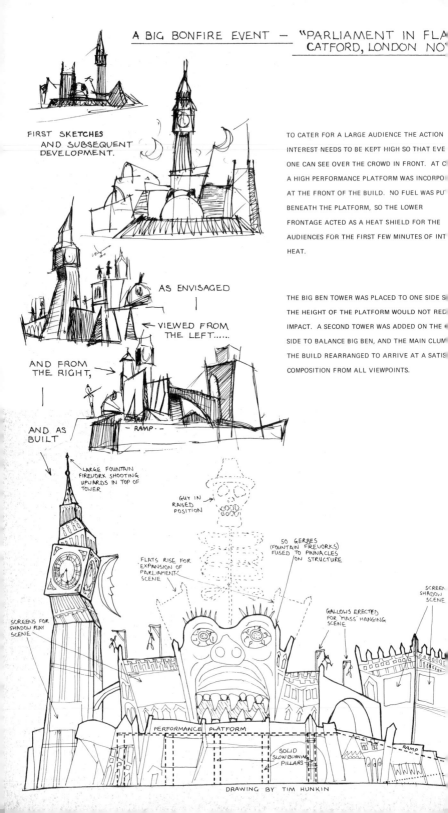

FIRST SKETCHES
AND SUBSEQUENT
DEVELOPMENT.

AS ENVISAGED

← VIEWED FROM
THE LEFT......

AND FROM
THE RIGHT, →

AND AS
BUILT

TO CATER FOR A LARGE AUDIENCE THE ACTION
INTEREST NEEDS TO BE KEPT HIGH SO THAT EVE
ONE CAN SEE OVER THE CROWD IN FRONT. AT C
A HIGH PERFORMANCE PLATFORM WAS INCORPO
AT THE FRONT OF THE BUILD. NO FUEL WAS PU
BENEATH THE PLATFORM, SO THE LOWER
FRONTAGE ACTED AS A HEAT SHIELD FOR THE
AUDIENCES FOR THE FIRST FEW MINUTES OF INT
HEAT.

THE BIG BEN TOWER WAS PLACED TO ONE SIDE S
THE HEIGHT OF THE PLATFORM WOULD NOT RED
IMPACT. A SECOND TOWER WAS ADDED ON THE
SIDE TO BALANCE BIG BEN, AND THE MAIN CLUM
THE BUILD REARRANGED TO ARRIVE AT A SATIS
COMPOSITION FROM ALL VIEWPOINTS.

LARGE FOUNTAIN
FIREWORK SHOOTING
UPWARDS IN TOP OF
TOWER

GUY IN
RAISED
POSITION

50 GERBES
(FOUNTAIN FIREWORKS)
FUSED TO PINNACLES
ON STRUCTURE

FLATS RISE FOR
EXPANSION OF
PARLIAMENT
SCENE

SCREEN
SHADOW
SCENE

SCREENS FOR
SHADOW PLAY
SCENE

GALLOWS ERECTED
FOR MASS HANGING
SCENE

PERFORMANCE PLATFORM

SOLID
SLOW BURNING
PILLARS

RAMP

DRAWING BY TIM HUNKIN

DEN PALLETS CAN BE VALUABLE
LDING UNITS TO CREATE
ENGTH, HEIGHT, AND WORKING
TFORMS FAST. USE PLENTY OF
GONAL BRACES TO STOP SIDEWAYS
LAPSE — HAMMER THE MAIN ONES
O THE GROUND BEFORE NAILING;
NT TO BACK DIAGONALS STIFFEN
STRUCTURE AND KEEP PALLETS
ILY ONE ABOVE THE OTHER. IF
STRUCTURE IS GOING TO BE
VY OR HIGH BE PARTICULAR
UT THE 'FOUNDATION' — ENSURE
T THE BOTTOM PALLETS ARE
ILY SEATED ON THE GROUND,
LEVEL. PALLETS BURN FAST —
NOT EXPECT THEM TO SUPPORT
HT FOR LONG IN THE FIRE —
OU NEED THE STRUCTURE TO
VIVE THE FLAMES FOR A WHILE
HEAVY JOIST TIMBERS.

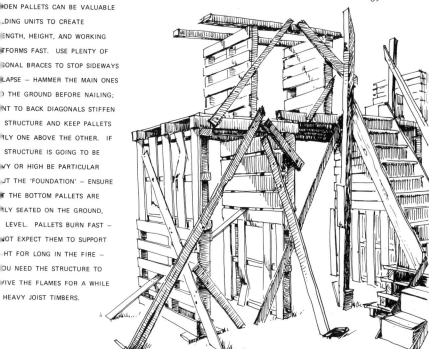

THE PAINTWORK CAN IMPOSE AN OVERALL ARCHITECTURAL STYLE ON ALL SORTS OF MATERIALS, AND IT CAN, AS IN THIS CASE, FURTHER DECEIVE THE EYE ABOUT THE SCALE AND PERSPECTIVE OF AN ALREADY ODD STRUCTURE. UNIFY EVERYTHING WITH A COAT OF WHITE, THEN BREAK UP OUTLINES AND PUT IN DETAILS WITH BLACK. LIMEWASH, APPLIED WITH A SOFT BROOM, IS CHEAP BUT UNPLEASANT TO USE — AVOID GETTING IT IN THE EYES OR CUTS. EMULSION IS BEST — IT CAN BE THINNED WITH WATER, SPRAYED, AND IS FAST DRYING. HOWEVER YOU GET WHAT YOU PAY FOR — VERY CHEAP PAINT HAS POOR COVERING POWER AND WILL WASH OFF IN THE RAIN; GOOD STUFF (i.e. EXPENSIVE) CAN BE THINNED BY 200% AND STILL COVER AND BE WATERPROOF. AN INDUSTRIAL SPRAYGUN CAN BE INVALUABLE, BUT NEEDS TO BE USED BY A CAREFUL OPERATOR TO BE TROUBLE-FREE.

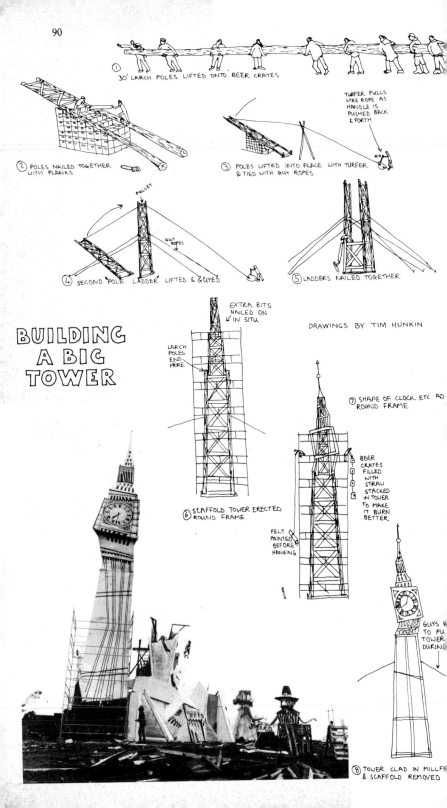

① 30' LARCH POLES LIFTED ONTO BEER CRATES

② POLES NAILED TOGETHER WITH PLANKS

③ POLES LIFTED INTO PLACE WITH TURFER & TIED WITH GUY ROPES

TURFER PULLS WIRE ROPE AS HANDLE IS PUSHED BACK & FORTH

④ SECOND 'POLE LADDER' LIFTED & GUYED

PULLEY

GUY ROPES

⑤ LADDERS NAILED TOGETHER

BUILDING A BIG TOWER

EXTRA BITS NAILED ON IN SITU

LARCH POLES END HERE

DRAWINGS BY TIM HUNKIN

⑥ SCAFFOLD TOWER ERECTED ROUND FRAME

⑦ SHAPE OF CLOCK ETC ADD ROUND FRAME

BEER CRATES FILLED WITH STRAW STACKED IN TOWER TO MAKE IT BURN BETTER

FELT PAINTED BEFORE HANGING

GUYS TO PU TOWER DURING

⑧ TOWER CLAD IN MILLFE & SCAFFOLD REMOVED

...Y AND START WITH A LOT OF MATERIALS — A LOT
...BEER BOXES, BRUSHWOOD, OLD CARPET, OR A LOT
...PALLETS — IT ALMOST DOESN'T MATTER SO LONG
...THERE IS ENOUGH TO DEVELOP A TECHNIQUE OR A
...DULE TO BUILD WITH, FAST AND CREATIVELY. IF
...INTRICATE DESIGN IS PLANNED IN ADVANCE TIME
...D MONEY MUST BE ALLOWED TO FIND AND MAYBE
...Y THE NECESSARY MATERIALS TO MAKE THAT DESIGN.
...RT MATERIALS INTO HEAPS CLOSE TO, BUT CLEAR OF,
...E CONSTRUCTION SITE WITH SPACE TO WALK BETWEEN
...EM.

...Y NOT TO FIGHT THE MATERIALS; ALLOW THE NATURE
...THE AVAILABLE STUFF TO MOULD THE CHARACTER
...THE BUILD.

...TAILS ON CONSTRUCTION VARY DEPENDING ON THE
...AL CLADDING MATERIAL, FROM A FLIMSY OUTLINE
...AME FOR A CLOTH COVERING TO STANDARD BUILDING
...CHNIQUES FOR A SOLID EXTERIOR. ONE OF OUR MOST
...FUL COVERINGS HAS BEEN 'MILLFELT' — THE HUGE
...OTH CONVEYOR BELTS FROM INDUSTRIAL PAPER MILLS —
...RDWORK TO PUT UP BUT STRONG AND BIG. HARDBOARD
...D PLYWOOD ARE IDEAL OF COURSE BUT ARE VERY
...FICULT TO GET FOR NOTHING ....

ABOVE: THE LAST 'PARLIAMENT
IN FLAMES', CATFORD, LONDON.
1981 ——————————

LEFT AND BELOW: 'PARLIAMENT
IN FLAMES', ACKWORTH, YORKS.
1979 ——————————

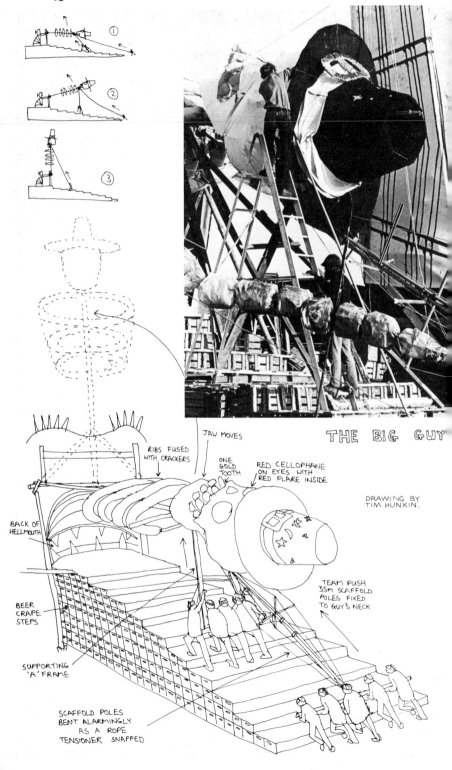

THE BIG GUY

DRAWING BY
TIM HUNKIN.

RIBS FUSED
WITH CRACKERS

JAW MOVES

ONE
GOLD
TOOTH

RED CELLOPHANE
ON EYES WITH
RED FLARE INSIDE

BACK OF
HELLMOUTH

BEER
CRATE
STEPS

SUPPORTING
'A' FRAME

TEAM PUSH
35M SCAFFOLD
POLES FIXED
TO GUY'S NECK

SCAFFOLD POLES
BENT ALARMINGLY
AS A ROPE
TENSIONER SNAPPED

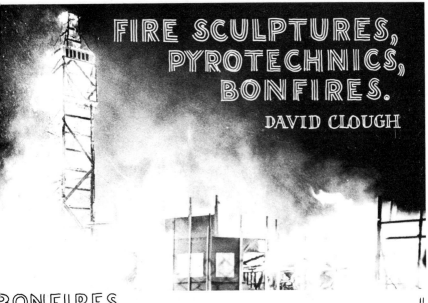

FIRE SCULPTURES, PYROTECHNICS, BONFIRES.

DAVID CLOUGH

BONFIRES

A BONFIRE CAN BE DEFINED AS ANY STRUCTURE DESIGNED TO BURN UNTIL
DESTROYED. THE SCALE CAN RANGE FROM A TINY FIRE OF TWIGS THROUGH
TO A HUGE, ARCHITECTURAL 'BUILD' CONTAINING MANY TONS OF TIMBER.
THE SUCCESS OF ALL BONFIRES DEPENDS UPON A PROPER BALANCE OF THE
SAME FACTORS:

  NAMELY: THE NATURE AND SIZES OF MATERIAL

       CONSTRUCTION

       IGNITION TECHNIQUE

       WIND, WEATHER AND ALLOWANCES FOR SAFETY

MATERIALS: THERE MUST BE A PROGRESSION IN SIZE FROM THE SMALLEST
TO THE LARGEST COMPONENT IF A STEADILY INCREASING FIRE IS TO BE
ACHIEVED, THE SMALLEST KINDLING SHOULD BE ¼" IN SECTION. A SMALL
QUANTITY OF THIS SHOULD BE FOLLOWED BY LARGER KINDLING, (UP TO 1").
THIS FIRE WILL RAPIDLY IGNITE SMALL TIMBERS, (UP TO 2½"), WHICH MUST
BE IN SUFFICIENT QUANTITY TO TAKE THE FIRE TO THE HEAT AT WHICH
BIGGER TIMBERS, (4" UPWARDS), WILL READILY BURN. ONCE LARGER TIMBERS
THAN THIS ARE BURNING THE DRAUGHTS CREATED WILL QUICKLY CARRY THE
FIRE TO THE LARGEST PIECES.

  RESINOUS WOOD SHOULD BE AVOIDED: IT MAKES POOR KINDLING AND
OFTEN BURNS WITH AN EXCESS OF SMOKE OR SPARKS. DEMOLITION TIMBER
IS DRIER AND EASIER TO BUILD WITH THAN UNCUT POLES. RUBBER, PLASTICS,
ETC. ARE NOT NEEDED FOR IGNITION IF A FIRE IS WELL BUILT AND THEY
ARE ALWAYS UNPLEASANT WHEN BURNING.

  WHEN MATERIALS ARRIVE ON SITE EVERYTHING SHOULD BE SORTED
INTO SIZES TO MAKE SELECTION EASY. TIMBERS LARGER THAN 2" IN SECTION
NEED NOT BE KEPT DRY IF THERE IS SUFFICIENT DRY KINDLING STORED AWAY.

TINY FIRE OF GRASS
AND DEAD LEAVES
OVER TWIGS. GIVES
WHITE SMOKE.
12" CONE

PYRAMID OF DRY
TIMBER. GIVES A HOT
TIDY FIRE. GOOD FOR
KEEPING WARM BY.
4' HIGH

FORMAL FIRE OF
GREEN BRANCHES WHICH
IF WELL IGNITED GIVE
A RAPID NOISY BLAZE
5' LONG

IN A LARGE BUILD MANY IGNITION POSITIONS WILL BE NEEDED. CRISS—CROSS NETWORKS OF MEDIUM AND SMALL TIMBERS SHOULD BE BUILT INTO ALCOVES UNDER THE STRATEGIC POINTS OF THE STRUCTURE. AT THE BOTTOM OF EACH ALCOVE, UNDERNEATH THE LARGER SIZE OF KINDLING, THERE SHOULD BE A SPACE JUST BIG ENOUGH FOR AN IGNITION BOX: A WOODEN CRATE OF FINE KINDLING WITH PARAFFIN SOAKED RAGS IN THE BOTTOM. FOR SAFETY AND WEATHER-PROTECTION THESE BOXES SHOULD BE STORED UNDER A HEAVY, WATERPROOF SHEET UNTIL REQUIRED.

WAX TORCH

ON BIG BUILDS WHICH TAKE SEVERAL DAYS/WEEKS TO CONSTRUCT IGNITION POSITIONS SHOULD BE MADE AT ALL POINTS OF THE COMPASS, SO THAT THE FIRE CAN BE IGNITED UP—WIND WHATEVER THE WIND DIRECTION. WAX PROCESSIONAL TORCHES ARE A CERTAIN METHOD OF IGNITION IN ANY WEATHER. IGNITION CAN ALSO BE BY REMOTE CONTROL: USE PYROTECHNIC FUSES (SEE PAGE 103) LEADING TO IGNITION BOXES WATERPROOFED WITH CLINGFILM. THIS METHOD IS PARTICULARLY EFFECTIVE FOR SMALL, SURPRISE BONFIRES. THROWING LIQUID FUELS ONTO A FIRE IS CLUMSY, DANGEROUS AND INEFFECTIVE BECAUSE THE FUEL GIVES ALL ITS HEAT TOO QUICKLY AND USUALLY FAILS TO SET FIRE TO ANYTHING ELSE.

ꓳNSTRUCTIꓳN

JUST AS MATERIALS MUST BE PROGRESSIVE IN SIZE, SO MUST THE AIR
SPACES AROUND THEM. BEGIN WITH A FRAMEWORK MASSIVE ENOUGH
TO ENDURE UNTIL THE HEIGHT OF THE FIRE. THIS IS THE SHAPE WHICH
WILL BE SEEN AMID THE LARGEST FLAMES. SMALLER TIMBERS CAN
THEN BE USED TO FILL IN THE STRUCTURE, AND TECHNIQUES TO
ACCELERATE OR DECELERATE THE 'BURN' CAN BE INCLUDED AT THIS
STAGE. 'CHIMNEYS' OF MEDIUM SIZED TIMBERS, PACKED WITH SMALLER
MATERIAL, CAN BE BUILT IN TO SPREAD THE FIRE QUICKLY. DECKS OF
HEAVY, SHEET MATERIAL CAN BE USED TO DELAY THE SPREAD OF THE
FIRE: FOR EXAMPLE TO TEMPORARILY PROTECT AN IMAGE SO THAT
IT MAY BE SEEN FOR SOME TIME BEFORE IT IS CONSUMED.
EVERYTHING MUST BE WELL FIXED: OTHERWISE FIERCELY BURNING
MATERIAL MAY COLLAPSE, BREAKING THE PROGRESSION OF THE FIRE.

   WHEN THE BASIC STRUCTURE IS COMPLETE ACCESS MUST BE LEFT
TO THE STRATEGIC POINTS WHICH WILL BE NEEDED FOR IGNITION.
THESE SHOULD NOT BE COMPLETED UNTIL LATE, TO AVOID THE DANGER
OF ACCIDENTAL OR MALICIOUS FIRING. SCRAP 'FELTS' FROM PAPER
MILLS ARE USEFUL FOR CLADDING. THEY ARE LARGE, CAN BE PAINTED,
AND THEY TAKE AN APPRECIABLE AMOUNT OF TIME TO BURN, EVEN IN
A BIG FIRE. (SOME ARTIFICIAL MATERIALS CAN BE USED FOR CLADDING
WITHOUT BEING OBNOXIOUS, PROVIDED THAT THE FIRE IS BIG ENOUGH.)
SMALL, HOT BONFIRES CAN INCLUDE NATURAL GREENERY IF A FIERCE
CRACKLING NOISE AND SOME SMOKE AND SPARKS ARE APPROPRIATE.

   THE SUCCESSFUL PREDICTION OF THE BEHAVIOUR OF ANY PARTIC—
ULAR BONFIRE IS A MATTER OF EXPERIENCE; BUT THE TECHNIQUE OF
THE PROGRESSIVE BUILD ENSURES THE BEST CHANCE OF THE FIRE
BURNING AS PLANNED.

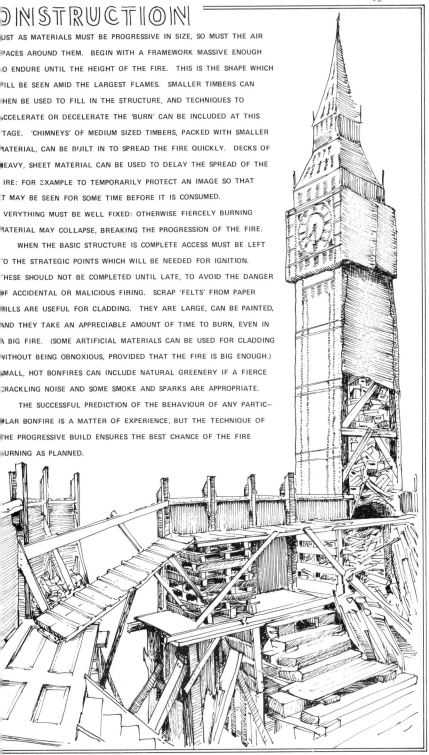

WIN
WEATHE
& SAFET

THE WIND CAN CARRY SPARKS HUNDREDS OF FEET. IN ADDITION
LARGE FIRES SET UP THEIR OWN CURRENTS, CAUSING SPARKS AND
SOMETIMES FLAMES TO TRAVEL LONG DISTANCES, EVEN IN STILL
AIR. SAFETY AREAS MUST BE CALCULATED ON THE BASIS THAT A
GALE MAY BLOW FROM ANY DIRECTION.

SMALL FIRES SHOULD BE ATTENDED, AT THE LEAST, BY BUCKETS
OF WATER AND WET, NATURAL FIBRE RAGS. THESE ARE ALSO
THE MOST EFFECTIVE WAYS OF DEALING WITH SPARK-FIRES ON
PROPS AND COSTUMES. SUITABLE FIRE EXTINGUISHERS SHOULD
BE PROVIDED WHEREVER ELECTRIC OR FUEL FIRES ARE A
POSSIBILITY. PEOPLE WORKING ON LARGER FIRES SHOULD WEAR
PROTECTIVE CLOTHING. A MODERATE LEVEL OF PROTECTION IS
PROVIDED BY THE FOLLOWING :–

> WOOLLEN, (NOT ARTIFICIAL), BALACLAVA HELMET.
> SPARK AND IMPACT PROOF GOGGLES.
> NATURAL FIBRE JACKET AND TROUSERS.
> WOOL, COTTON OR COTTON & LEATHER GLOVES.
> BOOTS WORN INSIDE TROUSERS.

CLOTHING SHOULD BE AS FREE AS POSSIBLE OF OPENINGS. WET
BLANKETS EFFECTIVELY SMOTHER FIRES ON CLOTHING.

THE LARGEST FIRES SHOULD BE ATTENDED IF POSSIBLE BY THE
FIRE BRIGADE AND BY THE ST JOHN'S AMBULANCE BRIGADE.
THE ROUTE TO THE NEAREST CASUALTY DEPARTMENT SHOULD BE
KNOWN TO EVERYONE AND A VEHICLE SHOULD BE READY WITH
IMMEDIATE ACCESS TO THE NEAREST ROAD. THROUGHOUT THE
SHOW EVERYONE NOT AT ANY MOMENT ACTUALLY WORKING
SHOULD BE INSTRUCTED TO RETURN TO A CENTRAL POSITION.
IN THIS WAY CHANGES OF PLAN CAN BE MOST EFFICIENTLY
COMMUNICATED AND THERE CAN BE LITTLE DOUBT AS TO ANY–
ONE'S WHEREABOUTS OR SAFETY.

GENERAL SECURITY ON THE SITE SHOULD ENSURE THAT NO
UNAUTHORISED PERSON COULD PUT THEMSELVES OR ANYONE
ELSE AT RISK. SOME SYSTEM OF IDENTIFICATION WILL BE
NEEDED TO ALLOW FREE PASSAGE FOR THOSE WORKING ON
THE SHOW.

A LARGE BONFIRE WILL COMPLETELY DESTROY THE GRASS
UNDER AND FOR SOME DISTANCE AROUND IT. THE PRESENCE
OF BURIED SERVICES SUCH AS GAS OR ELECTRICITY MUST BE
CHECKED OUT IN ADVANCE. ALL POSSIBLE DAMAGE AND THE
CLEARING OF DEBRIS WILL NEED TO BE PRE-PLANNED IF
INSURANCE CLAIMS OR LAW-SUITS ARE TO BE AVOIDED.

FIRE SCULPTURES

MANY TECHNIQUES AND EFFECTS CAN BE INCLUDED UNDER THIS HEADING — FROM SINGLE BURNING IMAGES TO A WHOLE LANDSCAPE TRANSFORMED BY MANY FIERY POINTS. THE EFFECT MAY BE ABSTRACT OR REPRESENTATIONAL, STATIC OR MOVING, SMALL OR LARGE. THE MOST COMMON TECHNIQUE IS THE USE OF FUEL AND WICKS TO CREATE SIMPLE AND RELIABLE FLAMES.

SOME FIRE SCULPTURES (e.g. STRAW FIGURES) MAY NEED FUEL ONLY FOR IGNITION, BUT MOST NEED TO BE COMPLETELY SOAKED IN ORDER TO WORK SATIS—FACTORILY. PARAFFIN IS THE BEST FUEL: IT BURNS CLEANER THAN DIESEL (LESS SMOKE) AND ITS LOW VOLATILITY MEANS THAT IT DOESN'T EVAPORATE TOO QUICKLY, NOR NEED IT BE DANGEROUS IN USE. PETROL IS TOO VOLATILE AND THEREFORE VERY DANGEROUS.

WICKS ARE BEST MADE OF NATURAL MATERIALS SUCH AS HESSIAN, COTTON AND PAPER ROPE. ASBESTOS ROPE IS RE—USABLE BUT IT IS EXPENSIVE AND MESSY TO WORK WITH. BECAUSE IT MUST BE STORED DRY IT MAY RELEASE FIBRES AND IN VIEW OF THE POTENTIAL HEALTH HAZARDS IT IS PROBABLY SAFEST TO AVOID IT.

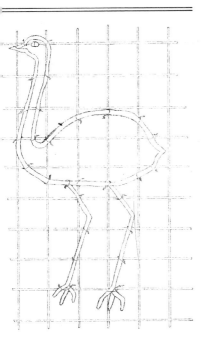

PAPER ROPE FIRE FIGURE.
HALF—INCH PAPER ROPE
  WIRED ON TO WELDED
  MESH SUPPORT.

SUPPORTING FRAMEWORKS CAN BE MADE FROM SCRAP METAL OF ALL KINDS, THOUGH WIRE NETTING WELDED MESH AND SCAFFOLD POLES ARE PARTICULARLY USEFUL.

THE WICK SHOULD BE FIXED TO THE FRAME WITH WIRE TIES, GIVING AS MUCH SUPPORT AS POSSIBLE, TO PREVENT IT FROM SAGGING OR FALLING WHILE BURNING. USE AN ACCURATE DISPENSER TO AVOID WASTE (PLASTIC DETERGENT BOTTLES ARE GOOD) AND SOAK THE WICK THOROUGHLY BETWEEN ½ AND 2 HOURS BEFORE FIRING TO GIVE AN EVEN COVERAGE OF FIRE. BUT TAKE CARE — IF IT IS SOAKED TOO LATE AND IS STILL DRIPPING WITH LIQUID FUEL, IT MAY BURN TOO FIERCELY, PRODUCING OVER—LARGE FLAMES; IF IT IS SOAKED TOO EARLY TOO MUCH PARAFFIN MAY EVAPOR—ATE BEFORE FIRING AND IN WET CONDITIONS THE WICK MAY TAKE UP WATER. PRIMED SCULPTURES WILL WITHSTAND A LITTLE RAIN, BUT THEY MUST BE COVERED AGAINST ANYTHING MORE THAN A LIGHT SHOWER.

IGNITION SHOULD BE FROM LOW DOWN AND UP-WIND, OR AT SEVERAL POINTS. FAST IGNITER CORD (SEE 102) CAN BE WRAPPED ROUND THE WICK FOR RAPID FIRING OF THE WHOLE SHAPE.

SCALE: IT IS IMPORTANT TO EXPERIMENT WITH THE BURNING WICK TO SEE IF THE FLAMES WILL PICK OUT THE INTENDED IMAGE: IT IS EASY TO BUILD THE SCULPTURE TOO SMALL, OR IN TOO MUCH DETAIL, SO THAT THE FLAMES 'BLOT OUT' THE IMAGE.

FIRE EFFECT

STRAW IS A CHEAP AND EASILY MODELLED MATERIAL FOR MAKING IMAGES: AFTER IGNITION THE SHAPE OF THE FIGURE WILL BE ILLUMINATED AS THE FLAMES SPREAD BUT ONCE FULLY ALIGHT IT WILL APPEAR AS A BURNING MASS. IT SHOULD NOT BE NECESSARY TO SOAK IT IN PARAFFIN, BUT SOME FUEL TO PRIME THE IGNITION POINT IS HELPFUL.

UNLIKE THE OTHER WICKS MENTIONED, STRAW SPREADS A MASS OF SPARKS WHEN BURNING AND GREAT CARE MUST BE TAKEN WHEN CALCULATING SAFE DISTANCES.

WAX TORCHES, AVAILABLE FROM SOME FIREWORK MANUFACTURERS ARE USEFUL FOR MANY KINDS OF ILLUMINATION (INCLUDING SHADOW PLAYS AND LARGE LANTERNS) AND THEY ARE PARTICULARLY SUITABLE FOR CARRYING IN PROCESSIONS AND FOR LIGHTING OTHER FIRES.

FOR EASE OF IGNITION DIP THEM IN PARAFFIN BEFORE USE. THEY DO NOT READILY GO OUT IF STAMPED ON, BUT CONTINUE SMOULDERING AND CAN EVEN RE-IGNITE IN A WIND. THEY CAN BE EXTINGUISHED BY WRAPPING THEM IN WET CLOTH, BUT THIS MAKES THEM DIFFICULT TO RE-LIGHT. A BETTER AND SAFER METHOD IS TO PLUNGE THE TORCH INTO A PART-FULL BUCKET OF PARAFFIN. THE BUCKET SHOULD BE FIRMLY SET (PREFERABLY DUG INTO THE GROUND) AND NOT CLUTTERED WITH TOO MANY OTHER TORCHES.

A VARIETY OF FIRE BRANDS CAN BE MADE USING PARAFFIN-DOUSED RAGS WITHIN A FINE WIRE-MESH 'BASKET'. OTHER TYPES INCLUDE FIRE BALLS ON CHAINS WHICH CAN BE WHIRLED IN A CIRCLE, AND FLAMES OF VARIOUS SIZES MOUNTED ON FRAMES OR SUSPENDED FROM WIRES.

THESE RAG AND WIRE CONSTRUCTIONS ARE DIFFICULT TO EXTINGUISH. WHEN MOST OF THE FUEL HAS BURNED OFF THEY MAY DROP FLAMING FRAGMENTS, SO ALLOW FOR THEM TO BURN OUT IN A SAFE PLACE, OR ELSE THOROUGHLY DOUSE THEM IN WATER.

STRAW FIGURE

JUNK WOOD FRAME

STRAW BOUND TIGHT WITH WIRE

FIGURE COULD BE SUSPENDED WITH WIRE OR CHAIN

WAX TORCH STORED READY FOR USE,

COTTON OR NATURAL FIBRE RAGS IN 6" DIAMETER WIRE MESH, SOAKED IN PARAFFIN

← HEAVY WIRE GOES THRO STICK TO HOLD MESH FIRMLY ON.

FIRE BRAND:

3FT STICK, LARGE FLAMES.

EXTINGUISH IN WATER

BEFORE RAGS DISINTEGRATE.

WHIRLING FIRE BALL

...KS ON A FRAME WILL BURN AWAY IN MINUTES,
FIRE–CANS MAY BURN FOR HOURS AND THEY
A VERY EFFECTIVE WAY OF TRANSFORMING
...PACE. USE THEM TO ILLUMINATE PATHWAYS,
...K AVENUES THROUGH LANDSCAPE, AND CREATE
...PES WHEN SEEN FROM A DISTANCE. (TO MAKE
...RIZONTAL IMAGES APPARENT CONSIDER THE
...SPECTIVE FROM THE POINT OF VIEW OF THE
...IENCE.)

WICK SHOULD REACH NEARLY TO THE TOP,
...ED FIRMLY SO AS NOT TO SINK UNDER THE
...AFFIN. A SCRAP OF HESSIAN CRUSHED IN THE
...JD AND PUSHED INTO THE TIN MAKES A GOOD
...K, BUT IF THE MATERIAL USED IS THINNER
... FLIMSIER A PIECE OF WIRE MESH CAN BE
...SSED INTO THE CAN TO SUPPORT IT.

IF RIM IS FAIRLY EVEN
EXTINGUISH BY EXCLUDING
AIR, E.G. WITH PAD
OF DAMP CLOTH.
CAN BE RE-USED IF
WICK IS KEPT DRY.

HALF FILLED WITH
PARAFFIN

FIRE CAN PROPORTIONS: AS HIGH
AS IT IS WIDE.
SIZE: TYPICALLY AN 8OZ FOOD CAN

A VERY LONG BURNING, BUT SMALLER, FLAME CAN
BE ACHIEVED BY USING A CLOSED CAN WITH A
HOLE IN THE TOP ONLY BIG ENOUGH FOR A PART
OF THE WICK TO PROTRUDE. EXPERIMENT WITH
THE PROPORTIONS OF THE CANS AND THE QUANTITY
OF FUEL TO ESTABLISH THE BURNING TIME.

A WORD OF WARNING: BECAUSE
FIRE–CANS CONTAIN A RESERVOIR
OF LIQUID FUEL THEY ARE MORE
DANGEROUS THAN PRE-SOAKED
SCULPTURES. IF A CAN IS KNOCKED
OVER, BURNING PARAFFIN WILL
SPREAD AROUND IT. THEY SHOULD
ALWAYS BE SITED WHERE ANY FIRE
SPILL CAN BURN OUT HARMLESSLY.

FIRE CAN SPIRAL

...PARAFFIN CONTAINERS SHOULD BE LABELLED. BUCKETS OF PARAFFIN HAVE BEEN MISTAKEN FOR WATER
...） THROWN ON A FIRE. A KETTLE WAS ONCE FILLED FROM AN UNMARKED CONTAINER AND THEN LEFT TO
...L ON THE STOVE UNTIL IT EXPLODED IN FLAMES. PETROL MUST NEVER BE PUT IN CONTAINERS SIMILAR TO
...OSE USED FOR PARAFFIN.

...HOT WEATHER LIQUID FUELS EVAPORATE MORE QUICKLY AND GREAT CARE MUST BE TAKEN TO AVOID
...IDENTS INVOLVING THE IGNITION OF CLOUDS OF VAPOUR.

...ATTEMPT SHOULD BE MADE TO RE-SOAK SCULPTURES WHILST THEY ARE ALIGHT, NOR TO RE-FUEL A HOT
...E CAN.

...EREVER PARAFFIN FIRES ARE USED THERE MAY BE DAMAGE TO GRASS UNDERNEATH. PARAFFIN STAINS ON
...NE AND CONCRETE TAKE A LONG TIME TO DISAPPEAR. CHOOSE A SITE WHERE ANY RESULTING MESS WILL
...T BE AN EMBARASSMENT.

...REIGN WORK: FOREIGN WORK CAN RAISE PROBLEMS OVER THE NAMING OF DIFFERENT GRADES OF
...L. TESTS SHOULD BE MADE TO ENSURE THAT THE FUEL IS SUITABLE, PARTICULARLY TO AVOID
...METHING WITH DANGEROUSLY HIGH VOLATILITY. INSUFFICIENT RESEARCH CAN LEAD TO THE
...CHASE OF USELESS LIQUIDS. A 45 GALLON DRUM OF 'PARAFFIN', BOUGHT BY US IN POLAND, WAS
...COVERED AT THE ELEVENTH HOUR TO CONTAIN A SLIGHTLY GLUTINOUS, NON-INFLAMMABLE
...STANCE. WE HAD BOUGHT ENOUGH LIQUID PARAFFIN B.P. TO RELIEVE CONSTIPATION ON A TRULY
...C SCALE ... ...

PYROTECHNICS

THE LAW

FIREWORKS MUST BE USED IN ACCORDANCE WITH
THE MANUFACTURER'S INTENTIONS AND CANNOT
SAFELY BE ADAPTED IN ANY WAY. ADVICE ON THE
FIRING OF FIREWORKS CAN BE OBTAINED FROM THE
MANUFACTURERS. SPECIAL STORAGE MAY BE
REQUIRED FOR THE HOLDING OF MORE THAN 5LBS
OF FIREWORKS. INFORMATION ABOUT 'REGISTERED
PREMISES' CAN BE OBTAINED FROM THE LOCAL
AUTHORITY (USUALLY THE TRADING STANDARDS
DEPARTMENT). FOR THE PURCHASE OF SOME ITEMS
A POLICE LICENCE IS REQUIRED.

THE SITE

THE SAFETY PRECAUTIONS DISCUSSED ON PAGE 96
APPLY WHEREVER FIREWORKS ARE USED, AND
SECURITY TAKES AN EVEN HIGHER PRIORITY. THE
FEWER PEOPLE THERE ARE ON A FIRING SITE THE
SAFER IT WILL BE. FOR STORAGE OF FIREWORKS ON
SITE USE A LOCKABLE AND SPARK-PROOF BOX, AND
NEVER LEAVE IT UNATTENDED. AN EXPERIENCED
FIREWORK OPERATOR MUST SUPERVISE THE RIGGING,
FIRING AND DE-RIGGING OF A SHOW. AFTER THE
SHOW IS OVER THE SITE SHOULD REMAIN SECURE
UNTIL IT HAS BEEN CHECKED FOR DANGEROUS REMAINS.
CO_2 FIRE EXTINGUISHERS ARE RECOMMENDED FOR
PYROTECHNIC FIRES.

DISPLAY OR EFFEC

FIREWORKS ARE EXPENSIVE AND SHORT-LIVED. FO
DISPLAY LASTING MORE THAN A FEW MINUTES YOU
MAY NEED TO SPEND HUNDREDS OF POUNDS TO AV
DISAPPOINTMENT. HOWEVER, SATISFYING EFFECTS
BE ACHIEVED ON A SMALLER BUDGET IF THE FIRE-
WORKS ARE USED NOT AS AN ISOLATED DISPLAY, B
AS AN ELEMENT IN A THEATRICAL EVENT. ALLOW
PLENTY OF TIME FOR REHEARSAL AND RIGGING. A
BARRAGE OF ROMAN CANDLES, WALLS OF SILVER
GERBS (POWERFUL SILVER AND GOLD FOUNTAINS),
EVEN JUST ONE GOOD ROCKET OR SHELL, IN THE
RIGHT CONTEXT, CAN BE MORE REWARDING THAN
DISPLAYS COSTING TWENTY TIMES AS MUCH.

REHEARSAL

ANY FIRE OR FIREWORK EFFECT MUST BE PRACTIS
UNDER THE CONDITIONS IN WHICH IT WILL BE USE
THE TIMING AND DURATION OF EFFECTS CAN ONL
BE ESTABLISHED BY FULL REHEARSAL. THIS SHOU
RESULT IN A COMPREHENSIVE RUNNING-ORDER IN
WHICH THE POTENTIAL HAZARDS, SUCH AS PREMA
IGNITION OF ONE PIECE BY ANOTHER, HAVE BEEN
IDENTIFIED AND ELIMINATED.
UNFORESEEN HAZARDS OR UNINTENTIONAL SIDE-
EFFECTS MUST BE UNDERSTOOD TO BE THE RULE
RATHER THAN THE EXCEPTION.

> THE PRECISE LEGALITIES GOVERNING
> THE PURCHASE, STORAGE AND USE
> OF FIREWORKS AND FUSES ARE NOT
> WITHIN THE SCOPE OF THIS BOOK
> AND IT MUST BE EMPHASISED THAT
> IT IS THE RESPONSIBILITY OF
> INDIVIDUALS TO ASSURE THEMSELVES
> THAT THEY ARE ACTING IN ACCORDANC
> WITH THE LAW.

IT MAY ALSO BE NECESSARY TO CONSULT OTHE
PEOPLE WHEN CONSIDERING THE USE OF FIREWO
FAILURE TO LIASE WITH THE FIRE BRIGADE, CO
GUARD OR MOUNTAIN RESCUE SERVICES CAN
RESULT IN RISK TO LIFE FOR DEDICATED PEOP
THE POSSIBLE PROXIMITY OF OLD PEOPLE, HOS
PATIENTS AND LIVESTOCK ALSO NEEDS CAREFU
CONSIDERATION.

(4) BURSTING CHARGE BREAKS UP SHELL & LIGHTS STARS INSIDE.

'SHOP GOODS' ARE THE SMALLER, LESS DANGEROUS FIREWORKS ON SALE TO THE PUBLIC DURING THE RUN-UP TO NOVEMBER THE FIFTH. THE SAME TYPES—FOUNTAINS, ROMAN CANDLES, ROCKETS, WHEELS, SET-PIECES, ETC. — ARE AVAILABLE ON A LARGER SCALE AS 'DISPLAY' FIREWORKS. MOST MANUFACTURERS SUPPLY THESE, USUALLY IN GOOD VALUE ASSORTED PACKS, THROUGHOUT A LARGE PART OF THE YEAR.

SOME TYPES ONLY APPEAR IN THE 'DISPLAY' CATEGORY; NOTABLY SHELLS. SHELLS, CASED IN PAPER OR PLASTIC, ARE FIRED INTO THE AIR FROM LAUNCHING (MORTAR) TUBES BY A 'LIFTING' CHARGE OF BLACK POWDER. A DELAY FUSE IN THE SHELL FIRES THE 'BURSTING' CHARGE WHEN THE SHELL REACHES THE TOP OF ITS FLIGHT. THE AERIAL EFFECTS THIS PRODUCES RANGE FROM PURE NOISE, (CRACKS, BANGS, WHISTLES ETC.), THROUGH TO MANY DIFFERENT SHAPES AND COLOURS OR STARBURST.

EFFECTS ARE DESCRIBED BY A SORT OF POETRY — GLOW WORMS, GOLDEN WEBS, SERPENTS, COMETS, TORBILLIONS, BOMBETTES, FLITTER, GLITTER — OR IN THE LANGUAGE OF THE CHEMISTRY LABORATORY. THEIR EPHEMERAL NATURE MAKES DESCRIPTION ALMOST ENTIRELY SUBJECTIVE, AND IT IS PREFERABLE TO MAKE CHOICES BY TESTING EXAMPLES.

WHEN TESTING A FIREWORK FOR USE IN A SPECIFIC CONTEXT EVERY ATTRIBUTE MUST BE OBSERVED. IT IS NOT SUFFICIENT TO OBSERVE THE APPEARANCE ALONE; YOU MUST ALSO ALLOW FOR THE DURATION, THE NOISE, AND THE SPARKS, DEBRIS AND SMOKE PRODUCED.

KEEP A RECORD OF GOODS OBTAINED AND MAKE NOTES ON PREFERRED EFFECTS. IT IS THEN SOME-TIMES POSSIBLE TO ORDER THE SAME SELECTION ANOTHER TIME, ALTHOUGH SEVERAL MONTHS NOTICE MAY BE NEEDED.

THEATRICAL EFFECTS: SOME MANUFACTURERS MARKET A RANGE OF PYROTECHNIC EFFECTS FOR STAGE, T.V. AND FILM USE. THESE INCLUDE BANGS, FLASHES, SMOKES AND OTHER EFFECTS, USUALLY FITTED WITH ELECTRIC IGNITION FOR PRECISE CUEING. IN ADDITION COLOURED FIRE, SMOKE AND FLASH POWDERS ARE AVAILABLE.

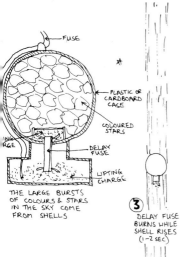

FUSE

PLASTIC OR CARDBOARD CASE

COLOURED STARS

DELAY FUSE

LIFTING CHARGE

THE LARGE BURSTS OF COLOURS & STARS IN THE SKY COME FROM SHELLS

(3) DELAY FUSE BURNS WHILE SHELL RISES (1–2 SEC)

(1) SHELL PLACED IN TUBE (THE MORTAR) & FUSE LIT.

(2) LIFTING CHARGE PROPELS SHELL & LIGHTS DELAY FUSE

BANG

INNOVATION

THE PARTICULAR USE OF A FIREWORK CAN ONLY BE REGARDED AS
SAFE IF IT CONFORMS TO THE MANUFACTURER'S INTENDED CONDITIONS
FOR FIRING. APPARENTLY SLIGHT CHANGES COULD RESULT IN A
DANGEROUS SITUATION. FOR EXAMPLE MULTIPLE ROCKETS FIRED FROM
A CONE CAN PRODUCE AN IMPRESSIVE AERIAL EFFECT BUT IT MUST BE
NOTICED THAT THE TECHNIQUE INVOLVES A CHANGE IN THE BASIC
FIRING CONDITIONS. A SINGLE ROCKET IS DESIGNED TO BE SUPPORTED
IN THE (NEAR) VERTICAL, WHILE REMAINING FREE TO RISE IN THE AIR.
IF A CONE IS USED IT IS IMPORTANT TO ENSURE THAT THE ROCKETS
ARE PLACED SO THAT THEY ARE ALL FREE TO RISE IN ANY ORDER.
IN PRACTICE ONE OR TWO WILL PROBABLY FLY FIRST AND THE REST
WILL ALL RISE TOGETHER, BUT BAD LOADING COULD RESULT IN THEIR
BECOMING TRAPPED OR TRAVELLING AT EXTREME ANGLES. ALSO, A
SINGLE ROCKET CAN BE ANGLED AWAY FROM SPECTATORS, BUT A
ROCKET CONE DISCHARGES ITS CONTENTS AT A SLIGHT ANGLE IN ALL
DIRECTIONS, THEREFORE IT MAY NEED A LARGER SAFETY AREA.*

*N.B. ROCKETS TURN INTO THE WIND WHEN IN FLIGH'

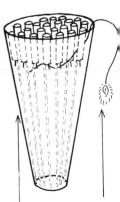

CONE - FIRED ROCKETS

PUT THE FUSE IN
AMONG THE ROCKET'S
THE FIRST FEW WIL
FIRE THE REST.
METAL OR STRONG
CARDBOARD CONE.
LASH IT FIRMLY
UPRIGHT AND CLING-
FILM OVER TOP
AGAINST RAIN.

FIRING AND TIMING

THE OPERATOR OF ANY PYROTECHNIC DEVICE SHOULD ALWAYS BE IN
SIGHT OF IT WHEN FIRING, FOR REASONS OF SAFETY AND PRECISE
TIMING. IF A FIREWORK DISPLAY SEEMS BORING IT IS PROBABLY
BECAUSE THE TIMING IS AT FAULT. A BANG A FEW SECONDS EARLY
OR LATE MAY BE A LOT WORSE THAN NO BANG AT ALL.

IT IS NOT ESSENTIAL TO HAVE SOPHISTICATED FUSING, WHERE MANY
EFFECTS ARE LINKED TOGETHER OR EXPENSIVE ELECTRIC CONSOLES
ARE USED. WITH THE AID OF PORTFIRES (SMALL FLARES USED FOR
LIGHTING) AND A WELL SET, WELL PLANNED SHOW, ONE PERSON CAN
FIRE MANY FIREWORKS SMOOTHLY AND SAFELY; AND IF SOMETHING
GOES WRONG (EITHER A FAILURE OR A PREMATURE IGNITION) THE
OPERATOR CAN TIME THE REST OF THE SHOW ACCORDINGLY. WHEN
LAYING OUT FIREWORKS IT IS ESSENTIAL THAT THE OPERATOR
HAS SUFFICIENT SPACE AND GOOD ENOUGH GROUND UNDERFOOT
TO WORK IN DARKNESS. IT IS NO GOOD TRIPPING OVER WHEN YOU
HAVE JUST LIT A FUSE.

POSTSCRIPT: THE VERY REAL DANGERS CONNECTED WITH PYRO-
TECHNICS MAKE IT IMPROPER TO TREAT THE SUBJECT IN ANYTHING
OTHER THAN A RATHER FORMAL FASHION. IDEAS NEED TO BE
EXCHANGED AND SKILLS LEARNED ON A PERSONAL BASIS, AND
DIRECT EXPERIENCE IS THE KEY TO SUCCESSFUL AND SAFE USE.

FLARES.

NAIL THRO AN UPRIGH
INTO WOODEN PLUG IN E

BENGAL ILLUMINATIO

GIVES
COLOURED LIG
BURNS DOWN LIKE A
CIGARETTE: BEWARE
RED HOT DRIPS.

LANCES
- SMALL FLARE
USED IN LARGE
NUMBERS TO MAK
PICTURES OR WORDS
IN POINTS OF LIGHT.

PORTFIRES
- HAND HELD FLAR
FOR LIGHTING
FIREWORKS.

BLUE TOUCH PAPERS: FITTED TO FIREWORKS WHICH ARE SUITABLE FOR CLOSE-RANGE IGNITION; ALSO TO THE DELAY FUSES ON LARGER, MORE DANGEROUS FIREWORKS. THEY PROVIDE A CHEAP AND SIMPLE METHOD OF LIGHTING NON-HAZARDOUS EFFECTS.

PAPER 'PIPE'

SEVERAL INCHES OF POWDER-COATED CORE BARED TO ACT AS A DELAY.

JOINTING –

① CORE BARED

PIPED MATCH: PAPER TUBE CONTAINING A BLACK POWDER COATED FIBRE CORE, IN LENGTHS FROM 6 FEET TO 50 METRES. GAS PRESSURE INSIDE THE PIPE GIVES PRACTICALLY INSTANTANEOUS IGNITION OVER LONG DISTANCES, SO SUITABLE FOR THE SIMULTANEOUS FIRING OF SEVERAL FIREWORKS. IT CAN WITHSTAND LIGHT RAIN, BUT IT IS NOT WATERPROOF AND SO LONG RUNS PRESENT A PROBLEM. SHORT RUNS (AND FIREWORKS) CAN BE PROTECTED BY CLINGFILM. A SHORT DELAY CAN BE CREATED BY BARING A FEW INCHES OF THE CORE – WHEN THE FIRE ENTERS THE PIPE AGAIN IGNITION IS INSTANTANEOUS.

② CUT OPEN AND INSERT

③ RESEAL WITH MASKING TAPE.

IGNITER CORD (POLICE LICENCE REQUIRED): A PLASTIC COATED FUSE AVAILABLE IN TWO SPEEDS, FAST (APPROX 1 FOOT PER SECOND) AND SLOW (APPROX 10 SECONDS PER FOOT). IT IS WATERPROOF, STRONG, RELIABLE AND CONVENIENT.

PLAIN ELECTRIC FUSE

'MATCHED' ELECTRIC FUSE TO IGNITE OTHER FUSES

'MATCHED' FUSE   IGNITER CORD
GOOD COMBINATION FOR
REMOTE-FIRED BONFIRES AND FIRE
SCULPTURES

ELECTRIC FUSES (POLICE LICENCE REQUIRED): TWO FINE WIRES LEAD INTO THE IGNITION HEAD, FIRED BY BATTERY OR MAINS OPERATED SYSTEM. 'MATCHED' FUSES END IN TWO SMALL TAILS OF BLACK POWDER COATED FIBRE: FOR PERFECT CUEING OF IGNITION OVER LONG DISTANCES.

PARAFFIN RAGS

SUPPLIERS CAN ADVISE OVER LICENSING AND USE.

LANTERNS
ALI WOOD

Almost any translucent hollow shape can become a lantern. Small lanterns, 1'-2' high - easy to make - look lovely in groups. Can be lit by one or two candles

Start with wire or withie structur bent to shape and joints fastened with masking tape. Soak withies in wat to make them more flexible: they keep their shape when dry.

The structure can be quite light - it does not need to support a lot of weight.

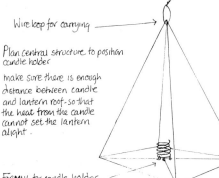

Wire loop for carrying

Plan central structure to position candle holder

make sure there is enough distance between candle and lantern roof - so that the heat from the candle cannot set the lantern alight.

FIRMLY fix candle holder - spiral of wire - twisted around candle for shape.

If the candle is to be left to burn down make a saucer of tin round the base o the holder to catch the candle dregs

the candle holder can be made from chicken wire pressed to sha and wired to withie structure.

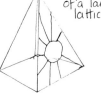

Any structural lines on the outside skin of a lantern will show in silhouette, so strengthening lattice work can make pictures or patterns.

Opening for lighting and replacing of candles

Bend wire into door frame (or use withie)

Wire loops so door can be fastened shut.

wire loop for hinge.

twist of wire to go through wire loops + fasten door shut.

fixed wire or withie strut accross top of door.

A simpler way

If the lantern is only to be used once - it can be covered with the candle in position already. Then cut a small hole in skin - just to light candle, and pin or glue up hole afterwards. OR leave the hole open if there is no draught or wind which could extinguish candle.

OVERINGS: When the structure is
mplete, cover it with good quality
sue paper, using copydex or P.V.A.
od glue.

uick method, but not waterproof:
near glue onto framework and press
tissue paper, leave to dry and
m off excess paper.

ronger rainproof method: place
sue on flat surface, and com-
etely cover with glue, using a sponge.
t paper carefully and lay over frame,
ue side in. Overlap pieces for
rength. work quickly before glue dries.
en covering is dry, paint with another
er of glue.

ute PVA with water-50/50-gives a
re translucent quality. Skin will stretch
t as it dries. Copydex dries slightly
lowish and rubbery giving a
onger more durable result.

en covering is finished, cut small
les in the top to let the heat escape.
nterns can be covered with fabric,
r more Strength. Down-proof cotton is ideal. Glue
Staple or sew it to the framework

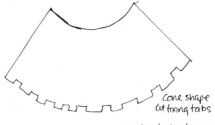

PAPER LANTERN TO SIT ON THE GROUND

Small lanterns can be made very quickly
from stiff paper folded and stapled into
shapes, and painted as for frame lanterns.

Cone shape
cut fixing tabs

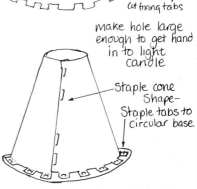

make hole large
enough to get hand
in to light
candle

Staple cone
Shape-
Staple tabs to
circular base.

Put a lump of clay in base to weight lantern
and to plant candle in.

These lanterns are not good in strong wind.

SMALL HANGING LANTERN   ~Make paper box

cut hole with stanley knife- to light candle +
to let heat escape

.wire loop for hanging.

use small ends of candles planted
in clay- or night lights.

NTING. For translucent decoration, coat paper
erns with oil (cooking oil, paraffin) then paint, using
based paints thinned down with white spirits. keeps
mboyant Enamels are especially good. Emulsion
nt (or any paint containing lime) will block the light
d dry as a silhouette. Fabric can be painted using
same methods- or use thinned down acrylic paints
t the fabric before painting with acrylics)

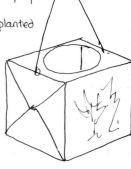

LIGHT SOURCES

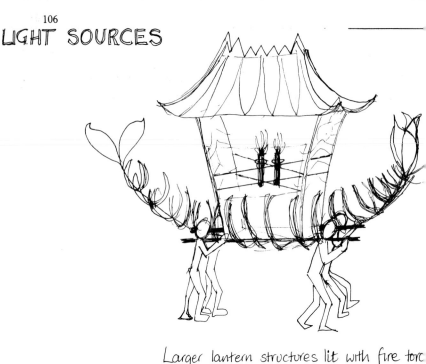

Larger lantern structures lit with fire torc
Structure is carried so it can be kept upric
and fairly steady. Make plenty of room for
inside. Fire torches give off a lot of heat, a
lovely flickering yellowish light.
Lanterns are very _inflammable_.
A constant check must be kept on them
when they are lit.

wire loop

Jam jar.

clay

If lantern skin is not windproof, and candle light
glow is required— use candles in clay in jars.

Electric lighting is better in some situations, although you lose
the flickering effect of flames. You can use mains electricity
on static images, or images which don't move far.

Alternatives; strap small battery torches inside the framework
the image can then have lots of movement without risk of fire
Torches with florescent tubes are most effective, giving an eve
glow of light. This method can become expensive and too heav
when used in very large images.

6 Volt batteries- strap all the weight of the battery to the operator, so only the weight of light bulbs is in the image. 6 volts will light 5-6 bulbs for several hours. (depending on wattage of bulbs)

Motor bike batteries are rechargeable, but must be kept upright to avoid spilling acid. Wrap in rubber inner tubes for protection.

You can buy rechargeable dry cell batteries from pot-holing shops, but they are expensive.

Car batteries (12 volt) will give brighter light for images that are seen from a distance. Use florescent tubes (caravan fittings). Use a long wire for movement- or transport battery on wheels. or build lantern on or around a car, using headlights for more illumination.

6 volt Bulbs

Bulbs wired in parrallel →

Crocodile clips

6 volt Motor Bike BATTERY.

You can make lantern structures and images as large as you want, but remember that structural bits on or near the lantern skin will show as black silhouette. So with a large lantern, if there are clumsy-looking structural bits, keep them well into the middle of the frame.

SHADOW PUPPETS

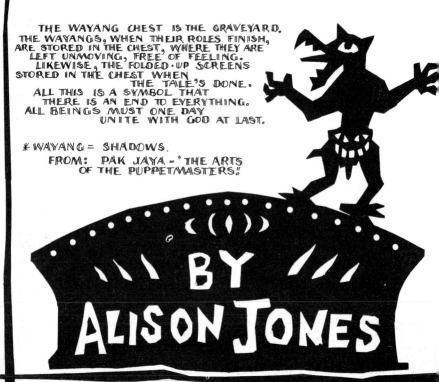

THE TRUNKS OF BANANA TREES THAT
THE PUPPETS ARE INSERTED IN
ARE SYMBOLS OF THE WORLD OF MAN.
MAN'S SPIRIT IS THE PUPPETEER,
SYMBOL OF TRUTH AND MEANING.
THE SCREEN'S THE UNSEEN WORLD ABOVE
MAN'S CHARACTERS THE WAYANGS,
AND THE LAMP'S RAYS THE ALMIGHTY.
THE AUDIENCE IS THE
ALL = PERCEIVING WISE MAN.

THE WAYANG CHEST IS THE GRAVEYARD.
THE WAYANGS, WHEN THEIR ROLES FINISH,
ARE STORED IN THE CHEST, WHERE THEY ARE
LEFT UNMOVING, FREE OF FEELING.
LIKEWISE, THE FOLDED-UP SCREENS
STORED IN THE CHEST WHEN
THE TAILE'S DONE.
ALL THIS IS A SYMBOL THAT
THERE IS AN END TO EVERYTHING.
ALL BEINGS MUST ONE DAY
UNITE WITH GOD AT LAST.

✻ WAYANG = SHADOWS.
FROM: PAK JAYA - "THE ARTS
OF THE PUPPETMASTERS."

BY
ALISON JONES

JOSEPH & MARY — Shadow Play

When Mary was big with child
   Joseph laid down his axe,
And they travelled thru the wild country
   To Bethlehem to pay their Income Tax.

Large, simple accessible puppet fill the screen.

Mary rode on a white mule
   With a shining silver horn,
And Joseph lead them, radiant,
   Thru bramble, briar & thorn;
Thru forest night in warm embrace
   They sang the dark til dawn.

Smaller Joseph, Mary & Mule figures. Concentrate on a good animated jungle (monkeys & snakes &c.......)

Volcanoes gurgled high above,
   And Mary raised her hand,
And Joseph & the mule dodged thru
   The fires of liquid land.

Firework ?

Across the plain the earth gave way
   Where swamps & monsters lie,
But Mary said to Joseph,
   "Our love is like the sky"
And they looked up into the blue
   And their feet stepped high.

Prehistoric zoo & maybe a cactus or two

Now Mary said, "My time has come",
   And her cry was deep & loud;
And in a cave was Jesus born,
   And outside a bright cloud.

Cave & blasted tree. Mary, J. & mule go in. Cloud opens to reveal angel in glory.

Everyone hums 'In the Bleak Midwinter' thruout (or medley)

They each carry one shadow-puppet in a cardboard tube, & work it on the screen when required.

Let the shadows dictate the pace (narrator leave space between verses).

Maybe sing 'Angels from the Realms of Glory' as angel emerges from cloud — & process off.

7'6"

4'

SCREEN MADE OF WHITE
COTTON STRETCHED OVER
THE AUDIENCE SIDE OF THE
FRAME, AND STAPLED TO
THE BACK OF THE FRAME.

SCREEN FRAMEWORK BUILT OF
2"×2" TIMBER, WITH 2"×1¼"
LEGS WHICH ENGAGE WITH
SIDE PANELS. (THE LEGS ARE
PERMANENTLY ATTACHED TO SCREEN.)

SCREEN ATTACHED TO SIDE PANELS WITH
8 COACHBOLTS WITH WING NUTS FOR EASE
OF DISMANTLING FOR TRANSPORT AND
STORAGE.

½" PLY

AUDIENCE   TWO SIDE SUPPORTING PANELS, MIRROR IMAGES
OF EACH OTHER, MADE OF ½" PLYWOOD WITH
2"×1½" AND 2"×2" TIMBERS FIXED

USING THE SHADOW SCREEN.

THE PUPPETS SHOULD BE LAID OUT BEHIND THE OPERATOR, FLAT ON POLYTHENE (OUTSIDE) OR STUCK INTO POLYSTYRENE BLOCKS (INSIDE)

TWO OPERATORS ARE BEST; MORE MAKES THE SPACE CRAMPED AND CHAOTIC.

LIGHT THE SCREEN WITH ONE WAX FIRETORCH — MORE THAN ONE GIVES DOUBLE IMAGES — HIGH ENOUGH TO HIDE OPERATOR'S HEAD.

WATCH FOR FIRE-RISK: LOW CEILINGS, CURTAINS INDOORS. LAY A DAMP BLANKET UNDER THE TORCH TO CATCH HOT WAX. HAVE A FIRE EXTINGUISHER AND BUCKET OF WET RAGS NEARBY.

FOR TINY SCREENS USE A CANDLE. FOR GIANT SCREENS AN ELECTRIC FLOODLIGHT WILL DO THE JOB — BUT IT LACKS THE WARMTH AND ANIMATION OF FIRELIGHT. TRY USING HAND-HELD FIRETORCH ON LARGE SCREENS, FOLLOWING THE ACTION FROM PLACE TO PLACE.

ALLOW PLENTY OF TIME TO PLAY WITH THE SHADOWS BEFORE THE SHOW. UNEXPECTED CHARACTERISTICS EMERGE, UNUSUAL MOVEMENTS ARE DISCOVERED AS THE OPERATOR DANCES TO THE MUSIC WHICH IS ESSENTIAL TO ALL SHADOW PLAYS.

MAKE PUPPETS LARGER BY HOLDING THEM FURTHER FROM SCREEN — BUT ALWAYS WATCH THE SHADOWS, NOT THE PUPPETS.

SHADOW PLAYS ARE BEST WHEN USED WITHIN THE FRAMEWORK OF A LARGER EVENT, EXTENDING ITS IMAGES AND MEANINGS.

OTHER SCREENS

SCREENS CAN BE ANY
SIZE, AND BUILT INTO
OTHER STRUCTURES
SO THEY ONLY
BECOME APPARENT
WHEN THE FIRE
IS LIT.

TRY USING A
MARQUEE ROOF. THE
ANGLE IS GOOD AND THE NOISE OF
PUPPETS SLAPPING AGAINST CANVAS
IS VERY EFFECTIVE INSIDE. LIGHT
IT WITH A TUNGSTEN-HALOGEN
FLOODLIGHT, OR A HAND-HELD
FIRETORCH.

A LARGE SCREEN CAN
BE MADE BY STAPLING
SHEET COTTON TO
TWO POLES. ROLL
CLOTH AROUND THE
POLES, STAKE THEIR
BASES AND GUY
THEM OUT. HANG
A CLOTH DOWN
TO HIDE THE
OPERATOR'S
FEET.

CUTTING AND JOINTING

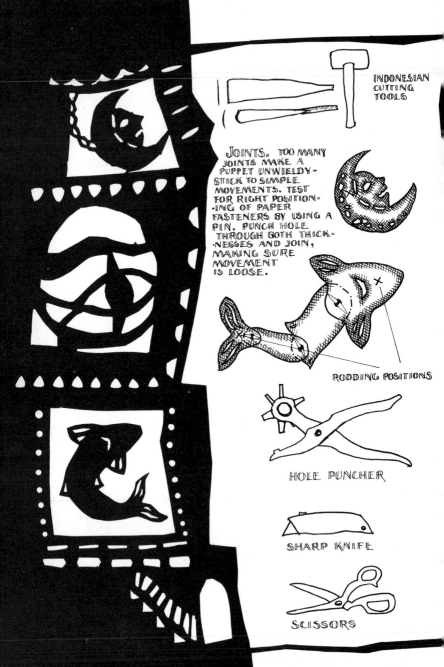

INDONESIAN CUTTING TOOLS

JOINTS. TOO MANY JOINTS MAKE A PUPPET UNWIELDY - STICK TO SIMPLE MOVEMENTS. TEST FOR RIGHT POSITION- -ING OF PAPER FASTENERS BY USING A PIN. PUNCH HOLE THROUGH BOTH THICK- -NESSES AND JOIN, MAKING SURE MOVEMENT IS LOOSE.

RODDING POSITIONS

HOLE PUNCHER

SHARP KNIFE

SCISSORS

LEATHER CUTTING TOOLS ARE GOOD FOR DECORATIVE CUTTING.

MATERIALS

CARDBOARD: MOST SUITABLE FOR SHORT-LIFE PUPPETS. STRENGTHEN SHAPES WITH WIRE STUCK ON WITH MASKING TAPE. EXTEND LIFE SHORTLY BY COAT OF P.V.A. GLUE OR VARNISH. NOT MUCH GOOD IN RAIN.

LINO: EASY TO WORK, BUT VERY DIFFICULT TO USE IN WET WEATHER. NEEDS STRENGTHENING WITH WIRE.

PLASTICARD: USED IN MODELBUILDING. RIGID, FAIRLY EASY TO USE, BUT EXPENSIVE. AVAILABLE IN DIFFERENT THICKNESSES.

THIN PLYWOOD: CUT WITH JIGSAW, QUICK TO WORK. MAKE JOINTS WITH DRILL AND HOMEMADE HEAVY WIRE SPLIT PINS. RIGID AND IDEAL FOR GIANT PUPPETS.

THREAD USED TO HANG LITTLE SHAPES

← THIS IMAGE IS ENTIRELY BACKED IN COLOURED GEL - TO MAKE A RIGID SHAPE; CARDBOARD SHAPES STUCK ONTO GEL WITH 'UHU'

COLOURING.
LIGHTING GEL (CINEMOID) IS BEST, BUT CHECK COLOURS ARE NOT TOO DARK TO LET LIGHT THROUGH. USE SELLOTAPE OR 'UHU' TO STICK IT TO PUPPET. GEL CAN BE USED TO STIFFEN VERY CUT-AWAY AREAS, SAVING WIRE. FOR SMALL COLOURED AREAS USE SELLOTAPE COLOURED WITH FELT-TIP PENS.

RODDING POINTS

THE WAYANGS ARE CUT FROM UNCURED LEATHER OF WATER BUFFALO SKIN

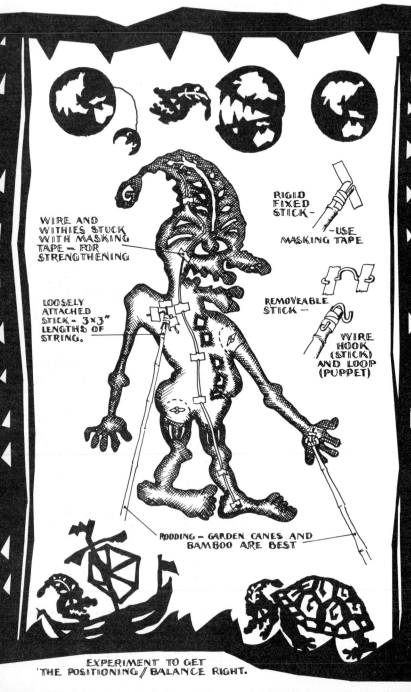

◄ RODDING & STRENGTHENING

WIRE AND WITHIES STUCK WITH MASKING TAPE – FOR STRENGTHENING

RIGID FIXED STICK –

– USE MASKING TAPE

LOOSELY ATTACHED STICK – 3×3" LENGTHS OF STRING.

REMOVEABLE STICK –

WIRE HOOK (STICK) AND LOOP (PUPPET)

RODDING – GARDEN CANES AND BAMBOO ARE BEST

EXPERIMENT TO GET THE POSITIONING / BALANCE RIGHT.

COSTUME
SUE FOX

EN THE COMPANY TRAVELS ABROAD THE 'CARNET'
NUMBER OF COSTUME TRUNKS. UPON INSPECTION
ROVE TO BE INDIVIDUAL CACHES OF ASSORTED
ND JUNK, PLUS A FEW HATS AND SHOES — ODDS
S TAKEN ALONG AS REFERENCE POINTS AND
TE SAFETY BITS, TO BE BUILT UPON OR ADDED
G MATERIALS AND OBJECTS FOUND IN THE NEW
N. ONE OR TWO BASICS ARE ALSO TAKEN: BLACK
TE CLOTH, WADDING FOR STUFFING PADDED
ES, FILLING OUT MOVING SCULPTURES.

CH INDIVIDUAL HAS ALWAYS DEVISED, AND USUALLY
IS OWN COSTUME. PERFORMANCE SOMETIMES
FROM COSTUMES, AS THEY ARE CREATED DURING
OLUTION OF A SHOW. IT WOULD BE INCONCEIVABLE
LFARE STATE TO DESIGN A PIECE, THEN CALL IN
E TO MAKE THE COSTUMES. THIS MEANS THAT
ES IN THE SAME SHOW CAN SOMETIMES LOOK VERY
ENT FROM EACH OTHER, AS EACH IS THE SUM TOTAL
INDIVIDUAL'S OWN AESTHETIC AND CURRENT
ONS WITH MATERIALS OR MAKING TECHNIQUES. YET
E COSTUMES ARE MADE TOGETHER THROUGH THE
ASIC PROCESS, UNITY IS USUALLY ACHIEVED IN THE
N APPROACH TO MATERIALS.

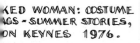

KED WOMAN: COSTUME
GS - SUMMER STORIES,
ON KEYNES 1976.

EVEN WHEN COSTUMES LOOK LIKE PIECES OF
MOVING SCULPTURE USUALLY THEY HAVE BEEN
COLLAGED TOGETHER. THE PRINCIPLE IS THE SAME
AS PICASSO USED IN TAKING A BICYCLE SADDLE AND
A PAIR OF HANDLEBARS AND TURNING THEM INTO
A GOAT. OFTEN THE PROCESS IS RULED BY THE
DEMANDS OF COLOUR. SCHWITTERS USED A FADED
BUS TICKET IN A COLLAGE — ONLY LATER DO YOU
REALISE IT IS A BUS TICKET — INITIALLY IT IS JUST
A RECTANGLE OF A PARTICULAR SIZE, COLOUR AND
TEXTURE.

BULLCALF: FROM NOAH'S ZO
BIRMINGHAM, 1982.

DANCE OF THE LIGHTHOUSE AND THE LINER:
LYME PARK FESTIVAL, 1981.

HUNTING THE STAG: BARON DUNDERBECK, LYME PARK FESTIVAL, 1981.

EACOCK: ST. ANDREW'S BEACH, SCOTLAND 1980.

120

COSTUMES ARE ALMOST NEVER TAILORED
GARMENTS MADE OF RECOGNISABLE FABRICS. RA
THEY ARE ASSEMBLED — TIED IN, ON, AROUND;
GLUED, STAPLED; EVEN WELDED OR SOLDERED.
WOULD ALWAYS SHOW THE SEAMS, THE ELASTIC
THE FALSE NOSE. THIS IS   COSTUME AS FEIGNE
DISGUISE — PLAYING AT — NOT WISHING EVER TO
TAKEN AS A NATURALISTIC REPRESENTATION.

BELOW: W.W.1 GOGGLES, NOSE
RING, SWIMMING CAP FOR
PROSPERO. TORONTO, 1981.

ABOVE: NOAH
ON HORSEBACK
BIRMINGHAM
1982.

SO A RIPPED—OPEN BRIEFCASE BECOMES A COW'S
[HE]AD; AN ARTIFICIAL CHEST STRAPPED TO THE HEAD
[BE]COMES A BISHOP'S MITRE; MOCK LEATHER SEAT
[CO]VERS FROM A SCRAPPED CAR BECOME A FIREMAN—
[AN]GEL'S COSTUME WHEN SPRAYED GOLD.

ABOVE: FIREMAN - ANGEL COSTUME,
EYE OF THE PEACOCK, 1980.

LEFT: ICE HOCKEY FACE MASK FOR
THE DEVIL, BLOOD PUDDING, 1979.

BELOW: CARPET SHAMPOOER HARPOON FOR
CAPTAIN AHAB, ULVERSTON CARNIVAL '81.

[A] COSTUME CAN THUS WORK ON MANY LEVELS,
[CARRYI]NG A MULTIPLICITY OF MEANINGS. A MELTED
[PLAS]TIC BUCKET MAY BE FASHIONED INTO A VERY
[BEAU]TIFUL CROWN, CREATING AN AMBIVALENT
[ATTI]TUDE TO THE ROLE OF KING AND MAKING A
[CLEARE]R STATEMENT ABOUT THE IMAGINATIVE RE—
[CYCLI]NG OF RUBBISH.

122

INDIVIDUAL PERFORMERS COLLECT AND
HOARD OBJECTS, MATERIALS, BITS OF OLD
COSTUMES. WHEN ASSEMBLED INTO NEW
COSTUMES THEY BECOME ELOQUENT STATEM
THEY REVEAL THE OBSESSIONS AND REFLEC
THE LIFE—STYLE OF THE PERSON. THEY MI
INCLUDE SPECIAL FEATHERS GATHERED FOR
CLOAK, OR FUNGUS FOR A BEARD, OR
BLEACHED BACON BONES FROM THE PEA SO
WHICH BECOME A DEVILISH NECKLACE. THE
SUM TOTAL OF THESE OBJECTS IS A PERSON
HISTORY WHICH GAINS PUBLIC STATUS IN
PERFORMANCE.

ABOVE: ASTRONOMER WITH FUNGUS
BEARD, ELECTRIC FLOOR POLISHER COVER
WIG, OLD BITS OF CAST=OFF THEATRICALS,
                SUMMER STORIES 1976.
BELOW: TWIN MERMAID FROM SCRAP MATERIALS, BARRABAS, 197

RIGHT: FEMALE JUDGE,
BARRABAS 1977.

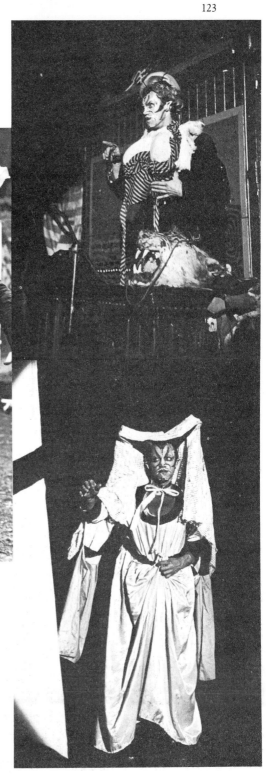

ABOVE: DEMON FIGURE
WITH FOLDED PAPER COLLAR,
INSULATING TAPE
DISTORTING EARS, WIRED
HAT, BARRABAS, 1977.

RIGHT: PREGNANT
WOMAN, BARRABAS 1977.

(ALL BORIS HOWARTH)

COSTUMES THUS REFLECT INDIVIDUAL TRADEMARKS OR HABITS. WHERE ONE GOES FOR A FAT PERSONA, ANOTHER IS NEAT AND DELICATE APPROACHES RANGE FROM LATERAL THINKING WHICH PRODUCES ABSTRACT IMAGES, TO LITERAL REPRESENTATION USUALLY PUSHED TO THE GROTESQUE.

PERFORMERS WHO HAVE WORKED CLOSELY TOGETHER FOR YEARS WOULD STILL FIND IT VERY DIFFICULT TO SWOP COSTUMES, AND PROBABLY IMPOSSIBLE TO FUNCTION IN THEM IF THEY DID. THIS IS NOTHING TO DO WITH PROPRIETORIAL CUSTODY — THE IDIOM MAY BE SIMPLY ALIEN AND IMPERSONAL, NO LONGER TRUE ON THE SHOULDER OF ANOTHER.

ABOVE: SALLY OCEAN, UPPENDOWN MOONEY, 1978

BELOW: DAME'S TRANSFORMATION COSTUME, SALT PANTOMIME, 1982.

ASSEMBLING THINGS AS WE GO ALONG KEEPS
COMPANY'S WORK ALIVE AND CHANGING. THIS
☐RASTS WITH THE MORE PLANNED, CEREBRAL
☐OACH OF THE DESIGNER, WHO HAS TO HAVE
☐ONCEPTIONS ABOUT HOW THINGS OUGHT TO BE.
☐ JUST AS THE MOTOR CAR BEGETS THE TRAFFIC
☐DEN, SO CURRENT THEATRE BUILDINGS PRODUCE
☐ WARDROBE PERSON. WELFARE STATE NEVER
☐S ONE. EACH INDIVIDUAL IS EQUALLY
☐ONSIBLE FOR HIS CONTRIBUTION TO THE PUBLIC
☐T — THUS AESTHETICS REFLECT POLITICS.

ABOVE: AN EVIL SQUIRE,
BARRABAS 1977.

BELOW LEFT: MADMAN MASKS,
SUMMER STREET SHOWS 1980.

BELOW: FLO ON THE FERRY TO SNAKE
ISLAND, TORONTO 1981.

CEREMONIAL FOOD SUE FOX

WE THINK OF OUR AUDIENCES AS GUESTS, SO IT IS ONLY NATURAL TO SERVE THEM WITH FOOD AS WELL AS FIREWORKS, TO OFFER SOUP AS WELL AS SONGS, DESSERTS AND DANCES, MERINGUES AND MYSTERIES. OUR SHOWS ARE HAND-CRAFTED EVENTS, SO WE CAN'T JUST CALL UP THE LOCAL HOT-DOG MAN. NOT THAT WE DESPISE BANGERS AND MASH: IF IT SUITED THE OCCASION WE'D SERVE IT, BUT IT WOULD BE FIRST-RATE SAUSAGE, AND WE'D KNOW WHAT WAS IN IT.

WHEN OUR EVENTS TAKE PEOPLE ON A DEMANDING JOURNEY — PHYSICAL OR EMOTIONAL — THEN THE FUNCTION OF THE FOOD IS SECURITY, AN ANCHOR OR REASSURANCE. (WE THINK THERE IS ALSO A LINK BETWEEN FOOD AND QUALITY OF PERFORMANCE: ON OUR RESIDENTIAL SUMMER SCHOOLS STUDENTS NOTICEABLY RELAX WHEN THEY DISCOVER THAT THEY WILL BE REGULARLY AND WELLFED: FOOD BECOMES A SAFETY NET TO THE TIGHTROPE OF PERFORMANCE.)

THERE IS NO SET PATTERN TO OUR USE OF FOOD AND FEASTS. JULY'S CARNIVAL OF THE SEA WILL REQUIRE THAT MORNING'S CATCH OF FISH BY LOCAL ANGLERS TO BE FRESHLY COOKED AND SERVED OUT OF DOORS IN THE AFTERNOON; A HALLOWE'EN BALL WILL DEMAND HUNDREDS OF SUGAR SKULLS, PARKIN AND MULLED ALE.

SKULL RECIPE

Almond paste moulded in the hand. Silver balls for eyes.

Looks good just yellow, but can be dipped in cooking chocolate. (expensive, time-consuming, can go solid if allowed to overheat).

FOOD CAN ALSO BE A CHALLENGING PART OF A SHOW'S JOURNEY: IT PRESENTS NEW TASTES AND OFTEN LOOKS UNUSUAL.

THE FOOD PICKS UP IMAGES FROM THE SHOWS, PARTICULARLY THE SHADOW PLAYS. THE NORTHWICH SUMMER PANTOMIME (SUMMER 1982) HAD A 'TREE OF LIFE' CAKE, AND FOR THE BIRTHDAY OF THE WORLD, A WORLD CAKE, BOTH MADE OF KOKONUT MIX.

'BARABBAS' WE MADE HOT LARDY CAKE FOR 50/60
PLE DURING THE SHOW IN A CARAVAN BEHIND THE
NES: FIVE TIMES A WEEK FOR SIX WEEKS IN N.E.
CASHIRE ON DAMP AUTUMN NIGHTS.

JAPAN WE SERVED 200 SMALL BOWLS OF BARLEY TEA
THE TOP OF A MOUNTAIN TO REFRESH THE AUDIENCE
THEY RESTED ON STRAW MATS AFTER THEIR CLIMB,
TCHING THE SUNSET JUST BEFORE THE SHOW BEGAN.
AUSTRALIA WE CELEBRATED THE NAMING OF 17
LDREN ON A SUNNY NEW YEAR'S MORNING WITH
ESH CUT MANGOES.

TRIED SERVING BORSCHT (RED CABBAGE AND BEET-
OT SOUP) TO YOUNGSTERS IN LIVERPOOL 8, BUT THEY
REW IT BACK AT US, THEN WENT ON TO FIGHT OVER
LPINGS OF MARINADED CHINESE SPARE RIBS.

LARDY CAKES — enough to fill 2 large roasting tins

lb white flour
oz fresh yeast
tsp. salt
oz. lard
oz. margarine
0 oz. dried fruit
6 oz. sugar
pts. warm water
tsp. spice: nutmeg
  and cinnamon
Cooking oil

Cream yeast in a little warm water with 1 tsp. sugar. Leave to stand. Mix flour, salt and a little of the sugar. Add the yeast, when frothing, with 1 tablespoon oil. Beat well, leave to rise. Knead well & divide into 2. Roll out 1 piece, spread half the margarine onto ⅔ of surface, sprinkle with half the sugar, spice and fruit. Fold over, re-roll and repeat, using half the lard the second time. Put into a deep meat tin, rub top with oil, slash with a sharp knife & rub in some sugar. Bake Nᵒ 7 or 8 (gas) for 40 mins. Repeat with second lump of dough.

ICARUS

Bread figures — one of Welfare State's first explorations into sculptural food.

HEAVENLY SPARE RIBS
(Chinese style marinade)

Mix together:

chopped garlic   soy sauce
Root ginger   2 dsst spoons of
sherry   5 Spice Powder

Marinade the ribs overnight turning occasionally.

WE RECENTLY DID A 5 COURSE FEAST
FOR 150 GENETICISTS IN CAMBRIDG

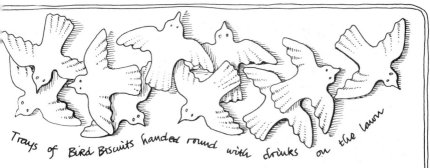

Trays of Bird Biscuits handed round with drinks on the lawn

PARROT BOUCHERE : Mix butter and flour until it resembles breadcrumbs. Add salt, then egg and milk. Mix to a stiff dough and let it rest in a cool place for an hour. Roll out and cut into shapes with a sharp knife. Place on greased trays, glaze & sprinkle sesame seeds on top. Bake in a moderate oven (gas 350° Reg 4) for 15-20 minutes. This gives about 6 oz. of biscuits.

oz flour
oz butter
small egg
tablespoon milk
99 yolk (glaze)
esame seeds
alt

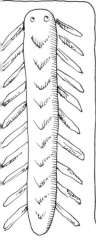

THE FEAST FOR THE 4TH INTERNATIONAL WORKSHOP ON RAT HISTOCOMPATIBILITY SYSTEMS WAS NEARLY A DISASTER (NOT THAT THE AUDIENCE KNEW THAT). THE BASIC ERROR WAS TECHNICAL: WE HAD TO COOK IN SNATCHES IN SOMEONE ELSE'S KITCHEN, WORKING ROUND THEIR SCHEDULE; THEN SERVING MEANT A 100 METRE SPRINT UP AND DOWN STEPS, THROUGH FIVE DOORS TO THE MARQUEE WHERE WE DID THE SHOW. WE SHOULD HAVE DONE SOMETHING SIMPLER, LIKE A GOULASH, INSTEAD OF DISHING UP SUCH DELICACIES AS BRIOCHE AND PRAYING MANTIS A LA CHANTILLY.

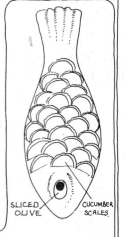

SLICED OLIVE   CUCUMBER SCALES

ELEBRITY CENTIPEDE
usage baked in a brioche dough: Mastering the Art of French Cooking: guin Vol 2 p.127 and p.399, garnished h match stick carrots.

MACKEREL PATÉ
24 oz. smoked mackerel   pinch ground nutmeg
2 x 5 fl.oz cartons soured cream   4 oz. butter
Put mackerel in a bowl, cover with boiling water for 5 mins. Drain. Remove skin & bones. Put fish in an electric blender, add butter, blend until smooth (or use wooden spoon). Beat in soured cream & nutmeg. Arrange on an oval dish in a fish shape. Cool until firm. This gives 10 generous portions.

ALDORF SALAD
ad celery   2 tsp.lemon juice
. apple   2 tsp. sugar
. walnut kernels
lsp. mayonnaise
the washed ry into small ces. Chop e. Cut uts into rters. Mix together.

PRAYING MANTIS À LA CHANTILLY
FEELERS- THIN STRIPS OF GREEN ANGELICA
BRANDY SNAPS - BOUGHT, NOT MADE, FILLED WITH PIPED CREAM
EYES- PLAIN CHOCOLATE POLKA-DOTS
LEGS- TWO ORANGE FLAVOURED MATCHMAKERS.
RECTANGULAR TRIFLE DISH

FACTORS TO CONSIDER IN DECIDING WHAT TO MAKE:

1. WHAT THE SHOW IS ABOUT?
2. NUMBERS OF AUDIENCE?
3. WHERE PEOPLE ARE — STANDING OR SITTING, INSIDE OR OUTSIDE ?
4. HOW LONG HAS AUDIENCE BEEN WITH YOU — ARE THEY EXPECTING A MEAL, OR WILL THIS BE A SURPRISE BONUS?
5. PLACE AND TIME OF YEAR — REGIONAL AND SEASONAL MENUS?
6. HOT FOOD OR COLD?
7. TO BE SERVED PROMPT ON CUE IN PERFORMANCE, OR AFTERWARDS IN SOCIAL SITUATION?
8. WHAT KITCHEN/PREPARATION SPACE AND WHAT EQUIPMENT IS AVAILABLE?
9. HOW MANY WORKERS TO PREPARE IT?
10. HOW MUCH MONEY TO SPEND ON IT?

ECONOMY. GET A CASH AND CARRY CARD TO BUY ITEMS IN CATERING SIZE, AT WHOLESALE PRICES. WE REGISTER AS THE COMPANY WORKS CANTEEN. IT'S NECESSARY TO SUBMIT BANKERS REFERENCES AND WAIT FOR CLEAR— ANCE.

NOTEBOOK. VITAL FOR ALL LISTS, RECIPES, COSTINGS, TELEPHONE ORDERS, ETC. MAKE A WORK LIST FOR THE DAY. AFTER 10 YEARS WE STILL DO THIS — COUNTDOWN OVER SEVERAL HOURS TO COVER ALL JOBS TO BE DONE, IN THE RIGHT ORDER. IN YOUR COOKING SCHEDULE AIM TO BE READY EARLY — IT ALWAYS TAKES LONGER THAN YOU THINK TO PRESENT, DECORATE, CUT THINGS INTO PORTIONS.

WORLD CAKE = BUILT WITH SPONGE CAKE - COVERED IN COLOURED ICING.

KOKONUT SQUIDGY MIX

Make up a jelly with 50% of the water usually needed, then add as much dessicated coconut as it will absorb. This gives a malleable edible icing which can be dyed different colours and is controllable to work with. Start with a lemon, orange or tangerine jelly for the best colour range.

BALINESE RICE DOUGH OFFERING

RICE SYMBOLISES FERTILITY. RE—BIRTH WITNESSED IN THE COOKING AS IT EXPANDS AND SWELLS. IN BALI, DEWI THE RICE GODDESS LITERALLY DWELLS IN THE RICE STALKS. AT HARVEST TIME THEY MUST BE CUT IN A CERTAIN WAY SO AS NOT TO OFFEND HER. WOOD-MOUNTED, RAZOR-LIKE BLADES (ANI ANI) ARE USED BY WOMAN WHO DEFTLY CONCEAL THEM IN THE PALMS OF THEIR RIGHT HANDS. ONLY 3 OR 4 STALKS AT A TIME ARE CUT SO THE RICE SOUL WILL NOT BE FRIGHTENED.

EQUIPMENT. EXCHANGE & MART IS A GOOD SOURCE FOR SECOND HAND CATERING EQUIPMENT. BUY GOOD HEAVY STEEL COOKING POTS, LIDS ESSENTIAL, AS LARGE AS POSSIBLE. THEY CAN LAST A LIFETIME IF YOU LOOK AFTER THEM. ALSO BUY THE BEST KNIVES YOU CAN.

FIRMS LIKE 'CALOR' HIRE CATERING SIZE OVENS AT REASONABLE WEEKLY RATES, FROM THEIR MAJOR DEPOTS; 6 BURNERS, DOUBLE OVEN DOORS, NO GRILL. THEY WILL DELIVER — OVENS VERY HEAVY — BUT USE YOUR OWN GAS BOTTLES TO SAVE MONEY. YOU CAN ALSO HIRE, AT MUCH CHEAPER RATES, A GAS HOT CUPBOARD. THIS EFFECTIVELY DOUBLES YOUR CAPACITY, SINCE YOU CAN BAKE IN BATCHES; IT IS ALSO USEFUL IN GIVING A WARM SURFACE FOR CROCKERY AND SERVING FROM.

YOU CAN ALSO HIRE ELECTRIC HOT CUPBOARDS, BUT THEY TAKE A WHOLE 3KW SUPPLY. IF THE KITCHEN IS PART OF THE PERFORMANCE COMPLEX YOU MIGHT GET JUMPS AND SURGES IN PA AND LIGHTING LEVELS AS THE THERMOSTAT CUTS IN AND OUT ... ... YOU MIGHT NEED A SEPARATE GENERATOR AND CABLE!

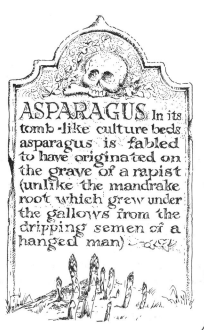

ASPARAGUS In its tomb-like culture beds asparagus is fabled to have originated on the grave of a rapist (unlike the mandrake root which grew under the gallows from the dripping semen of a hanged man)

OPULENCE: never be afraid to give very small portions of something exquisite; a taste of luxury.

1 basket mushrooms (2 to 3 lbs)   6 oz butter
salt & fresh ground black pepper   1 clove garlic
1 grated onion   2 tblspoons Madiera

Chop mushrooms finely. Melt butter in a heavy saucepan. Add onion, garlic and mushrooms, shake well and put on the lid. Leave over a very low light, stirring from time to time, until mushrooms give off liquid. Add the Madiera, remove the lid and let it reduce. Adjust the seasoning. Makes 36 portions (1 heaped teaspoon each). Use as a filling for a savoury.

PARKIN: cuts well, keeps well, tasty & inexpensive. Good in cold weather

2 lb oatmeal (fine)   1 lb lard
2 lb flour (½ white ½ brown) 4 eggs
24 oz. golden syrup   split almonds
mixed spice, ground ginger   2 lb sugar
and cinnamon   8 teasp. bicarb soda

Mix together all dry ingredients. Rub in the lard. Add beaten eggs & syrup. Put into deep sided tins, decorate top with split almonds. Bake 1 hour at N° 3.

PORRIDGE OATS :

included here only on account of its image value. Morally good, as all those Scotsmen with bare knees. Sacrifice, virtue & idealism all in one packet. Most palatable as FLAPJACK :

1lb margarine
2lb oats (muesli is better)
8oz white sugar
2 handsful peanuts (optional)

3 tblsp. golden syrup
2 tblsp. black treacle
mixed spice, cinnamon
pinch of salt

Melt margarine in a heavy saucepan & stir in everything else. Bake on 2 large greased trays for 30mins at N°3, then take it out, press down firmly with the back of a fish slice, then return to the oven at N°4 for another 5mins. Cut into fingers while it is still warm. Improves with keeping 3 or 4 days in a tin. 36 pieces.

POTECA — MOON CAKE. FOR AN EVENT FEATURING AN ILLUMINATED MOON FLOATING OUT IN THE DARKNESS ON A LAKE, WHICH GOT CAPTURED, THEN RESCUED, OUR FINAL DRY-LAND CELEBRATION INCLUDED A DELICIOUS MOON CAKE WHICH WAS SLICED UP AND HANDED ROUND.

POTECA : MOON CAKE

A Swiss yeast cake, filled with chewy walnut cream. Easy to make, inexpensive; preparation & cooking time 3 hours.

1½ oz fresh yeast
8 oz. white sugar
16 fl. oz. milk
8 oz. butter
3lb white flour
4 egg yolks, lightly beaten
2 teaspoons salt

FILLING :
6 egg whites
8 oz. castor sugar
12 oz. walnuts, finely chopped
grated rind 2 small oranges
     "   "   2 small lemons
For economy : you could substitute marmalade for the above ingredients

TOPPING :
4 to 6 tblsp. clear honey

DECORATION : Piped design of planets, comets & shooting stars

Mix yeast with 4 tblsp. warm water and 1 tblsp. extra sugar. Leave in warm place for 15 min. until frothy. Scald the milk in a saucepan, then on very low light add butter. When it has melted remove the pan from heat & leave to cool until lukewarm. Sift all dry ingredients, make a well & pour in yeast mixture, milk and butter mixture, & egg yolks. Mix into a dough, turn out onto a floured board & knead for 10mins. Put dough in a clean bowl, cover with a damp cloth and leave to rise in a warm place for 1-1½ hours, until doubled in size.
Meanwhile, prepare the filling: Beat egg whites until they form soft peaks. Fold in the sugar a little at a time; beat the mixture till it is stiff and glossy. Fold in walnuts, and orange & lemon rinds.

Turn risen dough out and knead again for 5 min. Roll it out to form large, long rectangle. Spread the filling on the dough. Roll up swiss roll style and carefully transfer to greased baking tray, seam side down. Pull ends of the loaf to form a crescent moon shape. Leave for ½hr. or so until dough has almost doubled in bulk. Bake in pre-heated oven N°7, 425° for 15 min, reduce heat to N°4 350° and continue baking for a further 40 min.
After removing moon bread from the oven, turn it over carefully and rap the underneath with your knuckles. If it sounds hollow, it is cooked. If not, return it to the oven, upside down, for a further 5-10 min. Before it cools completely, glaze with clear warm honey. When cold, add piped decorations.

A TOWER OF BABEL CAKE ... ... CUT AND SLICED AT HALLOWE'EN IN EXCHANGE FOR PEOPLE'S VILE MEMORIES WHICH WERE CONSIGNED TO THE FIRE FOR BURNING.

BREAD

PEOPLE NEED TO FEEL IT IS BEING BAKED BY REAL BAKERS AND TO SMELL IT BEING BAKED: HENCE THE DEVELOPMENT OF MANY BREAD SHOPS AND SUPERMARKET DEPARTMENTS WHICH BAKE ON THE PREMISES, IN SIGHT OF CUSTOMERS. RECENT "EAT BREAD YOU KNOW IT MAKES SENSE" SLOGANS ARE A REAL SIGN OF THE TIMES. BREAD WAS LOW STATUS; NOW A SOPHISTICATED REVERSAL HAS APPEARED — WE EAT DARK BREAD, FROM CHOICE, THAT FORMERLY WAS THE FATE OF THE PEASANT.

PANCAKES AND PITTA BREAD. STUFFED PANCAKES AVOID ROCK—HARD JACKET POTATOES FROM THE COMMUNITY BONFIRE. CECILIA NORMAN'S PANCAKES AND PIZZAS (GRANADA) GIVES USEFUL RECIPES, WITH BOTH SWEET AND SAVOURY FILLINGS. INGREDIENTS LIKE FLOUR, EGGS AND DRIED MILK POWDER CAN BE STORED AND CARRIED FORWARD WITHOUT WASTAGE. FILLINGS CAN BE SIMPLE: SPICED APPLE, VEGETABLE CURRY, HAM AND CHEESE, CHICKEN AND MUSHROOM SAUCE. PANCAKES CAN BE MADE IN ADVANCE AND STORED ʼIN FOIL TO REMAIN PLIABLE, THEN REHEATED AND FILLED WHEN NEEDED. SERVE IN A PAPER NAPKIN — NO CUTLERY, NO WASHING UP.

WEDDING BREAD:

usually baked with symbolic decoration in the bride's home, it is an integral part of the ceremony in Crete and the Ukraine. Decorative holiday bread is still common in many European countries — particularly at Christmas and Easter. An Italian fertility bread shows a three breasted woman. Welfare State has helped to arrange 3 marriages, and we used the following recipe for the bread:

6lb. brown wholemeal flour
2 tblsp. brown sugar
2 tblsp. black treacle
salt to taste: try 1 dsstsp.

4 oz. vegetable fat
6 oz. fresh yeast
2½ pts. warm water.

Use sponge method. this gives enough for 2 large plaques + plenty to spare for some rolls.

Work fast! The dough models well, but it is live & will continue to rise until in the oven. At one wedding the bride's mother was aghast at the sight of the bride's breasts swelling visibly in the kitchen.

MULLED ALE : Mrs. Beeton's recipe

Large quantities can be made in an electric Burco boiler, but keep a steady hand on multiplying the spices - it can get gritty.

1 quart ale
1 glass rum or brandy
1 tablespoon caster sugar

pinch ground cloves
" ground nutmeg
good pinch gr. ginger

Put everything except spirits into a heavy saucepan and bring nearly to the boil. Add spirits & more sugar if necessary. [It often is.]

IT IS A GRAVE RESPONSIBILITY FEEDING THE PUBLIC, ESPECIALLY OUTDOORS AND IN RELATIVELY 'PRIMITIVE' CONDITIONS. IT IS VITAL TO OBSERVE COMMON SENSE RULES OF HYGIENE AND TO BE AWARE OF THE FOOD HYGIENE REGULATIONS GOVERNING FOOD AT MARKETS, FAIRS, ETC. SEE THE APPENDIX FOR NOTES ON PUBLIC ACCOUNTABILITY, HEALTH AND SAFETY.

SERVING FOOD during a show to a large crowd outside can be difficult, whether you are selling it or giving it away. If there is a building with double doors opening to the outside, other than the usual entry/exit doors, claim this doorway for food serving (early on, before it gets designated as an entry for props, performers or musicians). Open the doors & secure them back, place your tables on inside to <u>cover the whole width</u>. Servers work inside & can have extra stock, boiling urns, money, knives all safely behind the good outside lighting is essential, & if the site permits, t for a one-way traffic flow system. This is the best way to avoid a free for all which can be distressing & devalues the food you are offering. Other solutions: a market stall rented from the council, covered o 3 sides with tarpaulins or plastic sheeting. A caravan with a large window adapted to a serving hatch. You may need pallets for customers to stand on to reach the window.

ON ST AGNES' EVE UNMARRIED YORKSHIRE GIRLS WOULD GATHER TO MAKE A DUMB CAKE. EITHER 3, 5 OR 7 GIRLS WOULD TAKE PART. EACH MUST TAKE A HANDFUL OF FLOUR AND LAY IT ON THE SAME LARGE SHEET OF CLEAN PAPER. NOT A WORD MUST BE SPOKEN. ALL ADD A SMALL PINCH OF SALT, THEN WATER, ALL TAKING PART IN WORKING IT INTO A DOUGH, ALL KNEADING AND ASSISTING IN ROLLING IT INTO A THIN CAKE, SUFFICIENTLY LARGE FOR EACH TO MAKE HER INITIALS ON. ALL MUST LEND A HAND LIFTING IT ONTO A TIN, CARRYING IT AND LAYING IT BEFORE THE FIRE. SEATED AS FAR FROM THE FIRE AS POSSIBLE EACH WOULD IN TURN RISE, CROSS THE ROOM AND TURN THE CAKE ROUND ONCE. ALL THIS WAS PREPARATORY TO THAT NIGHT'S DREAMS, WHICH WERE MEANT TO REVEAL WHOM THEY WOULD MARRY IN THE COMING YEAR.

Twelfth Cake.

Tennis Cake.

An unashamed food gig for 35 people a night .....

for a limited season! —
18 – 26 MAY at 8·30 p.m.
at Digswell House, Monks Rise
Welwyn Garden City.

"WHEN THE PIE WAS OPENED ---!"

GOLDEN EGGS
   see Middle Eastern Cookery — p.147
       "Baid Muttajjan"
MUSHROOM
   see "Opulence" above
SOUP
    see The Vegetarian Epicure p.71
       "Blond Lentil Soup"
PIE
   see Charcuterie & French Pork Cookery —
  p.88 "Pâté De Dinde" & make into a raised
                 pie.
SPARE RIBS
   see "Heavenly Spare Ribs" above
CREAM
   double & single cream, yoghurt and
   maple syrup
TO DRINK

     Cider : Devon home brew
     Beer : Bitter, Brown, Lager

FARE STATE INTERNATIONAL
WHEN THE PIE WAS OPENED ---!

DIGSWELL HOUSE : MONKS RISE : WELWYN GARDEN CITY

Menu

= The Blackbird's Golden Eggs =
Eggs gently smoked in OAK FIRES & enhanced with a nest
of PRETZELS & DARK SAUCE

= SEA-DRIFT SOUP =
Home-made LENTIL SOUP with Black Pepper & Green Herbs

THE PIE EXPLODES =
Marinated TURKEY encased in light Pastry with HOT ROYAL BEETROOT

= The Ribs of the Old Guard =
from the BARBECUE ~ Honey Glazed PORK SPARE RIBS

= CASTLES IN THE AIR =
A COLOSSAL EXTRAVAGANZA of Meringue & Piped Cream
Spangled with DREAMS & Bluebirds over

~ Plus Theatrical Refreshments ~
& a MUSICAL SIDESHOW by LOL COXALL & DAVE HOLLAND

= £2·50 =

ALL-INCLUSIVE : 5-COURSE BARBECUE, FREE ALE,
LIVE MUSIC, SONGS, DANCES & EXOTIC WAITERS

FOOD PANTOMIME =

SCENARIO

DESCRIPTION	MENU & THEATRE	METHOD	PEOPLE	LIGHTS	MISC.	MUSIC
Overture	MAID CLEANS TABLE		Janet			
Image I	Caged Bird on Nest	Shadow puppets	B & Lois	Tables Band Screen	Black & White	"Sing a S... Sixpen... Nostalg...
Entry I	Waiters take eggs from screen & serve					Proces...
Course I	Blackbirds Golden Eggs	⬭	John & Jamie	Tables	Giant Egg	
Image II	The Dinner Disasters	Shadow puppets Dandelion child	B & L Daniel	Storm lantern	Placard	Silent ... & effe... Song
Entry II	Dandelion bowlers					Process
Course II	Sea drift Soup	Seaweed pram	J & L	Tables		
Image III	The End of the World of Birds	Glove puppets & flying puppet	B & L & Janet	Blue & Turquoise	Placard	Accordeo... Tin Whis... Melodi...
Entry III	Pie-men	🥧				
Course III	The Pie Explodes	Marionette blackbirds	J & L & J	Tables	Giant Pie	
Image IV	Wasn't that a dirty trick to play upon the King	Big red puppets	B & L	Amber	Placard	
Entry IV	Funeral boat	⛵			9 Boats	Death Ma...
Course IV	The Ribs of the Old Guard		J & L	Tables	Rockets	
Image V	The Maids Dance Death by Blackbird	Real Head Puppets	B & L		Placard	
		Pier Diorama Fireworks	David			Song: Washing Li...
Entry V	Song The Meringue Princess (revives the Maid)	Dance	Dave H. Maggie	Ocean Lanterns	K & Q head on tray	Pantomime... Waltz
Course V	Castles in the Air	Puppets dance	David	Tables & stage		
Coda	Distant burning Blackbird Cigarettes & coffee	Asbestos string on wire with paraffin	B			Sing a so... of Sixpe...

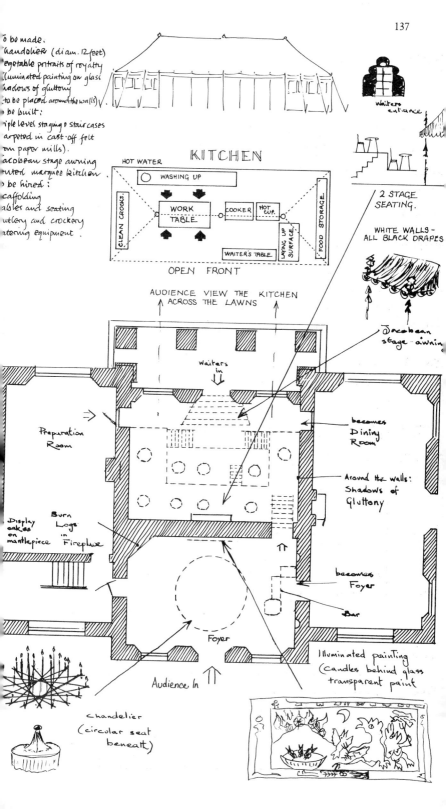

137

o be made.
handelier (diam. 12 feet)
egetable portraits of royalty
lluminated painting on glass
hadows of gluttony
to be placed around the walls)
o be built:
riple level staging o staircases
arpeted in cast-off felt
om paper mills).
acobean stage awning
uted marquee kitchen.
o be hired:
caffolding
ables and seating
utlery and crockery
atering equipment.

Waiters entrance

2 STAGE SEATING.

WHITE WALLS –
ALL BLACK DRAPES

Jacobean stage awning

KITCHEN

HOT WATER

○ WASHING UP

CLEAN CROCKS.

WORK TABLE

COOKER | HOT CUP.

LAYING UP SURFACE.

WAITER'S TABLE

FOOD STORAGE

OPEN FRONT

AUDIENCE VIEW THE KITCHEN
ACROSS THE LAWNS

Waiters in

becomes Dining Room

Preparation Room

Around the walls: Shadows of Gluttony

Display cakes on mantlepiece

Burn Logs in Fireplace

becomes Foyer

Bar

Foyer

Illuminated painting
(Candles behind glass
transparent paint

Audience In

Chandelier
(circular seat beneath)

PRESENTATION

Painted relief masks to hold individual pie-dishes.

Blackbird Pie

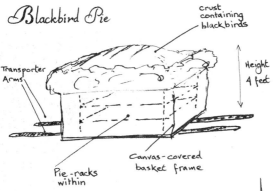

crust containing blackbirds

Transporter Arms

Height 4 feet

Pie-racks within

Canvas-covered basket frame

Ribs of the OLD GUARD: marinaded spare ribs, skewered onto the mast of a wooden carved ship, and served hot.

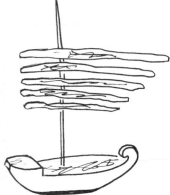

blue ostrich feathers.

blue & turquoise pampas grass.

disposable top of apricot-coloured crepe paper & turquoise taffeta. adorned with golden fruit

The Food.
meringues. boudoir biscuits.
whipped piped cream
glacé cherries
small pink & yellow meringues.
marzipan decorations of blue roses
green fish
blue stars.
blue birds.

little flowers
— pinks
or greenish yellow tiger lilies
Cement — butter cream.
Constructed on foil-covered bases.

turquoise & white taffeta.

PRESS. "THE CONFECTIONERY CARMEN MIRANDA SWAYED IN THROUGH THE FRENCH WINDOWS LIKE A PATISSERIE'S DREAM, HER HIGH HAT AND WIDE SKIRTS ENCRUSTED WITH ... ... MERINGUES, 'IT'S TIME FOR PUDDING', SAID A WAITER, SCOOPING OFF THE MERINGUE AND FILLING DISHES FOR THE ASTONISHED DINNERS ... ... THE DANCE STUDIO AT DIGSWELL HOUSE BECAME A BANQUETING HALL, WITH A RAISED DINING AUDIENCE AND THE THEATRE COMPANY DID THE REST. THEY WERE THE PERFORMERS, THE CHEFS AND THE WAITERS."
WELWYN AND HATFIELD TIMES. 25/5/79.

5

Events

There is wide variety of scale in Welfare State's work. Here, we print descriptions of three events, from domestic ceremony, through small-scale touring, to a large-scale international residency. These serve both to demonstrate this variety of scale, and to evoke some of the moment-by-moment feel of Welfare State shows and events.

(i) Naming, and other, Ceremonies

SUE FOX and LOIS LAMBERT

Welfare State International started doing ceremonies to celebrate the birth of their own children, and to focus on the naming of each child as an event to be shared with family and friends. In each case, none of the parents concerned felt, at that time, that an orthodox christening service or church baptism would be relevant to the views they held. Nevertheless, there were strong feelings about not letting the occasion pass unnoticed, simply because established ceremonies were inappropriate.

Since what was available would not do, we had to devise our own ceremony. An equally important personal factor was the feeling that, as a group of people spending our lives devising events and ceremonies for other people in strange places, we should not neglect those things close to home. We should use to the full our talents and resources and apply them to important domestic milestones in our own lives. Celebrations, we decided, should begin at home.

In a broader sense, we have thought for some time that a valid role for artists today is to reconsider, remake and invent new rituals, suitable for

ur own changing society. We get asked to help with special birthday
arties, and were pleased to have been involved in a betrothal and two
eddings. We master-minded the first wedding completely, the second
e helped to orchestrate in close collaboration with the couple who took
1e initiative in devising it. We have also celebrated the tenth anniversary
f another marriage. In these situations, there may only be three or four
f us, and the members of that small team become cooks, makers,
erformers and musicians, servicing the party for hosts and guests.

Welfare State has been researching for some time into funeral
eremonies, particularly those of Quaker, humanist and oriental
ultures, and we are named in the wills of several people as the managers
f their funerals. However, at present we feel prepared only to undertake
1emorial services, partly because of pressure of time, partly because of
1e legal complications surrounding funerals.

At the time of writing, we have organised eight Naming ceremonies, in
ourteen years. The first was in 1969 and in that case, as in most others,
iends, relatives, friends of friends, and neighbours became involved by
ord of mouth. The parents involved had either recently had a baby or
ad older children who were not baptised or otherwise named. Most
amings have involved about six or seven children – the maximum to
ate has been seventeen. With parents, children, relatives and friends,
1ere have often been as many as seventy people involved. Although the
ontent has changed and grown, and the namings have been performed
om the Yorkshire Dales to the middle of Australia, the underlying
rinciple has remained unchanged: to provide a non-denominational
1eans for the celebration of birth and the bestowing and proclaiming of a
ame.

Each new celebration draws upon the experience of the last. Thus,
ertain aspects are repeated in each successive naming, whilst others
hange according to circumstances and location. The essential elements
re:

i Arrival and welcome, perhaps with a specially-written Welcome
Speech.
ii Decoration and enhancing of the space. (Most namings take place
out-doors.)
ii A focused piece – a performance, a dance, a shadow play, a song, a
sculptural site to visit.
v Charging the space for the actual naming by parents.
v Celebrations and release, usually with fireworks and dances.
i Exchange of gifts.
ii Feasting and games.

Dates are arranged to suit the greatest number of people. Some
amings were a year or more in the planning, others took just a couple of

Holding them high in our arms we made the Declaration of Names.
Duncombe Park, 1979.

weeks. Venues are chosen for the personal association they have for the participants, and for their sympathetic qualities as landscape. A list of namings shows how flexible we have been to individual circumstances:

July 1969   A Hilltop on the North York Moors.
New Year's Day 1970   Inside the Wool Exchange, Bradford.
September 1972   A stone circle in Cornwall.
New Year's Day 1978   Underground limestone cave in Yorkshire Dales.
June 1978   Paved courtyard, Baltimore USA.
New Year's Day 1979   River meadow in New South Wales, Australia.
April 1979   Duncombe Park stately home, Yorkshire.
October 1981   Forest and shore, Suffolk.

In all this variety, however, there are recurring features:

i An open-air, sculptural, dramatic and participatory journey.
ii Earth and air, fire and water as real elements, often used to produce a memento of the occasion e.g. personal emblems in clay, fired on the spot.
iii Live music and specially-written songs and dances.
iv The liberation of doves.
v Photographs of the event.
vi A handmade, personal Book of Naming for each child, incorporating images, songs and stories and the names of other children named on the same day, and in whose making the family have taken part.

In 1978, we used the idea of two names for a child – the ordinary name by which he or she is known to the world at large, and the secret one which may be known only to his or her family. The latter was given under the protection of the sound of a crashing waterfall in the limestone cave.

What Do We Ask Of Parents?

Parents contribute to a Naming according to their interests and skills. Potters built a raku kiln for the firing of clay birds during one celebration, a blacksmith forged a flying dove for the entrance of a Naming site for another. Some people have made gifts in wood or metal for the other parents, some have made gallons of home-brewed beer, or painted lanterns, organised the catering tent, lent a hand with putting up marquees and screens, designed and printed the invitations, dyed fabric for parasols, done the driving, brought chairs from the village hall, supervised the barbecue, chopped wood for the fire, or sang and played music for the procession. There is space for as much contribution as parents want to make in devising the form, although usually, they look to us to give an initiative, which they then enthusiastically follow. On the other hand, we have been asked to give up leadership altogether. Some people near Sheffield who were enthusiastic about our work, approached us to devise a naming ceremony, and plans for venues and times were soon underway. Then we got a phone call to say 'Hope you don't mind about this, but we'd rather do it ourselves.' We had worked ourselves out of a job, but were quite happy to do this, for it was right and proper for that group to take charge of the naming of their own children. We had given them a structure to look at, use, discard or improve upon, and the confidence that, with their friends, they could get it on.

Coping with Misconceptions

It is essential to stress that in all these ceremonies, we do not take on ourselves the role of priest. We reject that kind of authority structure and require more active participation and responsibility to be taken by the participants. That done, we are happy to stage-manage and help the event to the best of our abilities.

Sensitivity towards the feelings of close friends and members of the family is most important in the preparation period. Older relatives, in particular, might feel that celebrations of this kind are just some kind of freaky party, and they may be reluctant to attend, afraid to be out of place. Do not underestimate their reticence and nervousness, since they have no yardstick against which to measure these occasions. In our experience, time and patience to explain everything carefully well beforehand are of great value. When it is explained what will happen when, where and why it will happen, and how serious are the commitments behind it, then usually all reservations are overcome. Relatives have often indicated, with hindsight, how pleased they were to have shared such a unique event. We try to let them know that we really want them to be there, that we need them. Often, asking someone to help with a job is the best way of breaking the ice, and we choose, if we can, something we know they are good at.

Legalities

Some people arrange their own wedding ceremonies, but for the mundane requirements of the Inland Revenue and the State, also go to the Registrar of Marriages. We try to suggest that they do this afterwards, not before, so that what they are doing, in effect, is saying 'We are already married. We had our own wedding last week (or whenever). Now we are simply coming to register this fact with the State.' It is exactly as you would formally register the birth of your child within six weeks, but without investing it with any sense of occasion, as compared with the momentous experience of the birth, and the celebration of the naming.

We try never to lose sight of the fact that what is done when is less important than how it is done. The spirit is crucial. In 1979, the Fox family visited Bali and were privileged to observe a naming ceremony at first hand. This is what I wrote at the time:

> The singers have been going for two and a half hours now, and are getting tired. The old woman, when she is not mocking the singers with cackles, lets out huge audible yawns. From time to time neighbours appear – the very same women who have freely given scores of their hours' labour to make offerings for the ceremony – attracted by the lamps and the chanting that carries over the still night air. It needed no translation. 'Call that singing?' or 'What a bloody racket!' or 'If you can't do any better than that, you might as well give up!' Laughter punctuates everything in Bali.

SUE FOX

On Easter Saturday 1979, six families and their guests gathered to celebrate the naming of seven children in the grounds of Duncombe Park in North Yorkshire. As we collected ourselves under the high cupola of the Tuscan Temple, many of us still strangers to each other, we looked forward to the day with a mixture of feelings. Some of us had been involved in the preparations during the previous week; building a giant of earth and stone in the woods, making and rehearsing a shadow play, erecting a huge bird whose wings spanned a wide avenue, whitewashing the old orangery where the feast was to be held, and killing and cooking the pig which would be served at it. So some of us knew the order of events. All of us welcomed the chance to dedicate our children in front of friends and strangers, a gesture of hope and blessing, protection too, in the face of the terrors of our present world, but we wondered how this day would be, here in the rather formal surroundings of these 18th-century grounds.

Our child, Richard, who was to be named today, was a lad of eight, and we had chosen him for our son when he was four months old. So this ceremony of dedication was especially important to my husband David and myself, since we had not been present at his birth. As a family we had been guests at a naming ceremony the previous New Year's Day, which had taken place at Yordas Cave, where a fifteen foot waterfall crashes down inside the cave and becomes a river which flows deep into the earth. There had been powerful forces at work and we had all been deeply affected by the event. The setting of Richard's naming was very different with its spacious walks and woods, gardens and fine buildings, the hand of man everywhere apparent. We wondered how Richard, old enough to play a conscious role in his naming ceremony, would hand the day.

It had begun simply in a hotel in the nearby village of Helmsley where participants were welcomed and given a chance to recover themselve after journeys of considerable length. We had driven together t Duncombe Park, and as we stood under the dome wating for everyone t gather, there was a sense of being outside the usual boundaries of time. had been a steep climb to reach this spot from the cars, and at the to there was an unexpected landscape that was at once natural and artificia A wide grass walk opened out in front of us, bordered by unkempt wooc on one side and tidy rows of evergreens on the other – a long vista with Greek Temple at its end, towards which we walked slowly chatting those we knew and also to one or two we didn't. The children playe around us, excited by the space, and with us also was a grea grandmother of ninety-two, who had come to take part in the naming her great-grandson George, the three months old son of Boris an Maggie Howarth. It was Boris who had planned the day, attending every detail of the preparations during the previous week, but now Bor and Maggie were parents for the rest of the day and our host was to t Jamie Proud, an old W.S.I. associate, who lived just up the road and wh guided us with a reassuring lack of ceremony.

Three musicians awaited us at the Greek Temple and led us towards tented space where we were to be shown a shadow play. With them carried on his father's back, was six months old Hannes, also to be name that day, who jumped up and down in his papoose trying to grasp th bird's nest in his mother's hat as she played the saxophone. This fami had come from Holland and already there was a sense in which we all fe that we were on a journey together, having come from very differe directions. This feeling was re-inforced by the shadow play in th darkened tent, where we were all brought together in a small space fc the first completely directed moment. It was the story of Gilgamesh an his search for Eternal Youth; he finds it, but loses it to a serpent wh finds it tasty, changes his skin and vanishes in thick grey swamps foreve So Gilgamesh lost Eternal Youth but found the salt of Life sweeter an danced with Death in Joy and Pain and Wonder.

For most of us this was our first experience of a shadow play and th moving images on the white screen lit by flaming torches had a subt effect on us as a group; the tent seemed like a portal to another wor where rare and magical things could happen. Jamie explained that v were now embarking on the next stage of our journey – A Quest throug the elements. Now, for the first time, we entered an area that was n tamed or landscaped. Having climbed with some difficulty up into th woods which bordered the tent, we had not gone very deep into th woods when we found ourselves approaching a tree which spread branches to form a dome, under which creatures of all sizes and shap

rown naturally out of wood and moss had been gathered together and
laced in a forest of jagged perspex pieces. Above them the tree suddenly
ecame a spring and all the branches came alive with streams of water.

Boris had written a short dedication for this space, which Jamie
elivered like a familiar fireside story . . .

> Noah dropped his telescope among the old certificates in the
>   cupboard
> And muddied his boots on the new found land
> But the eager angels still rode the surf
> And the speckled dew, like fishes' eyes
> Flashed beneath the indifferent stars;
> Rain washed the diamond roads
>   and flowers sang the pungent breeze.
> When the new morning rain had come
>   and gone again by dinner time,
> Noah smiled in his cup and replanted the
>   everlasting vine.

Some went forward and cupped water in their hands to drink, or
ashed their baby's hands or face; others seemed to decide that this was
fter all a space to dream in. No one told us what to do as we listened to
1e water cascading down from the branches of the tree, and at this stage
sensed an uncertainty as to what, if anything, had been required of us.

Now we followed the musicians to a huge recumbent giant built of
arth and stone, with a smoking pit of a stomach. Here there was no such
ncertainty; taut fishing rods, one for each child, reached into his
mouldering belly and one by one the parents pulled out a paper gift; a
inged ship, a lighthouse, a dove. Richard and four year old Kylie Stark
ere able to do their own fishing, but they needed parental help with the
eavy twelve foot rods, and there was laughter and supportive cheers as
ach child struggled to free the gift from the giant man.

Here too there was a story for us . . .

> There is a land of men – base-metal in their groins,
> Where no mortal treads. Upon their shoulders
> Perfection flutters like a silver bird.
> The shadow of hunting does not stain their pure breath.
> Sometimes this God-fired jungle flames with newer life:
> Phantom tigers tremble on the brink of dark pools
> Which reflect the lolling eye of greater heavens.

From the earth man we wound our way through the trees to a cleared
ircle where stood a kiln about four feet high and three feet in diameter,
uilt of twigs and bundles of straw to form a delicate criss-cross pattern.

It was topped with a nest. This kiln had been built for the occasion by Jil
and Peter Dick, local potters who had been involved as parents at the
very first naming ceremony in 1969 at which they had also built a kiln. As
we approached, the kiln was fired, and as the flames licked the nest each
family was given a brightly painted egg of paper and sawdust and invited
to place it in the nest. 'Come back later and see what hatches,' we were
told.

> Burning apples fall from orchards where not even God has been
> And from the sawdust egg the terracotta of our hearts
> Wings forth and beats the sullen air anew.

Water, earth, and fire; we went on our way with a sense of having set
something in motion. We soon found ourselves in a high wide avenue
across which stretched the wings of a huge white bird. Here we took our
children forward and holding them high in our arms we made the
declaration of names . . .

> Richard Soyinka Lambert
> May you dance in your visions
> May you sing your dancing visions to the world

Our hearts were full as we watched each child held high and heard the
names echo in that space of air . . .

> Hall George Daedalus Vanbrugh Howarth
> Kylie Ann Stark
> Hannes Antonius Van Raay
> Bryony Stroud Watson
> Katherine Bronia Witts
> Thomas Christopher Llewellyn Witts

> May their names sing as long as these brave trees
> May their lives echo on in the stars
> May our love give them help as they travel alone
> May our prayers hold their hand as they fly

As each name rang out a rocket exploded into the sky. Each stage of this
gentle journey seemed to have been preparing us for this moment.

> In the company of those we love
> Of friends who warm us
> And strangers who augment our little world
> We name our children.

We returned through the wood in high spirits having shared an
perience which had drawn us together and uncovered depths of feeling
at we were not used to sharing in this way. The floor of the woods was
ick with daffodils and as we approached the orangery underneath an
cade of white paper birds flapping in the wind, we could see that it too
d been filled with daffodils. Here the grand feast was spread out on
ree long tables, around a centrepiece which was a Norwegian
elebration Cake, a decorated spiral of almond paste eighteen inches
gh, surrounded by delicacies of all kinds, a leaping chocolate fish, rich

Delicacies of all kinds. Duncombe Park, 1979.

uit cake, apple pie. On another table lay meats; pork roasted with sugar
d mustard coating, liver and pork pâté; spicy chick peas, side dishes of
gurt, bananas, coconut, and with it all rich brown loaves of freshly
ked bread. There was nothing on these tables which had not been
epared carefully by hand especially for this afternoon – Jane and Lizzie
d been hard at work often until late at night cooking, mixing, testing
stes, shapes, colours, and it had been part of the business of the week to
ll and butcher the pig, reared by Jamie, which now provided us with all
e meats for our celebration. Even the mulled cider had been made last
inter by David Clough, Welfare State International's technical
anager, and the window ledges were decorated with brightly painted
ose eggs which had been blown and decorated by all of us, adults and
ildren, during the evenings of the previous week.

Now there was time as we spread ourselves over the grass terraces with our full plates, to relax and to talk more fully to other families and their friends. There had been a leisurely quality to the whole day and the feeling of timelessness persisted. No one hurried or worried us; no special behaviour seemed necessary and each event flowed easily into the next. The children were joyous, making friends with each other easily and soon had a game of football going which tempted several of the adults too. Those of us who had been making the preparations had been working hard up to the very last minute – I remember changing into my best clothes in the van on the way to meet the family at the hotel and contemplating my inevitably dirty fingernails with gloom, but once we had gathered there had been no more rushing about.

The children went off to follow a treasure hunt which had been laid in the woods. The final clue led them to a tall egg man in a top hat who led them a good chase before he allowed himself to be caught, and distributed the contents of his basket of chocolate eggs. The children cut the amazing spiral cake which was shared with everyone, old and young, and we all trooped back through the woods to the kiln to find that our eggs had given birth to a variety of small clay creatures – doves, winged horses, a bull, one for each child to be named. Back on the terraces we gathered around for the final event of the day – the liberation of doves. For each child there was a dove to be released and as each bird was held high and freed it circled once, twice, perhaps three times above our heads before it found its direction and set off with certainty for home. It was late afternoon now and the sun which had shone faithfully all day was now sinking behind the trees. It was time to go home.

We parted from each other having travelled together through territory that we do not often negotiate in our society, which packages and parcels out our experiences for us so that we lose touch with all that is profound or disturbing in our lives. We had confirmed and celebrated our shared humanity, making a public declaration of our love, our hopes for our children. There had been nothing strange or mystical about the day, we had not been seeking for a powerful magic in which to lose ourselves. All day there had been plenty of time to talk, to explain, to experience each focused moment in our own time. But what we had shared was important, and all the care and preparation that had gone into it was important too, an essential part of that committment we had demonstrated when we had held our children to the sky and declared our hopes for them. Nothing had been too much trouble for this celebration and every element of it had been prepared with care for this afternoon alone – the decorations in the orangery, the shadow play, the images and spaces in the woods, even the two chemical toilets which we had of necessity to erect in the woods, had been made as magnificent as possible, with white drapes, foliage and flowers.

We had prepared the ground as carefully as possible. We had let our

reams become concrete that day and the future seemed full of
ossibilities.

Today seven children have been named
From an infant of three months
To a boy of eight years strong
So here is a new beginning.
        May they dance in their visions
        May they sing their dancing visions to the world.

LOIS LAMBERT

(ii) The Barn Dance, 1981

BAZ KERSHAW

owards the end of Welfare State's 1981 *Barn Dance* the general lighting
ver the dance floor dims and a small harmonium begins to play 'Now is
1e Hour'. The moment is a risky one – it verges on sentimentality and
reatens to tumble the creative poise of the evening into hopeless cliche
 yet it was always saved from sentimental wallowing by a typical
1dacity. Two girls from the company join the harmonium and sing the
mg, quietly and gently, in *Maori*. And the strangeness of the tongue
shers the audience away from the easy stock response, encouraging
1em to listen and watch more carefully as John Fox walks into the
entral pool of light.
  By then everyone in the audience will have got to know John Fox
ersonally, as Councillor Brown: a shortish, stoutish, bluff Northerner
1 a brown suit (turnups, wide-winged lapels, waistcoat and watch
hain), crumpled brown trilby and big black boots. He has chatted all of
s up, with a broad friendliness which marks him, in one reporter's
ords, as 'a stalwart but by no means incorruptible representative of the
cal community': a key anchor role linking the ordinary world of the
1dience to the weird images produced by the company. But this final
ntrance reveals a transformation. He now wears an ankle length leather
oat, a wide brimmed leather hat, and carries in his right hand a leather

suitcase, all brilliantly decorated with multicoloured patterns. The witty, biblical allusion to Joseph is only part of the surprise; under his left arm he holds a rough but beautifully made model of an ark, which for a moment makes his new costume look like a sailor's heavy weather gear and reminds us of the many earlier nautical images of the evening.

He stops when he reaches the centre of the dance floor and gently places the ark on the ground. Round its upper decks are ranged twenty or so little candles, each standing precariously in a silver tinfoil holder. Initially the audience is amused, but then their focus, stillness and silence become complete as the song continues and as the new Councillor Brown takes out a box of matches, strikes one and invites them to light the candles. People happily oblige; people who at the start of the evening would probably never have imagined themselves kneeling carefully to light insecure candles on a model boat, being intently watched by two or three hundred others: old ladies, young businessmen, skinheads, punks, shy children.

Again, the trite and obvious connections with birthdays and Christmas always threaten to turn the moment into nostalgic mush. But the care demanded by the lighting of the candles, the genuinely benevolent smile of the ridiculously coated Councillor, the odd mixture of allusions in the total image, and, through all that, the clear impression that the people stooping over the model had crossed, were crossing, an important line on our behalf – all this evoked a powerful feeling that something valuable and rare was taking place. At the very least the stillness was a poignant climax to an energetic evening's dancing together, an acceptance of images and actions as strangely evocative as Councillor Brown and his ark, and a confirmation that the audience and company had created something unique and fundamental *together*.

2.

The overall structure of the Barn Dance was flexible, so that each night of the 22 gig tour was quite singular in its development. The dancing itself progressed through more or less the same tunes and dances, but dances would be added, subtracted or repeated according to the state of the audience. Similarly the songs and scenes performed by the company which interspersed the dancing could be introduced or left out according to need. That need was determined in response to the audience-dancers: Taffy Thomas, M.C. and dance-caller, decided on the shape of the evening as it developed, in consultation with John Fox and Boris Howarth. The significance of the event was in the action of company and audience together: the various ways in which objective events – performance and dancing – affected subjective relationships, the audience's 'sense of community' – through participation. The changes they went through to arrive at the collective silence and stillness described above were what the Barn Dance was 'about'.

The company's performance in the Barn Dance depended upon some of the formal skills employed by shamans – trance dancing, singing, puppetry, trickery, spectacle. And the imagery and symbolism of the scenes and songs derived more from the cross-cultural world of myths, dreams, hallucinations and visions, than from the everyday social experience of the audience. But the major success of the evening still rested firmly on the various ways in which the structure of the event and the forms of those images and symbols combined, to produce for the audience a simultaneous sense of shared meanings and unfathomable mystery. That combination was at the heart of the Barn Dance as a successful ritual-celebration of community, just as those qualities are at the heart of every successful community.

The tour opened in the Trinity School Rooms, Ulverston. The approach to the Rooms was as daunting as their name: cold, icy, ill-lit streets to a barren square – a total contrast to the scene inside. While I was explaining who we were to the man on the door I was offered a piece of blue cake, balanced on the end of a six-inch-wide, four-foot-long steel cutlass. On the other end of the heavy weapon, grinning in a splendid parody of a pirate's fighting gear – three-foot-wide hat, broadly striped shirt, big baggy pants and boots, long red beard and gold earring – was Taffy Thomas. 'Welcome aboard, shipmates', in a comic boom of a voice: 'Captain's guests', to the man on the door, smoothing over our explanations and entry. That clever and relaxed use of the overlap between fantasy and reality is a hallmark of Welfare State's work.

The visual impact of the hall and the hundred or so people already filling it was remarkable.

Every wall was brilliantly decorated with brightly coloured banners and flags, some glowing with lights behind them. The biggest showed a gold orange sun with ambiguous features. Others displayed skeletons, sinking ships, castles, trees of life sprouting eggs – strange and vaguely mediaeval images which were repeated in different forms on some of the eight huge Chinese-style lanterns hanging from the ceiling and throwing a warm glow on the people gathering below. Some were already forming largish groups of friends, acquaintancies, families round the edges of the hall. It was difficult to see any obvious outsiders – perhaps we were the only ones, Welfare State being based in Ulverston – but easy to see a complicated network of relationships in the ways that people greeted each other, often across the width of the hall. The mixture of different types, classes and ages was very wide (a second hallmark).

Lots of the kids were in fancy dress (pirates and cowboys abounded) and wandering among them, chatting and joking, were the performers. Tom Mix strode by on his high-heeled boots, a short man with a fifteen gallon hat and six shooters which would surely guarantee *his* death in a gunfight – the three foot long barrels needed an awkward and acrobatic draw to get them out of their holsters. Cinderella, looking down and out and sexily coy in an old liberty bodice, full see through skirt made of old polythene sheeting, a pair of good Lancashire clogs (much admired by the lady next to us), swept up the dog ends with a worn out broom, smiling sweetly. Robinson Crusoe in a tattered Safari helmet, tattered furs and khaki shorts, stood dolefully in the middle of the floor, lost apparently, bemused by the unusual crowd. A sexy Prince Charming minced past: fishnet tights, patent leather high-heeled shoes, bright waistcoat, tails, collar and dicky bow, a painted-on moustache suggesting Groucho Marx and a Chicago gangster. An odd white-faced fellow, looking like a cross between a sleepwalker and a motorcyclist carefully climbed onto the stage and closely inspected a fiddle – was he going to play? Councillor Brown himself came over and said he hoped we were all right and he thought things would start happening soon but he wasn't sure what exactly, though he'd make sure it was mostly legal at least. Dream figures – comfortable yet threatening, familiar yet strange – the focus of emotional and intellectual contradictions (a third hallmark).

Captain Cook/Long John Silver/the composite pirate announced, and demonstrated with Cinders, the first dance. Almost all the other characters were up on the stage. The sleepwalking-motorcyclist had tuned up his fiddle. The mediaeval old woman with a black ankle-length skirt had picked up the tenor saxophone. The emaciated judge in tights had a squeezebox. Banjo, drums, more saxophones, a clarinet: the first tune was well under way and twenty or so people dancing a simple square dance, and it had all begun with such aplomb and apparent casualness that the actual difficulty of what had already been achieved – a clearly excellent band, a smoothly and wittily organised dance ('All aboard for the first voyage' the M.C. pirate called), an atmosphere of contained and shared excitement – the underlying skill could easily have been overlooked. Professionalism: a fourth hallmark.

Two more dances followed, each a bit livelier and more complicated, each impressively introduced through nautical metaphors by the confident Taffy Thomas, each encouraging more people to dance. By the third one, there were over fifty people on their feet and established groupings had already begun to break down: local kids danced with camp followers, grannies with the odd rocker from a group that had shambled in late, a neatly suited middle-aged man whirled Cinders round until her clogs clattered.

4.

A barn dance alone is a social event which may confirm existing relationships within a community; it may even act as a quasi-ritual allowing a community to confront and overcome its latent tensions. But only under exceptional circumstances can it act as a model for the development of a community through factors external to that community. What Welfare State's *performance structure* added to the dancing were the terms of a different order of experience through which *any* group of dancers – from a fully integrated community to a disparate clutter of strangers – could choose to become part of a basic community-forming process. This was made possible because the forms of the company's 'interludes' both challenged and supported the audience.

For instance, two songs-scenes which were performed early in the evening of all the dances have a distinct mediaeval feel, as if we are being transported back to some vague root of lost cultural memories. The dancing stops, the lanterns dim, the spots came up on the centre of the hall, the harmonium begins to play a melancholy, wistful tune and into the light, stooped and slow and looking round with a wry smile, moves an old woman. She wears a long black tight skirt of rough material; black laceup boots show a little beneath the skirt; tight waist length black jacket over a dark blouse. On her head is poised a tall hat, dark again and reminiscent of a witch's tall hat. On a closer look it becomes a miniature spiral fairground slide draped in black netting under which tiny silver fish seem to swim.

On her bent back she wears a bulging sack, full of dead babies, we learn from the mournful, mischievous dirge that she sings (still stooped, still wry and wise in her direct gaze) about the 'Fairground of Dreaming'.

My hat is a fairground of dreamings
My handbag a bed for the dead
My stories will brighten your evenings
My songs they will lighten your head
Sing along
Sing along my children
Hear my accordion tune
The sweeties that hide in my shopping bag
Are acid drops found on the moon

The overall impression is part menacing, part heart-rending, part quietly humorous. If she had a name it would probably be Old Mother Death; but that name perhaps suggests a lack of the intimacy which was the main quality of Lois Lambert's performance, a distinct and direct invitation to share in her fearful mysteries, to reach into the dark to discover the cause of those deaths for which we might ourselves be responsible.

If you are lucky you are fixed with the old woman's final stare before the lights come up for another dance as she shuffles off, or before a lively drum beat strikes up and into the space gallops a vision from Picasso's Guernica: a wild, startled and startling horsehead with flaring nostrils,

A vision from Picasso's "Guernica". The Barn Dance, 1981.

glaring eyes, bobbing and swerving just above the heads of the audience
After the initial delighted shock, the equestrian vision turns out to be
wonderfully witty version of the old pantomime stock in trade: the on
man horse. But the usual stiffness of the standard model is replaced by
bouncy swerving fluidity of movement and life, reinforced by the bi
booted stamping gallop given to it by its rider: a rather blousey lookin
lady in a low cut silver bodice, golden hair and the kind of netted ha
which you would expect to encounter only at Sunday service. Again, th
visual wit, again the performance energy as the horse comes to a sto
and, pawing the ground in a scraping rhythm, its lady rider launches in
an up-beat foot-tapping Brechtian song:

> What did the wife of the soldier get
> From the ancient city of Prague?
> From Prague she got the buttoned shoes
> The silver-sequined buttoned shoes
> She got from the city of Prague.

What did the wife of the soldier get
From the rich town Amsterdam?
From Amsterdam she got the hat
It knocked them flat the new Dutch hat
That is what she got from Amsterdam.

What did the wife of the soldier get
From Paris the city of light?
She got the gown with the silken sheen
The girls went green at the silken sheen
And that is what she got from the city of light.

What did the wife of the soldier get
From the wilds of Russia?
From Russia she got the widow's veil
The widow's veil for his funeral
And that is what she got from Russia.

The final verse is sung slower, with a hint of hard sadness; then the drums start up their quick beat again, the horse rears back and begins to gallop in a big circle to be joined by a limping, staggering parade of wounded soldiers playing pipe and drums, which marches twice round the hall and out into the distance. The effect is poignant and shocking, hinting at images we've seen on film dozens of times. But the cliche of the routed army staggering home has been undermined by the directness, anger and invention of the parade; the song about death turned into a vigorous protest against one of its chief causes – the manipulation of men into soldiers and sailors.

The images and themes of these two songs-scenes are archetypally ambivalent. The characters and their sentiments are readily recognisable – the old woman, the abandoned lover – and they can thus confirm the audience's sense of identity in a communal response. But the emotions they stir are powerful and threatening, so the communal response is made in relation to the sense of an unavoidably destructive force. This ambivalence is fundamental to the community-forming process: the audience does not need to make explicit the meaning of the images because their archetypal significance is clear, yet some meaning or significance has to be communally recognised in order to deal with the threat that the images represent.

5.

This analysis is a result of retrospective luxury: in practice the dancing and the next scene animate the process at a relatively unconscious level. The scene may be a fantastic battle between a flying bomb-fish and a fisherman – which the fisherman loses – or a ludicrously spoof Barber of Seville scene in which Cinders shaves Prince Charming. Or it may be a long and delicate allegory performed by the sleepwalking-motorcyclist in which individual members of the audience help to bring about th happy marriage of the earth and the moon. Moments of tension ar created, and dissipated in pleasant surprises, shaman tricks, magic Thus the performances begin to imply that no matter how threatenin sections of the collective journey may be, it will perhaps end up well

Yet a couple of dances later two eight-foot-tall skeletons come jerkin on. Taffy Thomas hands out skeleton masks to the audience and withi minutes the dance floor is full of jiggling skeletons, arms and legs flun wildly anyway. An amazing sight, the exact inversion of the order of th barn dance, a release of the audience's wild, anarchic powers. Thi participation may be preceded or followed by a beautiful shadow-puppe show, lit by live flames: a respite from the dancing and a kind o summation of the themes of sailors, ships, journeys, flying to distan planets, confronting weird powers and death.

Still more barn dancing follows before the lanterns dim again and th audience now almost automatically clears the centre of the space. Tw drummers approach the spotlit area and set up a driving, insistent an urgent rhythm, before a truly impressive vision of a ship appears. It i eight feet or so long, an ocean liner with funnels smoking and porthole glinting with lights, and it sways backwards and forwards through th crowd to the centre of the hall at shoulder height, a long loose apro hanging down to the ground, hiding the dancer inside – the apro swishes as it swirls, like the wind and waves at sea, the smoke is blow about by the whirling, tilting, rocking energy of its wild voyage aroun and back and forth across the hall. It is obvious that dancing under th big ship, head hidden by the upper decks, vision drastically reduced must be extremely difficult and taxing. Yet the drumming goes on an on, and the ship swings within inches of the faces of the audience as i becomes manically possessed by forces apparently outside its control The combination of whirling dervish, Padstow horse, the Titanic, i unavoidable and, literally, mind-boggling. The life, the dancer, is *in* th ship – yet it is apparently in the grip of enormous external forces. Th contemporary image mingles with a sense of primal forces, yet there i never any doubt that the performance is merely a performance. So th 'sinking' of the ship is broadly symbolic *and* utterly real in the perceptio that it is the result of the dancer's exhaustion as he must stop, kneeling t rest from the extreme exertion.

The energy the ship has expended, at this stage of the evening, is ver impressive. The people are themselves becoming weary from th dancing, so they are engagingly co-operative when the Pirate and Ton Mix next ask them to sit in a large circle on the floor for a game of Pass th Parcel. Tom Mix is blindfolded inside the forming circle – whenever h shoots his gun the music will stop and whoever has the parcel strips off layer of wrapping.

The song is a Welfare State 'oldie' to a calypso rhythm:

> Where is the deadman?
> Where is the baby eater?
> Where is the deadman now?
> Inside the big house.
> Behind the courthouse,
> Under the fat dead cow.
> Where is the deadman?
> Where is the deadman?
> Up our nose no more.

Tom Mix stamps round the inside of the excited circle, no one in it eager to end up with the final layer; but in the end a boy of about ten tears off the brown paper to reveal a bottle containing an ark on a blue sea,

Councillor Brown, transformed. Barn Dance, 1981.

which, with Tom Mix, he carries round the circle so everyone can see. The effect is complex: the ship is safe, home and dry – but enclosed, caught, trapped; the voyage is completed – but diminished; the elements are stilled – but their energy is lost. The interpretive intellect fails under the pressure and gives way to a sense of poignancy – it is both the beginning and the end. We are beyond the deadman but the voyage, the dance, is finishing. A few moments later the harmonium begins to play 'Now is the Hour' and Councillor Brown enters, transformed.

6.

I have indicated that the Barn Dance animated a community-forming process between actors and audience, and that this process was a result of the dynamic produced by (1) the incorporation into the 'safe' form of the barn dancing of the 'threatening' images and action created by the company, and (2) the incorporation of the audience, through increasingly active participation, into the company's performance. The complexity of that dynamic seemed to make the community-forming process available to a wide range of different types of audience, as I hope the following four examples will show.

In Ulverston, for instance, the relatively close-knit nature of the audience produced a predominantly relaxed atmosphere that was nevertheless shot through with underlying tensions and animosities. This could be most easily detected in the initial hyper-excitement of the children, which was a result, in part, of the adults' nervous desire to make the evening a success, which in its turn led to tensions between subgroups in the audience, and between audience and company. As an outsider to both I would feel, perhaps inevitably, that the sense of community finally achieved in the lighting of the candles *contained* these tensions, rather than dispelled them. Yet my impression was that even if there were still signs of uneasiness at the end, then that was because the community had encountered some of its more basic internal instabilities more openly and directly than usual and that they had moved towards a better basis perhaps for sharing their lives.

A related, but very different, process occurred in other dances. In Fleetwood (12 March) an audience of about fifty were scattered around a circle defined by screens in the middle of the large dance floor of the Marine Hall. They were in groups of two or three – a young hippy couple, a mother with her two neatly dressed seven or eight year-old dancing-school girls, three giggling middle-aged spinsters – except for ten or so younger men and women on a works outing from the Milk Marketing Board. This group had seated themselves in a way that dissociated them from the event – almost *outside* the circle of screens. Consequently, the structure of the evening took place on two simultaneous levels: (1) the drawing together of the disparate groups of twos and threes and (2) the drawing into that process of the Milk

Marketing Board outsiders. In this case the tensions, animosities, fears, instabilities were at a much more obvious level than in Ulverston: there was no hint of community to offset the embarrassments caused by our sparseness in the big, empty-feeling hall. Yet the evening broke down physical and social inhibitions between strangers to create a sense of shared communal experience which was apparently *not* part of a wider local community.

By contrast, in Grizebeck Village Hall (10 April) there were three basic groups in the audience: the committee members who had organised the dance; the villagers who were not on the committee; and visitors from Ulverston and elsewhere, mostly friends and fans of the company. Of the latter the most obtrusive was a group of about nine punkish youths from an Intermediate Treatment Centre. At first the villagers showed some fear and animosity towards this group and to some extent, by implication, the other 'outsiders'. But two factors contributed to the overcoming of the tension created by this: first, all the 'outsiders' were willing to dance; and second, there were fewer villagers than expected because of a rival dance in a neighbouring village. The structure of the evening thus became the temporary incorporation of the visitors into the depleted community of the village. In the process the submerged animosities which had initially been directed at the committee members by the other villagers were dispelled in the desire to present a unified body which could exercise magnanimity towards the outsiders.

On the final night of the tour, at St Peter's Hall, Whitehaven (11 April), the audience was an incredibly disparate collection of some three hundred people rubbing shoulders in a smallish hall full of local animosities. Skinheads from the estate – out for heavy rock really – glared at the band and at the effete, suede-jacketed academic trendies from Lancaster. Local mini-skirted schoolgirls chewed gum and giggled as an uncle or a neighbour watched them refuse when gentle hippies invited them to dance. An old couple sat bemused at seeing so many oddball strangers in their hall, but apparently happy with the sense of energetic activity. Much later, Taffy Thomas told me that he thought there was no way of drawing this audience together. He had expected disaster: fights and broken bottles – so had I. The early dances of the evening were done with manic energy and incredible noise – shouts and whoops that made people jumpy and nervous. Only a slight accident – the wrong heel caught by the wrong toe in one of the many passings, and the evening could have crumbled into a chaos of outright, upfront conflict.

So what really happened that night was truly amazing. The frantic dancing lost none of its energy, but gradually gained in control as the audience participated increasingly in the Welfare State scenes. I had seen incredible combinations of energy and control in other kinds of dancing: Teddy Boys in a Hemel Hempstead club, punk head-banging in

Nottingham discos, Polynesian fire dancing. The purpose of these forms is twofold: to reach states related to trance and to affirm the solidarity of the group, and it normally takes time and united sub-cultural support to achieve. But in Whitehaven something similar was created in under an hour by a very wide social mix of people – and with it came an openness, warmth and acceptance which, especially considering the context, was very remarkable.

The truth is that, given the right circumstances, a kind of community can be created by a very disparate set of people in a relatively short time. It is not a community in the sense that Ulverston was: tensions created and contained through people knowing each other fairly well. Or in the sense that Fleetwood was: people moving closer together out of social embarrassment. Or in the sense that Grizebeck was: a community consolidating in order temporarily to incorporate others. In a way, the Whitehaven dance went through all these stages – or rather included them at different points for different people – and beyond. Of course this happens in traditional theatre – when it works well. But Whitehaven was very different. First, because the audience started at a potentially dangerous point – without agreed conventions – and second *because* they started at that point they were able to use Welfare State's songs and scenes to themselves create meanings together *during* the process of the event. That experience is unifying and enlightening – and I would argue that it was the source of the success of Whitehaven; it was what made the audience open and receptive, it turned potential disaster into miraculous discovery.

7.

John Fox is very lucid in his statements of Welfare State's basic aims:

> Theatre has a healing role. In terms of a group of people meeting together – they make a circle literally and emblematically, and the cast provides one part of that circle and the audience makes the rest. What drops into the middle is some kind of energy. That energy can have a healing effect on people. Now if you actually touch each other in different generations and different classes . . . I think that people who have eaten food together, have danced together, have held each other – it's more difficult for them to hurt each other.

He is also very clear about the ways in which the Barn Dance works to attain some kind of curative function:

> To get people together, to actually get them to talk to each other, to hold each other, to dance together, to experience together a mystery, to experience a dream . . . ideally we're working with images that are in the subconscious ... we take people on

a journey with us and if we discover anything on that journey and reveal it, that is an awakening of areas inside the audience and inside us. . . . I'm talking essentially about creative forces which are released, which essentially in the culture we live in are repressed.

The mystery he is referring to is, I believe, a central factor in the community-forming process of the Barn Dance and, like almost everything else in Welfare State's work, it depends on a paradoxical ambivalence. On the one hand, that mystery is threatening. Images of death, mutilation, isolation, overwhelming natural and unnatural forces pervade the Barn Dance both in the performance scenes and on the banners and lanterns which decorate the hall. The iconography, to use John Fox's term, is primarily negative and intended to stir fears and doubts. On the other hand, the ways in which the images are juxtaposed are so unusual that they allow the audience to make their own connections between them – to create the significance of the evening. And that is anything but threatening because it gives the audience power to control the imagery creatively – a freedom closely allied to playfulness and fun. This is reinforced, of course, by the use of familiar pantomime characters and idioms as the animators of the imagery.

In addition, the barn dancing serves to break down barriers between audience members and audience and performers; physical, social and aesthetic conventions are stretched and challenged within a recognisable and easily acceptable format. The dancing lulls the audience into a relaxed and receptive, but not unalert mood. Then as the evening progresses, the audience is confronted more and more directly and intimately by the ambivalent mystery of the event's iconography. The increasing levels of active participation in the scenes between dances is the basis of a further paradox: as the audience is more directly threatened it is more completely in control of the progress of the event. And this paradox is central to the significance achieved by the audience: a non-verbal significance developed through the evolution of collective responses to the increasingly encroaching but controlled mystery represented by the iconography. Welfare State's songs and scenes were brilliantly conceived to place increasing demands on the audience *as part of* supportive participatory experiences which augmented and extended the unifying function of the dancing. In other words, a relatively conservative social ceremony – barn dancing – was transformed by radical theatre techniques – the songs and scenes – into the experience of community-formation.

As in rituals, the significance of the total event is *implicit*: shared and known by the participants in non-verbal, non-intellectual ways. Non-participants may be aware of this significance, but they can not share in it. This is because participation in the event redefines the normal relationships between reality and illusion. Given the context in which the company works – tatty community halls, well-worn community centres, rough and ready spaces never intended for such rituals – that aim may seem preposterously ambitious. Yet because the Barn Dance is partly rooted in well-known social processes (through the dancing itself), and partly rooted in unknown psychological processes (the release of subconscious energy through public images in the company's performance), Welfare State could reasonably hope to bring social unity and visionary experience together in a satisfactory marriage.

In a time when enormous political forces are threatening to undermine and crush the development of unique communities the creation of that awareness is of central importance to our culture's future health. The Barn Dance was exactly what the Company's poster claimed: a knees up. But it was a knees up with an overwhelmingly urgent social and political purpose. And, amazingly, it succeeded in that purpose over and over again.

(iii) Tempest on Snake Island

PROFESSOR RON GRIMES

One of the best examples of an original, public ritual in recent times was 'Tempest on Snake Island', held just off the mainland of Toronto, Canada, by Welfare State in May 1981. Because of my work in ritual studies and theatre, I was invited to observe, interpret, document and participate in the event, which was a collaboration between Welfare State, the residents of Toronto Island communities, and the Toronto Theatre Festival.

Welfare State clearly prefers working outdoors with communities and neighbourhoods to whom they teach their skills, thereby demystifying technique, and with whom they create environments in which a primal sense of mystery can arise. One of the outstanding features of their activities is the way they connect art with ritual. Their celebrations are marked by an attunement to rhythm, space and construction not ordinarily found in modern theatre. They are not primarily concerned with plot, acting or character development. They are not just interested in rendering religious themes such as birth, re-birth, descent, death or

ιcred marriage in aesthetic fashion, but in dissolving the barriers which
ιolate art into aestheticism, and religion into sectarianism. Though the
ιoup evolved from the arts, not the church, they perform ritual
ιnctions traditionally done by religious institutions. Welfare State has
ιrong moral, ecological and political concerns, but is not at all political
ιitprop theatre. Its tone is humorous, gently ironic and playful, not
ιetorically revolutionary. No matter how religious or political its
ιages, its face always sports a bulbous red nose.

Having been invited to take part in the Toronto Theatre Festival, the
ιmpany sent two people to Canada to locate social and physical
ιvironments for the event. They chose to work with the Toronto Island
ιmmunity. The fifteen Toronto islands – the main ones being
ιnnected by walkways and bridges – are a ten-minute ferry ride from
ιwntown Toronto. They consist of eight hundred acres, thirty-three of
ιhich are residential. The 600-odd residents live in 250 houses on two of
ιe islands, Ward's and Algonquin. The land is owned by the city of
ιoronto. In 1968, the leases on the residential properties expired,
ιsulting in a protracted, widely publicised controversy in which the
ιlanders refused evictions from their cottages, which serve most
ιsidents as permanent homes. The Islanders are by no means a
ιmmunity of transients; the average Islander has lived in his or her
ιme twelve years, in contrast to the national average of four. But
ιansient traffic to the islands is heavy, especially in the summer, most of
ιpicnickers, cyclists and tourists.

Shortly before Welfare State's arrival, a lengthy Provincial Commis-
ιn Report recommended a 25-year extension of the Islanders' leases,
ιoof of the community's ability to mobilise itself quickly and
ιfectively, and in spite of strongly-held, half-informed views of the
ιlanders held by outsiders. It was partly as a response to this victory that
ιelfare State created 'Tempest on Snake Island'.

Snake Island is a fifteen-minute walk and one bridge-crossing from
ιards and Algonquin Island docks. It is roughly circular, approxi-
ιately five hundred yards in diameter, and is uninhabited bush. Since it
ιordinarily a lovers' nest, and is said to have been a native shaman's
ιaling site, it is liminal, sacred and ambivalent to some island residents.
ιis an anomalous place. Snake Island's spatial-symbolic position is to
ιard's and Algonquin, what the latter two are to the Toronto mainland.
ιThe first public summation of the theme of Welfare State's project was
ιamanism and technology'. Shakespeare's 'The Tempest' was chosen
ιa source of images because its characters, themes, actions and settings
ιclosely parallel those of the Toronto islands. The combination of
ιand magic and political intrigue seemed both to islanders and Welfare
ιate a clear match. The celebration involved roughly a hundred
ιanders, along with the company, in organising, making, animating
ιd performing. Two weeks were spent creating the environment and

building the structures. Five performances were done on five successive evenings for a sold-out crowd of two hundred a night.

No way of recounting 'Tempest on Snake Island' can evoke what the celebration itself did. Straight descriptive accounts of rituals, especially celebrative ones, are flat and boring. Treating the celebration as a story, when it was really a collage of collectively enacted images, would distort it. The problem of viewpoint is a drastic one in such events. To illustrate: no single performer ever saw the entire celebration either in or out of character. The most involved Islanders saw it from a perspective which combined being in character with management functions like ushering. The directors and conceivers of the event also performed and could not see it. Typical audience members saw it only once and therefore could scarcely get beyond 'What happens next?', atmosphere, or some intuited grasp of its sense. 'Tempest on Snake Island' itself can be treated as an interpretation of Toronto island culture, Shakespeare's play and universal themes such as Power, Life and Death, but full interpretations of the whole event did not occur even in the writings of drama critics, whose responses were generally laudatory, or about their private likes and dislikes.

Greetings and Garden Party

People purchased $8–10 tickets to 'Tempest at Snake Island' and gathered at the foot of Bay Street on the Toronto mainland at eight o'clock to be ferried to the Toronto Islands. The performance was advertised by the Toronto Theatre Festival as 'onstage', that is, not 'fringe' or 'open stage'.

These few facts – the ticket, time, and prestige of being selected for 'onstage' status, in addition to glossy, expensive pre-festival publicity, meant the audience came with theatrical, rather than celebratory expectations. Ticket costs selected for upper middle class, and going to an island by ferry for an outdoor performance attracted avant-garde theatre buffs or the adventurous. Only a few older people or children attended. Limiting the audience to two hundred, because of the size of Snake Island, probably prevented late deciders and the less organised from attending. That many were turned away left those with tickets feeling they held something special.

As one might guess from their name, the ethos of Welfare State is at considerable odds with that of 'North America's Largest Theatre Festival'. The festival programme, in glossy magazine format, contained not only schedules and advertisements but letters, seals and signatures from seven government officials, including those of the Prime Minister of Canada and Premier of Ontario. The festival was a new, complex bureaucracy replete with titles, relatively clear divisions of labour and considerable economic power. Welfare State, on the other hand, is nything but glossy. Its tone is that of the street, carnival, mumming, 'unch and Judy. Around its activities is an air of ragtag humour and isdain for roles and offices taken too seriously.

The first meeting of the public, whose expectations were conditioned irgely by festival publicity, previous outings to Centre Island and nowledge of the controversy about residence on the islands, occurs as pectators proceed past a ticket booth through sliding steel gates. Boris, ie only character whose name they will hear during the entire elebration, greets them. He is a dimwitted hunchback, full of friendly xcitability, who is subservient to the Master of Ceremonies who awaits ie crow on the ferry. Hopper, the MC, is dressed in a white suit, straw at, bright red vest and matching bow tie. Boris, his head and hunched ack covered in dirty, shapeless white and his face touched with white, ad and black, is a mediaeval buffoon. He lopes around the mainland ock greeting the audience and making foolish comments. The MC reets people a second time as they step aboard to the accordion music of bushyhaired Islander. Hopper chatters, improvises witticisms, iquires whether Boris is bothering them, and endears himself to people ith his Scottish accent. Meanwhile, Flo, a third character, is washing indows on the boat and joshing with the audience. A washerwoman hose wishes to be a lady of the night surely go unfulfilled, she is full of ugh humour, practical know-how and sports wildly patterned lothing, bedecked with loads of cheap jewellery and mismatched ccessories.

A film crew of three is obviously at work; their camera and iicrophone are omnipresent. Welfare State's business manager guards ie flowers and umbrellas. I am milling about openly taking notes. Iopper mounts the top deck and jokes about the film-making, recording nd note-taking. The camera has made the audience into momentary erformers, so Hopper has closed the circle by making us into erformers as well. Our documenting is not part of the show, but it is not xcluded from it either. The celebration will include whatever is noticed 1 the selected space and time, whether a real tempest, the city skyline, ie ship's captain or a note-taker. A modern, Western celebration, its vel of reflexivity is extremely high. At one point I am taking notes on a ameraman who is filming two women, one of whom is taking a picture of er friend who is photographing Flo! Some reporters, critics, actors and :stival personnel wear buttons or tags. A few in the crowd notice, and 1omentarily the limelight shifts: the critic must strike the attitude ppropriate to her role.

As the 'Ongiara' pulls away from the dock, the MC climbs to a level bove us where he can be seen clearly. The ship's captain is in the orresponding position on the ship's port side. We are confirmed in our ispicion that Hopper is our captain. As our speed increases, several irge grey flags unfurl. They are not part of the boat's usual emblems, the

Canadian flag and the Metro Toronto flag. On the former are stars, th moon, a unicorn, a caricature of Punch.

By now participants are calling for Boris by name; for them he i becoming a mascot. They are fond of him and show it by teasing. He ha bestowed on everyone a brightly speckled cloth flower. Ten minute later the boat docks at Ward's Island. As we disembark, we are greete by flute music and groups of island children clad in white tunics. Mos people see the large red and white sign on the Ward's Island Associatio Clubhouse: 'Save the Toronto Island Community'. Few notice th floppy straw basket which has been riding near the bow of the ferry. It i decorated with feathers and evergreen and contains two puppets, one of girl, the other of a drummer boy. Hopper removes the basket to the lea cart, where he deposits it at the front of the bails of hay on which thos unable to walk may ride. Those in love may also ride, he quips. Th children, along with the Girl, drummer Boy and flute band, lead th crowd on a twenty-minute stroll towards Snake Island, a place fe mainlanders have heard of. Here the colour-coded flowers will b required for entry so that gate-crashing does not push attendance beyon two hundred. Gulls, soaring overhead, have followed us down th asphalt road past expensive sailboats, picnic tables, a frisbee course, an decaying homemade water craft in the back yards of Algonquin Islan homes.

The initial interface of the largely mainland audience with Welfar State and collaborating islanders is disarming but basically reassuring However bizzare Boris and Flo seem, Hopper will guide and take care o us. Since mainlanders often use these ferries for going to the amusemer park at Centre Island, they are willing to trust they will not be hurt or le astray. Hopper is in charge, and so far we have been serenaded as guest Who can be suspicious when led by children, one of them a drumme Boy, the other an innocent Girl. And who can be afraid of a moroni hunchback if he knows how to obey orders and proves his kindness b distributing flowers? Thus far the event has elements of an outing, schoo play, and theatre performance, all relatively safe.

People are chatting pleasantly as they arrive at a white, arched bridg where the heavy railway flatcars and flutes stop. Across the water Snake Island, and most of us have already picked up the brassy musi which floats from it on the smoke of several grass fires. The bridg bottlenecks the flow of human traffic, and our MC takes the moment offer final reminders of two ordinary realities – the 'conveniences' an the flower-check.

Most are gabbing too much to listen. In single file we cross the bridg which is covered with feathered kites and immense parasols constructe of willow branches, binder twine and bits of coloured cloth. As we enter delightfully confusing garden, some recall scenes from *Alice Wonderland*. There is a unicorn watching slyly from the edge of th

learing. Here is one of the hostesses known as Graffiti Sisters in a pink
rinoline, with a necklace of bone and hat of gull's wings. There is old
Boris, snatching bites from one of the oranges he is juggling.
Windchimes rest idly over a fountain. Banners barely flutter in the pink
and orange of sunset. On them are fish, moon, rocketships and other
symbols. The Sisters, also called Aunties by our MC, are profusely
greeting the long stream of guests, as if this were a royal garden party of
some decaying monarch. But who is in charge of this island? Where is the
centre of action? The audience mills about in clusters. The Boy and Girl,
along with Flo, are playing in the band, but Flo is in a different costume.
So who is she now? Puppets are being hung from the trees; others already
hide in the bushes. One of them is a silver astronaut. A few spectators
venture closer and discover a frog, an old man, and some gaudy
papier-mâché ladies like these who are now playing croquet and
badminton with the guests. So much is transpiring that no one dwells on
details. All is atmosphere, friendly but topsy-turvy. The rules for
participating and spectating are not quite clear. Is it proper to dance?
Does the unicorn talk? A few strike out for the far side of the island but
are turned back by 'stage' managers posted by the Festival producers
from the mainland. They display a stereotype of mainland-style
authority by over-using walkie-talkies, sporting Festival badges, and
wearing white-billed sun-visors, though the sun has gone down.

Three times now we have been greeted, once on the boat, once as we
docked, and now this garden reception. The rites of decorum are
profuse, yet they do not re-inforce the conventions of polite social
gatherings, as do cocktail parties. Instead they make mockery of elevated
sociability, and disorient our sense of propriety. Why don't they get on
with the show?

Mummer's Tempest

A whistle blows. We turn towards a circle of stumps and split-log
benches where Prospero, whose identity only a few will ever infer, is
lighting torches. The crowd, amused but a little restless for a more
refined centre of attention, moves quickly. Then, recognising the shift
of convention from garden party to theatre in the round, some scurry for
front seats. Welfare State musicians and actors find their places. They
are in costume but not yet in character.

Our master of ceremonies has not changed costume. He beats a drum
and addresses us in a way that defines us as characters in a royal
ceremony,

> Lords and ladies, kings and babies . . . , I'm your life
> I am everyman's destiny.
> My hand is on your shoulder
> tomorrow, today & yesterday;
> I am the joker up your sleeve & the flea in your ear.

Already we have sensed that he leads us, but his hand has comforted, not tricked or irritated, us. He does not tell the audience that the ensuing performance is 'The Tempest, Inspired by William Shakespeare, refashioned by Welfare State International'. Instead he introduces the characters, who stare madly at us as they lumber, dart, whistle and buffoon: Prospero is a king who studies 'too much magic: the recipes of stars & songs of nuclear fission'. Sebastian, his brother and prime minister, turns out to be Boris. Miranda wears a tower on her head and tends the puppets. Ariel is a 'roaming angel from heaven'. Caliban appears in the mummers' play as 'a wild mermaid from the ocean deep, the fecund mother that everyman seeks'. And finally, we are introduced to the men who cast Prospero and Miranda adrift.

Perhaps our MC's joke is that, despite his introductions, he never gives us names, only hints, of characters who will not remain themselves the rest of the night. Our joke on him is that most Canadians do not remember Shakespeare, despite Stratford and high school. And even the few who do cannot decide which of these characters is Caliban. Eventually, most give up trying to discern either character or plot, because they are presented with allusions to a plot and only fragments of characters. The raucous action is done with such vigour and gestural hyperbole, that the audience attends to the cadences of actions and minimises attention to words. The mummers, with bugged eyes and deeply bent knees, fight, plot downfalls, get lost at sea, send spirits to wreak havoc, circumambulate an imaginary island, court and finally perform a marriage ceremony – all in fifteen minutes. And the audience laughs, even the children, because these outlandishly garbed characters sound so pompous as they fall over each other. Prospero has warts on his face and knobbly knees under his kilt. Ariel wears luminous, cross-guard orange and has handlebars for wings. Ferdinand's bare chest is slickly oiled; he struts like a banty rooster. Alonso and Stephano wear pieces of the Union Jack and King George's flag. The whiteface and make-up tell us this is clowning, but not of the circus variety.

The oratorical style is motley: a patch of poetry, a strip of song, a bit of incantation, a thread of romance and intrigue. The script matches the costumes. Literary analysis of it would only reduce it to remnants of meaning, because the words function just as one more gesture or one more musical instrument. This is not literary theatre; it contains no lines from Shakespeare. The script plays with images, clichés and political rhetoric: 'Fruit, wave & radio yearning for thunder' is jocularly dissociated imagery. 'I saw a salmon in a garden / Sing like gold / That I never heard' is a mixed metaphor parading as a paradox. And 'What right kicks a king off his stool?' is declaimed with sheer political pomposity.

So the mummers' play, on the one hand, caters to the audience by allowing it to spectate on a play, but, on the other, inverts expectation

y refusing the obligations to provide plot, character, or finely worked
:ting and poetry. And it works. We laugh at the non-fulfilment of our
:pectations. We do not know what to expect next.

viary

s the actors finish and hurry ahead into the woods, Destiny, as we now
now our MC, bids us to follow. Darkness is just descending. We pass
irough an aviary of bird puppets, most of them owl-like creatures made
om plastic milk jugs with candles glowing inside. Far in the
ickground we barely see Boris/Sebastian by a fire. He is yelling for his
.aster. We do not know why. Only a few people pause. Most hurry on,
:cause they hear an amplified synthesiser and sense something bigger.
   The aviary is one of two transition spaces designed as images for brief,
:ripheral sighting. We either shrug 'So what?', as one does when
umbling over a dangling modifier in a sentence, or we feel a suspicion
iat there is more to this than one can grasp. We are unsure whether the
:ene is a problem or a mystery. Are these birds, which any schoolchild
)uld make, more than they seem, or are they less? Is this art or the
arody of it? Is this a rite of passage or a mockery of it? Is anxiety or
xcitement the appropriate response? Are we expected to think about
iese images or respond without weighing our responses?

pace Station

he music pulls the crowd, and the crowd drags away the few stragglers
ho are trying to sense what connection the aviary has with the
ummers' play. Suddenly, the scale shifts towards immensity. We are
)nfronted with a series of spindly, white verticals which support mock
ectronic structures high above our heads. They could be radar screens
· TV antennae. The electronic sounds force us to associate them with
iter space. And now, far from being invited in close, we are kept back
y a yellow rope staked across the hundred yards of frontage. We are in
ir a spectacle.
   Prospero is walking, running, sneaking, then posing stock still with a
)ewing red flare. He darts in and out of abstract white shapes that
iggest icebergs perhaps or futuristic wreckage. They are decorated with
ny emblems the audience cannot quite see (lighthouses, a wedding
ike, aeroplanes, ships, satellites, spiders, a bomb, a moon, a
:ull-bearing kite, runic writings). Above him hangs a six-foot moon
iver, whose big nose, eyes, and mouth are lit from inside. To our right a
:w Caliban figure, a filthy, unshaven male in a hard hat, hides behind a
iabby little ark with dirty broken windows. He is utterly destroying (or
he making?) something with a screeching circular saw. The human
gures are shadowy, unhighlighted and utterly dwarfed by their
ivironment.
   From deep in the woods something huge stirs. The audience barely

sees it. It is a spider. 'Oh, my God. George, look at that.' 'I see it, honey. It's a beetle or a lobster of some sort.' 'Oh, it's creepy. How did they make that?' 'I could make one of those – just bamboo, plastic, wire and tape.' Momentarily, people become unguarded. Exclamations can be heard in the crowd.

A green follow-spot illuminates the giant puppet. Its half-dozen puppeteers roll it from side to side as its lower jaw and feelers find their way into the open near the space station where we wait in a torrent of synthesiser music from Haydn's 'Creation'. Prospero's magic island has become a mad scientist's laboratory and the scale of experimenting so vast that it is out of control.

A humanoid creature, illuminated from inside and followed by a white spot from without, floats out of the bush on the backs of black-faced, darkly-clad puppeteers. We forget Prospero and Caliban as we look far above their heads towards the action in front of silhouetted tree tops. The figures clash again and again. The beast's claws and beak almost rip off the head and arms of the rotund spaceman. The final battle, amid the death cries of puppeteers, leaves the beast dead. Then the spaceman lumbers off. Are these two creatures fragments of Prospero's imagination? Or are Prospero and Caliban puppet-servants of these two creatures? If this is a cosmic morality play, what is the moral?

Without warning, a rocket-puppet soars from the ground, hits the moon, and falls. In response the moon slides out of the sky, lands gently on its back and tips on its side facing us. A wave of silence and sadness ripples over the spectators. Then two toothy monsters dance slowly out of the woods. Are they dragons or crocodiles? They approach the moon curiously and begin to shed tears made of ribbons studded with pieces of broken mirror. With their mouths they gently lift the white sliver of moon by its tips and bear it funereally into the grove, as the Boy and Girl walk past us through the forest of antennae playing a sad, flawed version of 'Startune' on their brass instruments.

For a few moments we stand still, as their music fades. A twelve-year old points through the trees at the CN Tower, 'the world's tallest free-standing structure', and remarks, 'That looks like part of the play, eh?' Some in the crowd are excited, hungry to be fed more spectacles. Others are pondering. The structure of the event is disorienting our various maps of reality. How did we get from old fashioned crinoline and English mumming to twenty-first century technocracy? Where are we – this is not England nor a space station? This is Snake Island, near metropolitan Toronto. But who ever heard of Snake Island, and which way is Toronto from here? Disoriented on an uncultivated island, we depend on the great tower for orientation. Is this how Babel was used?

The flow of the celebration is segmented yet simple, complex, yet connected. We go from discrete space to discrete space. We witness this; it ends; we go on to that. We are surrounded with isolated arenas of

tion and paradoxically juxtaposed symbols but not provided with
onnective tissue. We must make our own, but those who would use
hakespeare to do it only arrive at remnants of meaning. Some find their
maginations drudges of entertainment or advertising industries:
'The big human-looking creature must be the Michelin Man.' His
iend remarks,
'Yeah, it's just escapist entertainment to trick you into forgetting
hat's back in Toronto, in the real world.'
In Shakespeare's 'The Tempest' Caliban says to those recently
hipwrecked on Prospero's island, '. . . The isle is full of noises, /
ounds, and sweet airs, that give delight, and hurt not' (Act III, Scene
). As a result, they follow Ariel's music, not knowing they do so in
ervice of Prospero's magic. By analogy mainlanders lured by the craft of
Velfare State and Islanders, are at once relatives, rivals and now
hip-wrecked 'trickees'. Of course, 'Tempest on Snake Island' is
ntertainment, but in service of what, of whom?
The images at the space station are simple and emblematic, like
lustrations from *Mother Goose, Alligator Pie* (Dennis Lee) or *Where the
Wild Things Are* (Maurice Sendak), but their meanings are enigmatic and
omplex. They are easy to feel but hard to think. We are not given a story
ne to connect them. Our only connection so far is perambulatory. We
alk together from site to site. But does this action constitute celebration
ny more than carnival hopping or shopping centre strolls? In a culture
tually undernourished but inundated with a surplus of fat, discon-
ected symbols, how is a celebration on Snake Island any different from
visit to Canada's Wonderland amusement complexes? In short, what
eparates the trickstering of 'civic shamans' like those of Welfare State
nternational from the huxtering of image marketeers? I see two crucial
ifferences. One is the de-mystification of technique. When people first
y the creatures, they often react with wonder ('Wow, it's scary'),
ystification ('Gee, how could they make such things?'), puzzlement
What is it?'), and finally, de-mystification ('I could make one of those
yself'). The celebration undermines an ideology of mastery, of either
he technological or fine arts varieties. Islanders regularly felt this in the
reparation process, and mainlanders sensed it in the performances. A
econd factor is self-critical iconoclasm, illustrated by the next scene.

hipwreck Beach

estiny, our guide, is now high on stilts, as if he grew to match the size of
he creatures and to dwarf the children. People are relieved when they
oot him again. He and the Aunties crowd us onto platforms, stumps,
ld tyres and logs on a bit of beach hidden behind Caliban's ark. We sit
acing the brilliantly lit Toronto Skyline which is punctuated, as always,
y the phallic-needle shape of the CN Tower.
The male version of Caliban is combing the rubbish on the beach. Old

reflectors, a greenish blue rubber ball, dead fish, straw, feather, driftwood and scum have washed up underfoot. His grimy face peers at us from beneath the visor of a dull silver hard hat. He wears a dirty karate gi and moth-eaten longjohn underwear and has built a model tower of junk. He has constructed something else but hidden it with a black plastic sheet. The smoke of his hobo's fire burns our eyes.

Far to our left the Hunchback, perched on a fat tree fallen into the lake barks,

> Roll up, roll up, you skinny carcass.
> Roll up, you bag of bone.
>
> Step this way to the wheel of fortune.
>
> The wheel spins upside down.
>
> The world's on fire in the iceman's kingdom.
> The world spins upside down.

Caliban milks the audience for applause and laughter as he improvises. He mocks us by sitting in his found chair as if joining us to watch the city-as-set. He baptises us with droplets of dirty water from his ball which he stuffs inside his shirt. He swordfights an invisible assailant, swinging his sword-tower over our heads and finally smashing it to bits. He tends his fire and with trampy pomp eventually reveals his cardboard City of Toronto precariously balanced atop a spool of telephone cable. As we hear a woman's voice singing across the water, 'God be praised, all will soon be over. . . . Where are the tears of Friday evening? / Where are the snows of yesteryear,' Caliban is walking into Lake Ontario floating a model of the city towards the real one. In this moment, we wonder which is 'real'?

Suddenly a dinghy rows round the fallen trees. Death and three Madmen approach the model city. A bamboo bomber sways atop the little mast, so we easily guess what they will do with their torches. The crowd cheers enthusiastically as their city goes up in flames.

The images seem stereotypically clear, yet what is done with them contravenes what would be done with them in Shakespeare, circuses or McDonald's. We feel we recognise the gestures, yet as we reflect on them, we are not sure what values we are affirming. Should we cheer? Who is hero and who villain? Unlike stereotypes, the images seldom preach. Instead they precipitate questions, not during but after celebration.

Caliban slides back to shore through the filthy waters. He retrieves his punctured ball. It is a world – with a hole in it. He finds a cradle – with the bottom out of it. As he exits, his mime has transformed the ball-world

His cardboard city of Toronto. Tempest on Snake Island, 1981.

:o a baby lying in a cradle. Is this the basket we brought with us on the
·ry? Caliban exits to the singing of 'Grey Flags'

> Grey flags tear in the west wind.
> Red crabs die in the rock pools.
> Old moons fall to the seabed.
> An eagle soars from the ashes.
> An eagle soars from the sea.

Caliban's gestures alternate among allegory, clowning routine,
provisation. He re-cycles garbage and yet destroys what he builds with
He is both ecologist and technocrat. At the space station the humanoid
>n but the moon was lost. At the shipwreck beach Caliban, another
manoid, wins, but the city is lost. The world-baby is saved, but the
adle has no bottom. So easy optimism and cheap resurrections are not
esent. By winning one has not necessarily won. The audience has just
en tricked by the use of clowning conventions to cheer the destruction
their own cultural achievements. Yet, Metro Toronto still sits across
e harbour, dwarfed by distance so it is usable as mere fool's backdrop.

What control we have been given over the city's image! But what will we do with it? Have we become a pack rather than a group? How could we dissent from the crowd? How can we control the bombardment with images? Does it really matter that most neither interpret nor criticise but just respond by cheering or walking? How does one know which images are major ones and which, minor?

Oracle

We carry these questions from the littered beach down a runway of black and white, candlelit lanterns past a tree-house separated from us by a bramble thicket and known only to its makers as 'Oracle'. This is the second transition space, but this time some people pause longer unwilling to be drawn on too rapidly by the audience. Others walk past it as they would a carnival sideshow, thinking the real action is in the big top. And others are searching for breathing room, hoping to re-possess themselves after being tightly bunched together with strangers. As we were climbing up from the beach, we heard what we now discover to be the Boy's trombone, picking up strains of 'Grey Flags'. Now he is astride a low branch of The Tree. Above him sits the Girl in a cosy bower of driftwood and remnants of persian rug, dropping cardboard animals into an eggcarton ark. She is strongly lit to radiate. A child madonna? If the scene is Edenic, or if this is the outcome of Caliban's world in-a-cradle the presence of the ark and the sound of the music remind us of the destruction of the Flood. Did the Flood precede her, or will it follow her? Is this the ark from the space station? There are no children in Shakespeare, why here? Are these the children of characters from the Tempest? Or are they the characters *as* children?

Shakespeare's tempest and the Biblical flood have now become cross-tabulated. Having watched this scene several times, I can hardly resist interpreting the Girl as an Eve-figure or a Marian resonance especially if I recall Caliban's baptism of us a few moments ago – first by water, then by fire.

Shadow Tempest

The crowd enters a semi-circular corral, opening towards the city and constructed of split timber. Hefty emblematic lanterns gradually brighten above our heads. We notice a lighting technician hut, ten microphones, and raised platform. We suspect we are near the heart of things – the back room of the Wizard of Oz. We are being handed punch by the Aunties and shown to rows of chairs in front of an elevated shadow puppet screen, which blots out part of the Toronto nightlights. All the characters we have seen are gathering, some as musicians, others puppet animators.

The 'Shadow Puppet Tempest' is the second play, and again we are seated. People are noticeably more comfortable this time. Performers are

hind a screen, not almost spilling over into our laps as in the
ummers' Tempest'. Musicians gather at the side of the screen and
gin playing gamelan-style music. A flickering torch behind the screen
ates a mysterious aura. The scale and colour of the event are greatly
duced in comparison to previous ones, but the idiom is foreign,
vanese.
The scenario which follows is punctuated by haunting musical sounds
d utterances that hover on the threshold between chant and the
nguage of trance:

> The king rocks a cradle and mucks about with rockets, producing a
> plague of spiders, a tempest. Final rocket hits the moon. It falls.
> King sends it back on another rocket. Sleeps under the moon by the
> cradle. Wild woman & boy steal crown & puts King & cradle into a
> boat. Cloud over moon. Tempest. Boat wrecked on an island. King
> dances with native spider & chains it to palm. Passing cloud reads
> '20 years later'. King grows beard. Baby becomes girl. Boat arrives
> with wild woman & young man. King fires rocket at cloud to make
> tempest. Boat founders & woman & man spill. Man awakens &
> finds girl. King puts spider as hump on man's back. King stalks
> Wild Woman & holds rocket to her throat. Girl & man with hump
> dance clumsily. King uses rocket to knock off spider. Spider flies off
> on rocket. All dance & sail away. Moon from behind cloud.

'The Shadow Tempest' does not repeat the 'Mummers' Tempest' any
re than the latter repeats Shakespeare's 'The Tempest'. Despite our
ing given no title and no names, we feel the play is vaguely familiar. It
ssesses a strong archetypal quality. We begin to sense the resonance of
tifs which, one might say, recur without being repeated. Some
mples will illustrate this principle.
In the mummer's play, Miranda carries Ferdinand on her back. He, in
n, is laden with garbage bags. She sings, 'I saw a spider through a
st/ Soft as skin/that I never touched.' The untouched island girl longs
experience, which Ferdinand, the city boy from the mainland,
ovides. In the shadow play the spider of experience is native to the
nd and is enslaved like Shakespeare's Caliban. This spider becomes
hump on Boy's back.
In the mummers' play Caliban is a wild mermaid on the island, while
the shadow play, Wild Woman comes from beyond the island. In fact,
r role parallels that of Prospero's conspirators: she and the Boy steal
crown.
In the space station a rocket shoots down the moon. In the shadow play
moon is shot down, then put back up, where it serves as
ardian-overseer of the action.
On the shipwreck beach Caliban, a maker, discoverer and re-cycler of

garbage, finds a cradle. In the shadow play the King brings the cra
with him to the island (as we have done with our basket of two puppe

These ways of allowing symbols to shift shape, context and th
meaning prevent their reduction to intellectual allegory. A rocket,
instance, is in one action a symbol for technology, in another it i
substitute for Ariel. A ball means in one moment 'world', then in
next, 'breast'. A spider means 'Ferdinand', then 'killer', then 'burde
These are resonances, not codes, either conventional or esoteric, thou
participants may in the face of a given gesture feel they are seein
familiar convention or suspect they are not being given some secret k
'The Shadow Tempest' is not a 'reflection' of 'The Tempest'. Rather i
an evocative shadowing of other parts of the celebration, concentrati
almost entirely on the dance of opposites (King/Wild Woman: Boy/G
Rocket/Moon) and the web of connections and obstructions in wh
they are entangled.

By the end of the second tempest all the major associations of
celebration have been made: Masculine/King/mainland Toronto/rock
tower, on the one hand, and Feminine/girl/Toronto Islands/cradle-mc
on the other. Participants, of course, are not *thinking about* the
connections, rather they are seeing them *made* and even helping eff
the wedding of opposites.

Wedding Dance

As we begin shifting chairs to the periphery of the corral, our Desti
announces to us that the moment of the wedding has arrived. Calit
and Prospero set fire to two life-size skeletons, one male, the oth
female, raised high on the beach so we can see Toronto through their
cages and pelvic bones. At the same time the Boy and Girl approach
slowly from the feet of the flames. He is a silvery astronaut,
countenance hidden behind the smoky face shield of his helmet and
back aflame, as if he has just climbed out of a burning spaceship wree
She is a flower child, carrying a garland in stark contrast to
anachronistic hatchet. As they lay their implements on the ground, flu
stop playing 'Anna Marie', and the band begins 'Swedish Masquerad
At first we watch the wedding dance of the children, but imperceptit
Islanders and Welfare State people are inviting guests to dan
Spectators cease huddling around the blazing fire-barrels and ventu
towards the centre of the corral. Circle dances, polkas and ree
accompanied by resounding brass and percussion, have soon surpris
most people into participating despite their self-consciousness.

The bridge from performance into celebration has been made, and t
tone of the evening changes radically. We no longer need Hopper as t
focus of our trust, and he remains out of character from now on, as
virtually all the other characters. He has turned over to us the char
promised at the beginning of 'The Mummers' Tempest'. 'For yours

She is a flower child. Tempest on Snake Island, 1981.

e Kingdom, the power, the judgment/For this day alone: the account's
your hands.' The slippage of dramatic roles and increase in the level of
dience participation are tentative first steps towards ritual, away from
eatre.

Relations between mainland Metro and the Islands are highly
oliticised. During the week of the celebrations, for example, Islanders
ocked the erection of a bike-rental shed, insisting Metro had no
ilding permit. Each regularly obstructs the other to signal continua-
on of the tenancy feud. But 'Tempest on Snake Island' was a gesture of
other sort, possible only through the mediation of outsiders, the
elfare State celebration-makers. The islands are the toys of Metro
oronto. They are for recreation, relief from the city. One goes to them
be entertained. What is risked in 'Tempest' is the perpetuation of the
ave-as-entertainer syndrome familiar from Roman circuses to all-black
views for white audiences in the States. When performers forget their
ace, and intermarriage, symbolic or otherwise, occurs, solidarities are

weakened. Mainlanders may lose their commercial-technological sup
iority and Islanders, their moral superiority. The circle dance, 1
instance, re-aligns the vengeful circumambulations of Prospero in t
mummers' play ('twice round the island to settle the score') into
momentary re-union. No celebration, much less one event in it such
the wedding dance, actually constructs a bridge, but it at least illustra
the gestures around which reconciliation might begin.

As the wedding dance ends, Ariel does a bit of magic to conclude t
'insubstantial pageant'. Amid his scurrying and whirly whistle, he rais
a bike wheel on a pole (a resonance of the wheel of fortune on t
shipwreck beach). Out of a cardboard skyscraper (cf. Caliban's c
aflame) he fishes a tin can and out of the can, a moon which a Graf
Sister, mounting a tall ladder, hangs from the wheel. Then, out o.
barrel he pulls long skinny arms with a white hand at the end of each. 1
coaxes viewers to hold them. I expect an octopus, but he hoists out t
attached body: a grinning globe of Earth. From its grinning mouth
pulls a paper bird.

Launch

Quickly, Miranda gives the Boy and Girl the two puppets of themselv
as they and Ariel lead us out of the corral down to a clean, sandy bea
where a glowing ship – at once a wedding cake and tower – is moore
The bird and two puppets are put on the boat, and to the wail of bagpip
it is launched from the island towards the mainland docks. What w
come of the fledgling marriages of Miranda and Ferdinand, Girl a
Boy, Girl puppet and drummer Boy puppet? Is this tower-cake
beautiful wedding of images or a grotesque grafting job like the 'orient
cactuses one sees in dime stores? The puppets are in need of animatio
and our hope is a mere paper bird on this foolish ship.

We are not left to see how far the boat goes. Our moment's meditati
is past, and the bagpipe is calling us to follow it beneath a bower
shimmering white cut-outs of boats, flying frogs and other isla
symbols, and then down a path strewn with brightly batik-cover
lanterns. Without ceremony the crowd re-crosses the white bridge a
gathers around a brass band and catafalque bearing a green papier-mâc
island around which coils a fat snake, eating its own tail. Like it, we ha
come full circle, but what are we to make of such a circle
self-sufficiency? self-consuming? Self-nourishing? By re-cycling do
merely eat our own waste? Or do we become whole?

Procession

We are handed torches and white silhouettes lashed to poles – eagl
frogs, moons, boats, snakes. And to the samba-like rhythm of 'Mag
Island Meringue', people dance, skip and walk in procession back to t
ferry dock. Participants take turns shouldering the canopy-covered bi

ome think of carnival in Rio; others, of the shadows in Plato's cave.
lost let their feet think.

At the docks we are greeted by the stench of diesel and the drone of
ngines. As the guests board, the celebration makers sing 'Now Is the
Iour', a South Pacific bon voyage song. Meanwhile, a flying frog,
ymbol of the Toronto Island Community, is set afire. And Caliban lifts
ιe Girl above his head so she can release a unicorn that soars aloft on a
alloon. Mainlanders hesitate to leave, swallow lumps in their throats,
nd cheer. Finally the engines rev and the water churns. The celebration
f Snake Island is over.

Je are always driven to ask of celebrations and other kinds of rituals
vhether they work and what they mean. But such questions are no less
ricks than magic is. 'Tempest on Snake Island' worked. It galvanised a
roup of Islanders and Mainlanders, entertained and enlightened
pectators, salvaged a lot of thrown-away junk, taught numerous skills,
enerated several thousand dollars of income, facilitated important
ontacts, initiated ritual processes with ongoing possibilities, and so on.
ll this, and more, comprise the effects, though not the meaning of the
elebration. Its most significant social intention is articulated by Ariel in
he last line of the Mummers' Play: 'Once around the Island for
Destiny/And never again for spite.' But surely spite is not forever gone
etween the Islanders and Metro. Like the Mummers, they have already
one several times round the island for vengeance. And they will go
ound again. 'The wheel spins and turns again/ And another trick's
arnt in the mirror-black night.'

At the end of the shadow-play, the spider flies off on a rocket to the
Moon again. Then 'all dance and sail away', and the Moon comes from
ehind a cloud. Like the moon's phases, the cycle will go on, but it has
urtured a new symbolic form. At least there is now a paper bird's worth
f hope that spite will not return. Welfare State has not provided an
nswer to the social-political problem, but has transposed it to a more
ensual medium, that of a nursery rhyme celebration rite in which people
re more free to imagine alternatives (from *Beginnings in Ritual Studies*,
Jniversity Press of America 1981).

6

The Tips of a Thousand Icebergs

(i) Ark

JOHN FOX

March 20th, 1983. The first day of spring.
On one time-scale an interval year.
15 springs ago we started.
After 15 more springs the year 2000.
A time for reflection.
A time for stories.
And if the stories are seeds for action, what kind of action shoul
they provoke?
But reflection is not easy.

A few days ago on Mothers' Day, my twelve year old daughter got u
before 7 a.m. to silently garland and decorate the bedroom around he
sleeping mother, as a waking surprise. The same day she produced
book from her school bag and gave it to me. Whilst in the library at he
new comprehensive school she didn't see much that took her fancy, bu
did see a book she felt her Dad would like, and brought it home for me.
was 'The Day of the Bomb' by Karl Bruckner. Written in 1961,
describes the dropping of the first atom bomb as seen through the eyes o
a four year old girl, Sadako Sasaki, who subsequently grew up in a pos
war world surrounded by a black market, shortages and bitte
competition. The in memoriam at the end of the book reminds us that i
the world (in 1961) there are a thousand hydrogen bombs lying i
readiness and that the destructive force of one such bomb is a thousan
times greater than the uranium bomb which destroyed Hiroshima in
matter of seconds. In 1983, of course, the numbers are . . .
   And my New Internationalist tells me that global military expenditur
is now running at over one million dollars per minute and topped the si
billion dollar mark in 1981, equivalent to 110 dollars for every mai
woman and child on earth. And that 49.5 million people are engaged i
military activities world wide.
   So reflection is not easy.
   How many more fathers on Mothers' Day are reduced to inertia b

ıch artificially induced fear? It's no wild alsatian snapping behind in a ırk lane . . . . but it breeds a cerebral panic. Once in Briston 1972 the :ones rained down on the roof of our parked caravan. My daughter then ˙as the age of Sadako Saski. I lay over her to protect her from the flying ɔlinters of glass from the skylight.* Next night, at the same time the ɔmpany were out with pick-axe handles. Are we bullies? Masculine and ʒo bound . . . or does circumstance force us that way . . . ?

Fifteen years ago it all seemed very clear.

On St. Valentine's Day in February, 1968, we recreated the Dresden ᴋrestorm in the middle of a straightforward public dance in Bradford. It ˙emed morally satisfactory to remind and shock an audience . . . after ll the British had killed more at Dresden than were killed at Hiroshima . . and poetically it was appealing . . . there *was* a carnival on in)resden at the time. So out came the imagery and the thunderflashes. ˙oggle-eyed, green-lit airmen in flying helmets appeared over balconies. ₊ parachuting harlequin leapt from the roof. Men in white coats ollected her body. They sprayed disinfectant over a dozen large papier ιâché clown heads bouncing on the spring floor. They collected the orpses. A thousand paper hearts fluttered from the ceiling. (Parodying oppies in the Albert Hall, they contained the facts of the raid). With the ırens and the smoke, and the unprecedented attack, the audience were ysterical and nearly panicked totally.

I don't believe anymore that you can do things that way.

You become part of the problem and not part of the solution.

There has to be another way.

The occasion for provocation has to be picked with care. The ossibility for healing must be looked at first. The spectacle must be a ehicle for change.

Such was Greenham Common. 30,000 women, a long way from the 'ommercial Mothers' Day, offered a different method . . . a different nergy. Organised participation with art, gesture and life as one.

In November (1982) some of us visited the peace camp at Greenham. Vhilst they were engaged in their ten year epic struggle, we were doing ıur six weeks gig a few miles away at Bracknell organising 'Scarecrow oo', an event for Hallowe'en and November 5th. In this the world ιade from a cracked and converted septic tank is balanced preca- ously on the top of the tower of Babel. A Babel of cracking material- ˙m and obscene consumption. A monument to the greed of our ırrent capitalist system (or cistern). After the rescue of the world, ˙irty bikers surrounded the tower, their girlfriends on the pillion ˙ielded fire brands and the phallus was fired.

Actually it was pointed out to me that at the time of the raid, I wasn't there at all. I was in ˙e pub. It was a woman who took charge of the situation, herded the other frightened ιothers and young children into one caravan and took cover until all went quiet. So much ˙r the memory of a male egoist!

Earlier, ghost children in a burning wasteland had followed th
indefatigable spirit of Cordelia, their Japanese candle lanterns dwarfe
by the blaze of crashed Falklands helicopters. Later a great silve
whale dowsed the embers of the dying tower and from the steam clou
mushrooming to the sky rose a lantern tree. At its base a Trojan fo:
tottered, its spindly wooden puppet legs feeling the soft earth an
searching for the World, its Mother planet (see second illustratio:
back cover). Happily and sadly we danced round the Earth. We dance
a hymn to the spirit of Gaea.

We danced with the Fall Out Band.

The big scarecrow competition drew a hundred scarecrows from th
people of Bracknell.

But there were questions.

The belief was of participation and the release of creativity of al
through workshops at our site. (A six week residency and th
organisation of an Arts Centre at South Hill Park.)

So it was a people's fire festival in theory.

And what were they burning?

I wanted it to be the externalisation of their fears objectified in th
accessible form of a scarecrow.

I guess we have stopped questioning the meaning of burning Gu
Fawkes (except in a few Protestant enclaves), and the last remainin
universal Fire Festival in Britain (excluding 'Up-Helly-aa' in Shetlan
and Allendale) has just become a habit. Not necessarily a bad one if
gives families fun, (although some women in Sheffield claim that suc
'wanton' burning is all part of the male ego aggro spirit) . . . but w
wanted to give this November 5th in Bracknell a different focus.

A large percentage of people in Bracknell (part of the 49.5 millio:
make parts for the Ministry of Defence – control systems for rocket:
Citizens are fully and happily employed. The local papers can't afford t
report Greenham . . . some twenty miles down the road.

So could the scarecrow be a focus to release creative energy, to get th
people working together and be a symbol of hidden schizoid fears? Fc
even the daughters of fathers who work making bombs, must as
questions like Sadako Sasaki. . . . Can the farmer's men of strav
warding off their black crows, become the hollow men of a New Tow:
pretending cruise missiles don't exist? Would the burning of the hollov
twisted, schizoid un-nameable, made by, for and with the people, be
useful public exorcism? Not really. Despite the contradictory Mammo:
Dangler of a rich prize and a holiday in a Motel (in the third world) mo
scarecrows were sub-telly. Blue Peter loved the knitted dolls, and th
craft teachers on the programme exposed their pom-pom eyes to th
nation with giggles.

No terror allowed to children.

No terror between the jam sandwiches.

And the bikers' girls, nice as they were, and wielding fire brands yet ere still only riding pillion.

But down the road before a different fire . . . a hearth fire . . . twelve omen camped outside twelve miles of barbed perimeter wire. 'We do agic as well,' they said, and offered me some stew. Previously I had had oughts of scarecrows burning round the camp and rattles and drums as e Chinese army used in Korea.

An un-nerving circle of counter-fear.

'But', said Helen John, 'they are just like us. The men who built those los can just as easily take them down again. They are just ordinary iman beings like us. And the moment we think they are special ogres, e make the problem something else'.

And she offered me some stew.

Her colleagues pointed out the symbolism of the web. 'With wool we n weave tapestries in the wire. The spider can wait.'

My thoughts of burning scarecrows went away. The spectacle . . . the pocalypse Now' syndrome, maybe the 'Fitzcarraldo' syndrome . . .)esn't change much. Art outside life doesn't change much.

Chastened, but elated, I drove back to Bracknell.

Next week we took them one of the 'Japanese' candle lanterns – a oah's Ark. They erected it on a tripod next to the perimeter fence. ake it down,' said the policeman, 'you are not allowed to build ructures here.' (By now their caravans had gone. Tents were not lowed. The only shelter in the freezing cold was polythene sheeting spended on rope between bushes.)

The women looked at the policeman and pointed out the erect flagpole side the wire. 'There's a structure' they said. 'When that comes down e'll remove the ark.'

The lantern winked knowingly in the cold air. The Ark stayed.

Tonight I'll read my daughter a story.

I'll thank her for 'The Day of the Bomb' and tell her that although ories must provoke action, we must not panic, or we lose *twice*. We ive sometimes to make an umbrella and shelter together underneath. nd see that the Ark is our planet World and it's not really a glass fibre ptic tank after all. . . .

(ii) Golden Fleece

I was lecturing in Adelaide, Australia at an INSEA conference: T▌
International Society for Education through Art – a body of academic
teachers and jet set social workers containing very few artists ▌
aboriginals, when Mobil Oil offered a commission for a 'Happening
Kings and Barons and their jesters, it seems, have gone upmarket on th▌
tiny planet, but surprisingly, within the cracks of modern patronage,
have had as much discussion about responsibility and change within t▌
community round a table of businessmen, as I have had with artists
'Finding imaginative solutions . . . dipping down into the collecti▌
unconscious is like finding oil' I said somewhat glibly to Mobil. 'Y▌
research and you drill, but you can never be sure what you are going
come up with. And here I cannot predict. There is too much consum▌
Art in Adelaide already. A happening will be just another gimmic▌
Another packaged and saleable commodity. But trust me please and w▌
. . . and we will see what drops in.'
It happened a few weeks later in Semaphore, a small seaside town fi
miles from Adelaide. A commuter base, a delapidated resort and an ▌
storage depot . . . a place with its own work magic. I couldn't buy
simple picture postcard. Nobody local it seemed, wished to celebrate t▌
promenade in their own backyard. Then one evening an oil tank
overturned. Painted with the emblem of a Golden Fleece it overturned
Black Dyke corner. The driver was killed and black blazing oil pour▌
round the white holiday yachts in a nearby harbour. Things, as ofte
came together.
Here I was, a wide-eyed pom on the worn jetty of an early coloni
stepping stone, on the stone of Semaphore, already tinged wi▌
nostalgia, with the classical solidity of its Customs House and the sto▌
tower, whose dropping ball signalled 1.00 p.m. every day. First, t▌
instant patina of 100 years, which we Europeans prefer to call Histor
then, fire on the water, through the new Imperialism of Oil. A Gold▌
Fleece at the bottom of the Black Dyke and a forgotten mongrel
celebrate.
Image, poetry, source, rationale and method fused almost sim▌
taneously. Eventually not a set of postcards, but a calendar emerged.
paintings, domestic icons of Semaphore were printed and distributed ▌
Mobil Oil as their national Australian calendar for 1980, which was al
widely distributed free in Semaphore itself. Not stations of the cross
the Mediaeval Cathedral, but curious equivalents in the Modern Sta▌
. . . technicolour fleas on the back of an enormous multinational . .▌

In Australia 11 million people live in an extended village round its
ge. Inside there is desert. A flat eroded stone thousands of miles
ross, one huge prehistoric pancake. Between 'seasonal' cycles over a
ven year span, between drought and rain, a flower may flourish once in
lifetime. My calendar became, in part, a graphic debate about the
lationship between old and new settlers, multinationals and tribal
tterns, history and timelessness. . . .
Like all intellectual poms I wanted to rub shoulders with the
original. Beset with guilt and curiosity we Europeans are fascinated by
e remnants of ancient tribes. Aboriginals have been in Australia for
0,000 years and we have nearly wiped them out. Just as we (and our
ty of life) have virtually wiped out all nomads, gypsies and Indians and
e dignified forests and animals of the Earth.

But just why do we want to rub shoulders –
What are we looking for?

Maybe we seek a centre and a balance. A placing of our shod feet on the
in of the earth. An extension of our limited consciousness to discover
r role in the cosmic order. Once Europe had its mystics . . . now the
ost popular sport is fishing. More effective than the Church of
igland, fishing is Europe's Shinto religion of the masses. We have
ard it said that Red Indians could talk to salmon and that they
iderstood (and so did the salmon) how many to talk into the net to
aintain their own flesh and the ecological balance. We have heard it
id that the aboriginal has had no property . . . that his lifetime is a
ilkabout round the sacred water holes of his ancestors who live forever
the dreamtime campfires of the dome of stars in the sky. His paintings
e not designs to end up on whiteman's tea-towels but repositories of
owledge and the maps of a journey. It is as inconceivable for the
original to own land as it is for the land to own the aboriginal.
Yet now multinationals dynamite the Sacred Mountain of the tribes
r uranium. The Rainbow Serpent is trucked, on unsafe ships, to the
ltonium reservoirs of Windscale. We need more electric power. So we
ed more political power. We need more shareholders, we need more
mbs. The aboriginal sings the history of the lizard and the green ant.
hen the typhoon struck Darwin, that concrete emplacement in a
b-tropical swamp, there were no aboriginals in town. Weeks before
ey had sung the history of the ant and knew their unusual behaviour
edicted a coming typhoon. They had knowledge . . . . we have power.
ie electric power to spark the video to cerebrate with National
ographic cassettes depicting the sad entertainment of a disappearing
ecies of primitive man and animals. Kodachrome awareness. Our
iderstanding is cerebral. Our behaviour is neurotic. We seek, grab,
tionalise and package.

One image on the Mobil calendar showed, in the desert, a Ran
Golden Fleece exploding in a fish-laden sky. It depicted the Story
Burke and Wills who botched up an early European expedition into t
desert of South Australia. They were dying from lack of food and wat
. . . although unknown to them they were surrounded by sustenan
They just didn't know where to look for it. . . . They couldn't see it, f
it or smell it. They had no intuition. In the distance aboriginals appear
offering gifts of fish. Most Europeans were, and are, too frightened
trust. Their double standards, their hypocritical politicians, their ar
dealings, their bullying muskets, their violence breeds a one w
communication. It breeds fear in the participant and fear and pity in t
recipient. Burke and Wills died because they were too frightened
accept the fish.

But one man, Mr. King, a carpenter on the expedition . . . a man w
thought with his hands and was neither leader nor politician . . . he s
other possibilities. He ate the fish and he lived with the tribe. He settl
with an aboriginal woman. They had children and they survived.

I met his descendant. The happiest man I ever met. A fitter and mo
bike stockman who had roamed the wire fences of white man's territc
helping to contain the hordes of alien cattle. The Range Rover of his b
was plastered with car stickers saying 'EAT MEAT YOU BASTARDS THIS
CATTLE COUNTRY'.

But one day he dropped out. He married an aboriginal woman and h
a child. In the desert of South Australia he built a shack from discard
corrugated iron. He built a small windmill, enough to power a sm
fridge and a small TV. With rain collected on the roof and a simp
irrigation system he grew a few vegetables. He lived in three rooms a
once a month shot a Kangaroo for meat, not sport. He had everythi
material he needed, little money, but considerable art.

He had placed his shack next to a Talc mine and with the offcuttir
carved small primitive statues . . . like black/grey Epsteins. These
placed in his garden occasionally selling one to a passing tourist like n
Also on slabs of Talc he carved poems.

One was to the memory of a white man from the Talc mine who h
killed himself by lying on the gravel slope in front of a giant digg
dumper. First he had removed the chocks from underneath the hea

eels and as it had started to roll forward very slowly he had carefully
ked a point in its path. 'I won't sell that carving' said Talcman. 'It's a
mn to an unknown man. . . . If he did nothing else in his lifetime at
st one person remembered him.' I then asked him why he had
)icted a Roman soldier in the work. 'That is the centurion who refused
spear Christ' he said. 'They were both victims of the Roman Empire
. and the man who killed himself was also a victim, of himself and the
tem. He couldn't handle his fear. He'd made an aboriginal girl
:gnant and he couldn't come to terms with that. And he hated his job
i couldn't come to terms with that either. Death was the only certainty
his confusion.'

Talcman and Dumpertruckman have become for me small symbols of
r age.

The deaths, the machines, the vanity, the lies, the costly wastage of the
lklands war, these were a macro/mirror image of Dumpertruckman.
When one individual is psychotic it is disturbing, but when a whole
tion goes that way it is a profound tragedy. The reverse side of creative
covering is the death wish and currently our culture is steering itself
o suicide.

So maybe Talcman shows us a way out. New alliances, simpler living,
)re honesty, a unity of existence and a joy and truth in creating. Maybe
: next INSEA conference will be at Talcman's shack – and Mobil Oil
ll ask his black wife to sing 100,000 years into a year.

Maybe *there's* an alternative calendar of change.

Maybe.

(iii) Safety Valve

According to much contemporary analysis (see Marcuse, Gorz, Ba█ and the pamphlets of the Green Alliance, for example), change is in ` air. The basic thesis is that late capitalist industrial society is coming an end. Now ecologically based values on a global pattern must t█ precedence for the sheer survival of us all. The old concepts of work, █ leisure as negative work, must be replaced through the compl█ re-integration of culture into everyday life . . . thereby enabling us al█ live in smaller, more caring communities where we will be more fulfi█ and more productive, even, than we are at present.

In such a new civilisation, the old forms of art will wither away and will rediscover an accessible and useful art through the individual a█ collective liberation of the imagination. In such a culture, Art will not the lackey of class interests, investors, anaesthetists and Uncle Tom█ but rather the joyous centre of a spiritual consciousness.

I love these romantic projections and I agree with them. I'll even put sequinned blinkers when my theatre (old style) friends pass me by. █ the practice always seems harder than the theory.

First in our existing cultural pattern, there is a King and a Jester, a█ the King is no Fool. His sharp knives will readily sever the Jeste█ tongue should the latter become too outspoken. Secondly, cerebrati█ and ideology are little use unless they trigger life-enhancing action, a█ action, like charity, art and hypocrisy, begins at home. One of █ Western diseases is that too many decisions are made by people who ca█ think with their hands; our grandfathers and grandmothers had toolk█

d musical instruments in the cupboard. Now we've handed over our
ritage to professional thinkers and entertainment stars; experience
comes vicarious rather than direct . . . we lose touch with reality and
allow self-perpetuating, dangerous, abstract games (like economics
d defence policy) to be played in our name by inaccessible 'experts'. By
d large, we don't build our own houses and we don't make our own
tertainment.

I have spent hours in dreary back-rooms in pubs arguing about Art
d Society when in two hours we could have re-decorated such brown
les. Weekly we get requests from young students *writing* theses about
he Fringe', most of whom (and whose tutors) have never seen our
rk, who don't *do* theatre and who find it easier to get money to write
ademic irrelevancies than artists do to create art.

ange can only begin with self.
So what has Welfare State International done to help eat out the belly
the old dinosaur? Have we built any useful rafts, or ivory, or golden
wers on the rafts inside the carcass in the last 15 years?

t's invent a character . . . JUDGE JACKASS THE APPLEMAN.
e'll give us a fresh Granny Smith for the Clear Truth and a core up the
m for a Rationalisation. Well, your Honour . .

We *always* believed in alternatives. We stole our first publicity paper
. . . it was a wonderful silver . . . and proclaimed that we presented
'An entertainment, an alternative, and a Way of Life' (1968) *No
apple?*
We got a whole mobile village together. Caravans, tents, circus tents,
generator . . . a travelling terrace street of thirty people . . . 9
children, 20 married and unmarried men and women who lived on
£18 a week each and made a lot of art all over Europe. *Apple. . . .* and
we called it a 'Microcosm of Possibilities'. *Core.*
Once, we spent £500 (fuel, breakdown trucks, drivers' wages, train
tickets) transporting one woman and her child and her caravan five
hundred miles to work three days on a gig. It would have been
cheaper to have put the whole company in the Hilton Hotel. *An apple
for the truth and three penalty cores for blind ideology.*
We got our own 'school' together. (See Catherine Kiddle's book
about it.) We didn't send our own two children to the State system
until they were nearly ten . . . the verdict of most teachers has been
that 'they were too busy learning to have time to go to school.' *Big
Apple.*
From an early age, our children have been playing music regularly in
the street with and for other adults and children. The commonest
reaction is 'Aren't your kids talented!' 'No', we say, 'Every child is

talented, given the right environment to grow in . . . why is it t
your child has gone to school for six years and cannot play
instrument at all?' *Apple*.

'. . . That's the most political thing we do . . .' *Little core*.

5. We fly to big international festivals to create simple models of sim
celebration. In Japan, the village people loved us because with
directness and visual style, we demystified Big Art. *Apple*.

To get there costs thousands of pounds, uses up many tons
precious kerosene, as well as polluting the atmosphere. *Apple* (
truth).

We offer a different kind of nomadic culture because we insist o
small group of us working with a small exchange group of indigen

artists and residents. So together, we make something totally new a
transnational. The children travelling with us are our best diplom
(unpaid) and we believe we achieve more for understanding than c
thousand paratroopers. In the new culture, aircraft carriers will
converted into mobile Art emporiums, and Trident will be melt
down to produce a mountain of Tin Whistles as big as the Houses
Parliament. *Apple*.

We see these as anthropological experiments . . . starting blocks
change, transition statements at this moment of time in wo
culture. *35 cores up the bum*. Sorry, we are clowns really . . . o
kidding. *Apple*.

6. We blocked the drains at Birmingham Rep. *Apple*.

We were making four sand sculptures round the edges of the stud
theatre for the audience to move round in groups . . . as in a wh
drive. The management, the unionised electrician and the do
keepers, insisted that the 20 cwt. paper bags of sand be stored outsi
the building. It rained and the bags burst.

Since 1980, we've run six week long residential summer schools in the Lake District on the practical methods and philosophical implications of our work. So have shared our experience there with over 120 practitioners and art administrators who have gone to many parts of the world to create their own events, and sometimes their own summer schools. *Apple.*

/e find a lot of people have immense potential but often their energy is locked. Through carefully graded 'making' exercises and working

uickly as a group to real deadlines, we generate trust and confidence, nabling participants to risk failure. Exercises have included:

a Divide the group into smaller units of three to five. Then, using sellotape and newspaper only, construct a sculptural costume on one member of the group. In twenty minutes, construct an environment or procession or dance or story to relate to the other paper figures of other groups. Sometimes a theme is given, e.g. The Queen and the Reptile.
b In two hours, as an individual, make the smallest celebration in the world.
c Sit in a circle. (Chance positions.) In two hours, make a present for the person on your left. (Objects or performances to be presented publically or privately.)
d Outside in the landscape, in groups of six, create a ten-minute event around the themes of an animal, a hundred yards and a launch; or a large head, a dwelling, and the wind.

And so on. The exercises build to greater complexity. Later on, those who wish to, 'write' their own scenarios until finally we may end up with a two hour event which takes two or three days to make and ends with full celebration including dancing and food.

This way of teaching suits me better than teaching in a Fine Art department in a Polytechnic. I once did this as Senior Lecturer for three years in Leeds. The students were great, especially when creating actual contexts to real deadlines outside the Department. Out of those years and out of the tuition of myself and others, including Jeff Nuttall, Roland Miller and John Darling, some very exciting performance and other work has developed, (e.g. D D'Art, Hesitate and Demonstrate, Kevin Atherton) but eventually stasis ruled. A cabal of senior management and threatened Fine Artists made a ruling that one had to teach from 9.30 a.m. until 4 p.m. IN THE STUDIOS. I resigned. It was like asking a farmer to grow turnips in a greenhouse. You'd get some

weird turnips. And so you do in Fine Art colleges. Inbred enclaves divided by hardboard partitions where Ego, not Identity, is force-fed through competition, exams and an entire lack of context and function. *Apple for awareness but a core for arrogance.*

A bit dangerous to say these things because these days such criticism can be used as an excuse for stopping art education and turning it into, anything, Industrial Design etc . . . Rather, I advocate *more* art education, but of a different form, more radical and more of it, from the early days of school.

I am looking for more of what one student described at a Summer School: 'My own experience of uncovering the unconscious, childlike spontaneous energy and vitality and creativity, working in a harmonious, not a chaotic way; extraordinary interaction between people who had never met before. It was a heightening of consciousness of individual potential, not in a religious or spiritual sense, but in a sense of moving with the Universe, with the chi, the tao, a letting go of conscious control . . . increasing awareness of the nature of control within our society restricting, dominating, suppressing the creative, the unexpected . . . Not so different from what Sir Herbert Read was looking for in

Education Through Art' in 1945. But in 1983, we are still light years off getting there.

Judge Jackass the Appleman hasn't said anything for a while. In fact, he's asleep.

I blow a raspberry on my soprano sax . . . Suddenly without appearing to think, he leaps wildly from the top of his Tree throne and swings his bulk on a pendulum of rope round the perimeter of his papier mâché cosmos, bouncing back to earth, his little flailing legs half walking and half dancing. He shouts 'PARAMPARA PARAMPARA!' and proclaims:

The times are out of joint.
The danger is great, the doubt is deep.
Confusion makes my Judgement steep.
But, you must go on,
To work more change.
Here is an apple from the Moon,
Plucked from its backside with a spoon.
A golden apple
No snake in sight.
Take it now.
Bite in the light.
Give it away and make a wish,
Pretend its the Core of Genesis.
Bye. . . . . .

And he was off, into the void, dancing man-like with a chorus of vegetables, creatures and stars. Goodbye Judge Jack Ass.

I am amazed and gratified . . . Is this a sign? *A huge apple core crashes from the heavens in a flourish of thunder and lightning.*

Is this some justification for the work? Are we worth our annual grant of £90,000 of taxpayers' money? That's probably about what they spend on burglar alarms in Liverpool schools. 82,000 children a day die of deficiency diseases in the developing world. (see 'The Future in our Hands' by Erik Damann, Pergamon International Library, 1979.) With postage, we could give them a pound each. This book cost £5000 to produce. How many trees are crying for the paper in its body? Is our strategy right? In the long run, is the book a tool that will liberate more healing energy? I hope so. Anyway, where can we hide with our little apple?

It costs more to let go than to hang on. If you want to build a log cabin in Britain now, you have to have land, permissions, carpentry skills, time and an income. So if you earn £6,000 it will cost you at least £30,000 to let go. If you were in parts of the Southern hemisphere (say New Zealand or Australia) you could do it for a quarter of the cost (and whilst building you would be warm and fed: drop a packet of muesli before breakfast

and, in subtropical zones, you have a banana tree by noon). So should w
persist in our search for a 'new' culture in Western Europe? Is it better t
eat out the brain of the old European dinosaur or pierce its so
underbelly in the distant south?

In Nimbin, a well-established alternative community in the North c
New South Wales, Australia, for example, they have community house
and farms, home birthing, new planning laws (with governmer
approval), they make their own celebrations and they fight multination:
timber exploiters with massive passive resistance. Here is the only plac
we have worked where Europeans have created alternative Naming
AND alternative Funeral rites.

If you can judge a nation's attitude to the living by the way it buries it
dead, then Britain is not good. In Nimbin, for a young child Emma kille
in a car accident a few months after her naming, the women washed th
body, and made burial garments, the woodman (who had planted a tre
at the Naming) made a coffin, an artist wrote a ceremony, the songma
sang a lament and the community buried the child in a 'sacred' place o
their own land. Can you imagine that happening in Britain? Here aga
we hand over these rights (and rites) to remote professionals an
specialists. Sometimes they are good but often not. Again our materi.
concern is excessive and our spiritual orientation and its practic.
application is minimal.

In 1979, the Fox family intended to begin again in Australia in Sout
Tasmania to research alternative theatre from the Living end rather tha
from the Theatre end. We planned to build this with a growir
community of mature people who had left the cities of the mainland, b
family ties and illness obliged us to stay in Britain. For three and a ha
years now, we have been settled in Ulverston, a small market town (po
12,000) in Cumbria on the north side of Morecambe Bay (opposi
Heysham nuclear power station and next to Barrow-in-Furness, whe
they build Trident). And in a way, we *have* begun again. Not now th
mobile village of the Burnley days, where we lived for seven years :
'hippies and gypsies' on the wrong side of the Ring Road, but respectab
householders, sharing dreams and worries with real neighbours in a re
terrace next to a central car park. They are avid followers of our work ar
have started to write their own plays and poems and stories.

We go out carolling together with home-made lanterns. Th
Christmas, our Guizers (The Gill Mummers) busked the carol service
the Market Cross. Father Christmas (Peter the Window-cleaner) g
stuck in a chimney pot while cleaning windows; the Mad Doct
(George, of the 'Pot and Pan' shop) cut him out with a spell of 'Ea
Peasy Glaxo Oil' and returned him to his mother Molly Masket (Denn
the Director of the local Rennaissance arts association). And St. Geor
(Nick the Press photographer, whose shiny helmet was a Polaro
camera) recorded the scene for posterity. The photograph w

auctioned. Said St. George: 'With this snap we'll make a profit/We'll auction it off for a British rocket.' The Lord of Misrule has risen again. We made two pounds seventeen pence at the carol service. Then there's Carnival Night, when 800 people dance round the World on the tarmac outside our front door. And the Raft race, when solid Macho energy is released through home-made craft on Britain's shortest canal and this year, the night before that race, there will be a gentle lantern parade and a September carol sung in the streets. (A builder has already made sixty lanterns and asks me every week for our photographs from Japan.) Maybe the source is under our feet after all.

Peter the window-cleaner knocks at the door. He used to work at Vickers in Barrow building submarines. He tells me a story. . . .

BOB THE BALL-VALVE
by P. Croskery

I remember when working at the shipyard a man we used to call 'Bob the Ball-Valve'. Bob was a bit strange, or that was the impression most people got. Bob had acquired his name because of his peculiar relationship with the valves he sorted out, but to Bob they were more than just valves, they were his personal friends. He would talk to the valves like lost friends, he even called them by names.

Anyway, one particular Monday morning Bob didn't turn in to work, which was strange because he took his job most seriously. Several people were asking for Bob that morning as an important job had come up and two very special valves were needed, and only Bob knew where they were. Dinner time came and Bob still hadn't arrived. Things by now were getting desperate, so the foreman decided to send me and my friend to Bob's house to see what had happened.

Now Bob lived somewhere on Walney, but no-one was quite sure where, as he was never married and lived an unexciting life outside work. After asking around, we finally found a person who knew the rough location. We finally found the place, a small house by itself overlooking the channel. In fact, it was quite strange, as if nobody had ever been to visit the house before. We got out of the car, walked to the door, knocked and waited. A voice shouted, 'Wait a minute.'

'That's one thing', I said to my mate, 'he's still alive.'

Just then, the door opened. Bob peered out. 'We thought you were dead, Bob.'

'No such luck, eh!' Bob replied.

'No need to be like that, we were only joking.'

'Anyway, what brings you two here?' Bob said.

'They are all running around like crazy, back at work, they can't find some valves, and wondered if you knew where they were?'

'There you go' Bob said. 'I have one day off and everything comes to a halt. I am only noticed when I am needed. Anyway, I am finished with that place, I am never coming back again.'

He then slammed the door in our faces.

Over two weeks passed, and Bob had still not returned to work. By this time valves were being put on the wrong boats, some were lost, still nobody could sort the problem out. If only they hadn't relied on Bob so much. So I decided to go and see Bob once again.

When I approached the house this time, the front door was ajar, but still no sign of life. I entered the hall, and was astounded by the sight I saw. Within the house, a maze of pipe works. Every size, every colour, every shape you could imagine, like a thousand coloured snakes, they weaved their way through ceiling, walls, and floors.

'Bob,' I shouted, 'Bob.'

'Yes,' came the reply behind me. I turned to see Bob closing the door.

'What brings you here again?' Bob asked.

'I was just worried about you', I replied.

'Worried? Don't worry about me, I have no more worries. Come I'll show you.' He led me to a room. I couldn't believe my eyes. Towering above us a huge golden valve shone like bright sunshine.

'What do you think of that?' Bob said.

Still astounded I asked what it was. 'This is my way to a new life. Through this valve there is happiness for me!'

He asked me to stand back, and started to turn the huge golden wheel on the valve. As he turned, a light appeared from the centre of the valve, immersing the room in waves of coloured light, and a strange sense of peace overcame me. I heard laughter and children singing, sounds not associated with Bob's dull life. By now the light had obscured my vision, but a shape could be seen approaching the light. A voice then said 'Stand back.' The light was drawn back into the valve with frightening speed, and all that had been there had disappeared. I was on my own.

I ran from the house, scared, and returned home trying not to believe what I had seen. Next morning, I returned to work as normal and avoided any questions asked about Bob, still not sure if I had dreamt the whole thing. The weeks went by and the events of that night became unreal. I had almost dismissed it from my memory. It was Tuesday morning when I came to work, and something strange was happening. A crowd of people had gathered round the edge of the dock. An ambulance was there and people were pushing to see what was happening. I moved through the crowd to see for myself. As I got nearer, men were turning away silently, and there the reason lay in front of me. A man's body, perfect in proportion, with golden skin and an expression of pure happiness on his face.

I remember Judge Jack Ass's Golden Apple.
I give it to Peter.
'Make a wish. Pretend it's the core of genesis.'
Art and the apple are back with the people.

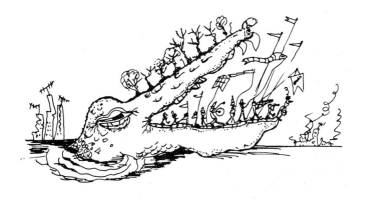

7

Techniques of Survival –
Statements of Hope

Welfare State in the 1980s

BAZ KERSHAW

Just because everything is different
doesn't mean anything has changed.
(*Southern Californian Oracle*)

(i) Moving into the open

At the heart of the Welfare State project rests a series of paradoxes that
inform every aspect of the company's ever changing practice. The
paradoxes are what make the company's performances simultaneously
simple and complex, tacky yet beautiful, accessible yet opaque. They are
what gives the most successful work its 'magical' quality. More prosaic-
ally, but perhaps more centrally, these paradoxes are the foundation for
the irony and the humour which continually connect the work to a spirit
of resistance that aims to change the world. But like all paradoxes, as
soon as you try to explain them away they assert their irreducible
presence, and as soon as you attempt to grasp them they can dissolve into
next to nothing. Nevertheless, in order to see the full significance of
Welfare State's work, particularly in the 1980s, it is necessary to grapple
with their implications. For the paradoxes are the product of the
company's increasingly determined attempt to mount a socio-politically
critical practice in an ideologically hostile environment. They are the
sharp edge of a radical knife that aims to cut through the hegemonic
bindings of a pathological 'normality'.

In the opening chapter Tony Coult rightly suggested that Welfare
State's descriptions of itself capture the high-risk nature of the
company's project. Tony wrote that chapter in 1983, when memories of
the inner-city riots and the Falklands War were still palpably tinged with

he smell of burning. At that historical moment it may have seemed
particularly absurd to describe yourselves as 'pathological optimists', as
Welfare State continued to do. So for Tony, and for me as co-editor, the
concepts of Change and of the Imagination as the source of change were
called on in an attempt to by-pass the absurdity and to connect the
company's practice to a radical refusal of the status quo. Now, at the start
of the 1990s, in the third term of Thatcherism, as the crumbling of the
Berlin Wall pushes the world into a new political era and as the
ideological paralysis of post-modernism seems to be tightening its grip on
Western culture, our analysis seems too deliberately tentative. The
smokescreen may have been necessary then, but in today's climate
perhaps it's healthier to be out in the open, which, both figuratively and
literally, is where Welfare State have usually been.

Now, in 1990, we must open up the argument by noting that the
central paradoxes of Welfare State's best work crystallise all that is
positively dangerous in the company's creative practice, in that they
suggest an impossible mission caught in a web of self-contradictions and
vicious circles. In the company's policy statements they are usually
signalled by the yoking together of unlikely bedfellows: pathological
optimists, civic magicians, holy fools, engineers of the imagination. The
phrases stick in the mind by conflating universes that are usually kept
separate – the essential feature, according to Arthur Koestler, of all that
is creative.[1] It is the same with the imagery of the shows and processions
and sculptures: nature and technology collide in the image of the
blackbird that is a bomber, in the phoenix driven by a coal mine, in the
crocodile with nuclear missiles for teeth. And similar techniques inform
the music, which slips easily between continents, cultures and historical
periods, combining tribalistic drumming with state-of-the-art electronic
manipulations. And now the same pattern can be read in the company's
most fundamental operational procedures, inscribed in its decision to
put down roots in Ulverston, on the edge of the most polluted sea in
Europe, if not the world; in the no-man's-land halfway – in John Fox's
iconographic geography – between the two worlds of Wordsworth and
Windscale.

To my mind the move to Ulverston is the single most important event
in the company's twenty-two year history. It signals an absolute distance
between the nomadic caravan-trailing of the 1970s and the jet-setting
international festival-hopping of the 1980s – without, of course, denying
the continuing significance of either. This could be clearly seen at the
weekend-long twentieth birthday party that the company threw for
friends and colleagues in 1988. There were at least four 'generations' of
creative people there: the counter-culturalists in their forties, the punk
paraders in their early thirties, the post-modernists in their teens and
twenties, and the children, always the children. But there was little sense
of any 'generation gaps' in this. What was on show (for itself) was a

A phoenix driven by a coal mine. D. H. Lawrence Festival, 1985.
(Maker: Tony Lewery. Photo: Vicky Carter.)

continuity, an evolution, a hope-filled potential for re-generation. But
nevertheless there was a *difference* in the history, and the difference was
in the building where the party took place. It contained offices, a library,
a kitchen cum canteen, a music room, workshops, storage spaces, a large
yard in which were parked the company's various vehicles – and,
incidentally, the motor-caravan of its first administrator! And the building – the Ellers, a former primary school – belonged to the company.
That possession signifies one of the paradoxes at the heart of Welfare
State, circa 1990: the company so famous for its resistance to perma-
nence, its embrace of Change, its opposition to institutionalisation, had
now got a mortgage and taken up residence in a former institution. What
the Ellers so clearly signalled was that Welfare State had become an
anti-institutional institution.

Of course, it had actually always been that, from the moment it
accepted its first Arts Council grant. But the relationship between the
two worlds – the ever-changing company and the company that was
always there – had altered, and it had altered because the Ellers
represented a new style of negotiation between the company and its
socio-political context. In 1983, in the last chapter, John Fox wrote of
becoming a householder in Ulverston that '. . . we *have* begun again . . .
with real neighbours in a real terrace next to a central car park.' The

ontext makes it clear that the 'we' he has in mind is actually the Fox amily, and emblematically, the company. The purchase of the Ellers radicates any doubt about the emblem: Welfare State had made a major ommitment to the neighbourhood, to the community of Ulverston, and to the sub-region of South and West Cumbria. In order to achieve that at a level which could be read without ambiguity and with some hope of making a significant impact on the culture of the locality the company eeded to become a local institution, but a local institution with distinct international interests and concerns. The interests materialise in the regular invitations to craft performances for festivals, and (more recently) to run training programmes, in other countries. But the concerns connect all the company's interests to a commitment of a very different order. For they signal another of the paradoxes at the heart of the company's practice which (just as the paradox of the anti-institutional institution is written into the actual building of the Ellers) is inscribed in the social, political and geographical landscape which the company has chosen to inhabit.

The crucial nature of that landscape in the international context can be indicated by a single fact: North West England, and especially South and West Cumbria, has a greater density of nuclear installations per head of population than anywhere else in the world. Furthermore, the range of those installations reflects and is the source of the whole spectrum of nuclear practice, for good and for ill. From Ulverston you can see Heysham nuclear power station across Morecambe Bay. Just a short drive south-west is the town of Barrow-in-Furness, which is dominated, economically and physically, by the huge shipyards which first made Polaris, and now make Trident, nuclear submarines. Another thirty miles up the coast is the Sellafield (formerly Windscale) nuclear pro-essing plant. As if this were not enough the Cumbria fells to the north of Ulverston were particularly badly contaminated in the fallout from Chernobyl in 1986 – in 1990 some of the hill farmers are still not allowed to sell their lamb. Like attracts like, as they say. But the true fatuity of that old adage is demonstrated by Welfare State's commitment to the nuclear-staturated region. The company that for years has devoted itself to constant re-creation, to re-generation, to a creativity that aims to eliminate the boundaries between art and living, to life-enhancement, chooses – *chooses*, mind – to settle more or less at the centre of one of the most dangerous, that is, potentially death-dealing, areas of the planet. The second main paradox: the company lives where death has its dominion.

I hope it is clear that this is not a romanticism of Welfare State's current situation. The risks are real enough, as recent reports on cross-generational transmission of cancer-prone genes make all too abundantly clear. Yet at the same time Wordsworth *was* just up the road, and there is something of Conrad's Marlow in Welfare State's determi-

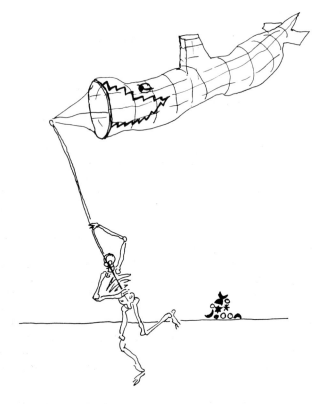

nation to stare into the heart of darkness at the horror. But there is als
rather more than just the shade of Mr Kurtz. For not only have Welfar
State settled into the community of Ulverston and undertaken a seven
year project in Barrow, they have taken on the local culture in its ow
terms, and if they have partially transformed it, it has partly transforme
the company. The emergence of Welfare State the institution has bee
part of this. But at a much more fundamental level the company
practice has been modified by the commitment to the locality, whilst
the same time remaining true to the creative and ideological principl
that were there, at least in embryo, at the start. It is this development th
I wish to chart in the rest of this chapter, for it represents what I take to l
the central paradox of the Welfare State project. For its flexibility, i
chameleon character, is precisely what gives the company an unchangin
identity that articulates its underlying principles. We need to investiga
that chameleon nature, with all its potential for contradiction, in order
try to describe how the principles and the practices combined in th
1980s to make Welfare State what it is: still, after 22 years, one of th
most extraordinary performance companies in the world.

(ii) Swimming against the tide

elfare State is an impressive inventor of hybrid arts forms and genres
d a constant innovator in opening up new contexts for creativity. Even
e briefest glance at the up-dated chronology in Appendix 2 reveals a
story of continuous experimentation in every aspect of its practice.
nis has produced an extraordinary variety in the scale, types of playing
ace, operational modes, and cultural contexts in which Welfare State
s worked: from one-man backpack storytelling to giant processional
agery; from cathedrals to the London docksides; from touring shows
the company-owned 'second smallest theatre in the world' (the
intern Coach) to long-term community residences; from international
stivals to intimate domestic settings. But the most characteristic span is
ated by the nature of the invented forms: street opera, sculptural
hancement, daylight oratorio, celebratory bands, town-hall tattoos,
hedral lanterns, touring barn-dances, and so on. Much of this is, of
urse, part of the pragmatic business of public relations hype, the need
excite the interest of new audiences and keep at least two steps ahead of
e funding bodies. But it also represents an almost pathological need for
ative unorthodoxy that Welfare State shared with other alternative
mpanies, a restless seeking for originality and uniqueness in a culture
nich in the 1970s was most often characterised in terms of standardis-
on, machine-line repetition, technological sameness.

Lantern coach panto. *Jack and the Beanstalk*, 1986.
(Performers: John Fox, Tim Fleming. Photo: Westmorland Gazette.)

Giant processional imagery. Barrow-in-Furness Tattoo Day, 1987.
(Makers: Andy Plant, Alice King, Les Sharp, Ali Wood.
Photo: West Cumberland Advertiser.)

This tendency of Welfare State continued into the 1980s, but it
notable that the company's increasing shift towards a commitment
community, to working with people as much as for them, has coincid
with the onset of the post-punk, post-modernist 'free' market. As t
high streets and shopping centres have been flooded with consumer
commodities, as late-capitalism has established a widening span of wh
Ivan Illich calls 'radical monopolies'[2] – so that no part of our bodies, c
environment, our social and private activity, has escaped the raveni
attention of industry and commerce – as we have less and less call
create anything for ourselves, Welfare State has increasingly insisted
stimulating the desire for creative outlets of 'ordinary' people. This c
be read as the company coming rather late to the community a
movement which it had previously tended to avoid, but such a readi
would miss the point of the development. For the shift towar
community-based creativity is not a narrowing of the company's acti
ties, but a widening. And it is a widening in at least three senses. Fir
simply because Welfare State has kept up, and more significant
combined, its commitment to the spectra of scale, playing spaces, cultu
contexts, operational modes and hybrid forms noted above. Secor

:cause the focus for many projects has shifted from producing an
twork to enhancing the process of living in a particular community
rough the production of artwork. And third, because this last shift has
d Welfare State to become more overt and precise in establishing the
cial and political significance of each project, particularly in respect of
e ways in which it relates to the immediate concerns of a locality. And
hen those concerns are intimately locked into the great global issues of
ar times – economic, ecological, political – as they are in Barrow-in-
Jrness and South-West Cumbria, then the thematic and ideological
ope of the company's practices may at times seem genuinely awe-
spiring.

In the quest to identify the underlying principles of this chameleon
nge it makes sense briefly to investigate in more detail three of Welfare
ate's projects which are on the cusp, so to speak, of the new develop-
ents. Through a close-reading of the points of transition perhaps we
n pinpoint the characteristics that form the common ideological
drock of the company's wide-ranging practices. As it happens, the
mpany was beginning to make these moves at the time when this book
as first being collaged together, so of course there are portents of the
pansion scattered throughout the text. However, it is only with the
xury of hindsight afforded by this revised edition that they can be
aced in a more revealing perspective. For as the company moved into
e 1980s, it had to engage increasingly with the contradictions of neo-
nservative capitalism in order to survive. One of its techniques of
rvival, I will argue, is to turn those contradictions into paradoxes
aich illuminate the context of the work and allow the company to avoid
e ideological paralysis of post-modernism by suggesting positive
ernatives. So this new chapter provides a welcome opportunity to
aw out the principles behind Welfare State's extraordinary progress
to the 1980s.

(iii) A full-scale model of 'Titanic' endeavours

an interview for *Performance Magazine* in 1988 John Fox explained
at:

> There's a clear line really between the work we did in the seventies
> and the work we're doing now . . . The last really big show in
> London was the raising and sinking again of the *Titanic*, which was

an allegory about the state of Western Culture. It did have some, l
not enough, community involvement, so it became a model of c
visions.[3]

Raising the 'Titanic' was staged on the dockside of Limehouse Ba
in the East End of London for twelve nights in August, 1983, a
commission for the London International Festival of Theatre. Some
young adults and 60 children from the locality were involved through t
work of 'The "A" Team', a multi-media community arts company bas
in Limehouse. More local people were recruited through a commun
video and photography project and via the Chisenhale Dance Proj
based in Tower Hamlets. Hence the complement of non-profession
contributing to the project numbered over 150 people. Welfare Stat
professional team of performers, makers, technicians, enginee
designers, stage and publicity managers, cooks and community c
ordinators, all directed by John Fox, numbered around 60 people. T
show accommodated 325 spectators on each of its slightly-chilly (blan
ets courtesy the Red Cross) late-summer nights. The critical recepti
was very enthusiastic ('the best party in town' claimed *The Guardia*
but the show would have sold out anyway, on the reputation of t
company (infrequently seen in London) and through its animation of t
networks of the East End community. Despite selling every ticket, t
cost of mounting the project almost bankrupted the company.

However, the potential bankruptcy seems rather paltry given t
social and cultural context of the show. Limehouse and Tower Haml
in 1983 provided examples of the worst housing and economic dep
vation to be found in any working-class inner city area in Britain – rott
1960s tower blocks, rubbish-strewn and pot-holed streets, rotten
thickened by the constant stream of commuter traffic getting through
quickly as it could, many people obviously living on (and over) the ec
of constant poverty. At night the atmosphere was punctuated w
monotonous regularity by squealing police-car sirens. Yet edge-on to
Thames, just backing onto the show's dockside site, was a row
colonised old warehouses, their four-stories-with-river-views conver
to luxury bolt-holes by the commercial and political élite. And porte
of greater things to come were already happening downriver at the Isl
Dogs, where the first stirrings of that latest paean to capitalism,
Docklands Development, was heralding the yuppie future. Not to be
out of the new 'renaissance', Tower Hamlets Council was curren
considering potential uses for Dock B, Limehouse Basin: should
become yet another developer's dream of an exclusive waterside encl
for Thatcher's children, or could it be turned over to the local cc
munity for uses to be determined by its members?

Welfare State has never been committed to agit-prop directness
issues such as this. John Fox has always aimed to imbue the compar

tal endeavour with his own mode of poetic dreaming. Usually the
reaming has projected a kaleidoscope of mythological images onto a
ulti-faceted screen in order to subvert any totalising reading of each
ent. This has infuriated some critics – obscurantist, arcane, deliberate
ystification, they cry – while enticing others through its promise of
terpretative freedom. As the company moved into the eighties yet more
nfusion/attraction was layered on by the creative conjugation of the
sthetic forms of performance and the social forms of dance, dining,
ening stroll, mountain climbing, what have you. That potential
iring of presentation and participation had always been part of the
mpany's total aesthetic – compare and contrast, for instance, the
ming ceremonies with the epic journeys of Lancelot Quail. However,
was not until the early eighties that they began to be seriously
mbined in large scale events. What is exceptional about Raising of
itanic' in the company's canon, from the point of view of aesthetics, is
at it used a sandwich format to layer social and aesthetic conventions. It
gan in the early evening with a real open-air market with local
mmunity-produce on sale, continued beyond dusk with a two hour
ectacular variety-style show, and ended often after midnight with a
gh-energy dance for the audience. A provocative unity was given to this
ur hours of media-mix by a straightforward, central and over-riding
etaphor – the Titanic was Western Civilisation. More specifically,
estern Capitalist Civilisation.

The metaphor, in one way or another, insinuated itself into every
ement of the event. So the opening market-place featured stalls in the
ise of lifeboats, peopled by the local community as survivors and/or
ctims and serving delicacies such as freshly-grilled shark steak. In the
ild evening air, besides the hubbub of many milling people, there was
enty to distract and entertain the customers: the natural pleasures of
e dockside location, the smells of barbecued food, the music of the
tanic syncopators, and brief informal introductions to the perambulat-
g characters of the show – the first-class passengers, the Purser, the
ptain ('Do join me at my table for dinner.') And the dockside
thering was treated to a good menu of performance entrées, such as the
ummers-style Three Men in a Boat Versus the IceQueen Berg (performed
the Limehouse Club Players), a comic broadside swipe at naff
vivalist theatricals. While, by way of contrast, Marcel Steiner's resus-
tation of the Captain's Ghost in the Smallest Titanic in the World (a two
ater pros-arch theatre built on a motorcycle sidecar) was an ironic
odel of pathetic neo-naturalist self-justification.

None of this, however, prepares the audience for the pragmatic climax
the market sequence. A huge motorised crane drives slowly through
e sea of stalls and spectators, wheezes to a halt at the far end of the dock
d, following instructions called between the Captain and a minion in a
all boat on the water, majestically swings its lengthening boom out

A good menu of performance entrées. *Raising the 'Titanic'*, 1983.
(Performer: Limehouse Players. Photo: Alex von Koettlitz.)

A seventy foot long apparition. *Raising the 'Titanic'*, 1983.
(Makers: Tim Hunkin, Andy Plant, Les Sharp. Photo: Edwin Lewis.)

over the glinting expanse. Then slowly and painfully, as the crowd gathers along the dock-edge to get a good view, the long arm of the crane hauls up out of the limpid depths a skeleton *Titanic*. The seventy foot long apparition, water pouring through flapping seaweed, is gradually cranked up into a steep slant: it represents only the stern-end third of the great ship, but still it towers high above the level of the dockside. It is an amazing theatrical coup (no-one does such things better than Welfare State), partly because of the sheer spectacle, but mainly because the image suggests so much more is hidden in the depths. The syncopators play a celebratory number, the lifeboat stalls clear the decks (there is a poignant irony in this), and the Purser and Captain usher the audience into the specially built 325 seat canopied auditorium set back from the dockside. And as dusk falls (the metaphorical use of natural light is impeccable) the show that will call up the dead to bear witness to the end of Western Civilisation begins.

A large and yellow forklift truck buzzes in, swaying wildly under the weight of an enormous ship-deck container, which the Captain signals to be placed between us and the dockside. It returns three times, with more containers, to make the set: a two-storey metallic metaphor of the decks (and depths) of the *Titanic*. This is followed immediately by the first of the ten songs of the show, written by John Fox: the Lookout's Song.

> Lookout, lookout, I'm the lookout man
> Listen to my song
> I'm the Ballad Monger
> But I cannot sing for long
> And I sing of right and wrong . . .
>
> Tonight you lose your lover
> Tonight the banks will sink
> Tonight the ghosts of ghosts arise
> Tonight we're at the brink . . .

It is sung in a plaintive cry by Luk Mishalle, brilliantly accompanied on banjo by Hassan Erraji, a blind Moroccan musician. The audience have seen that he is blind by the way that Luk has gently guided him across the rough concrete of the dock/stage. The audience may also know – though it doesn't matter if they don't – that the lookouts on the *Titanic* did not have binoculars, owing to a tiff between officers. So there is an appropriateness in the lookout singer having backing from a blind man, both at the level of historical detail and at the level of metaphorical meaning. Already there is the implication that the hierarchy that built, launched and sailed the *Titanic* must have been creatively disabled, possibly even crazy.

The show that follows uses song and broad comic acting to create a rich pattern of paradoxical points. So in the first scene, the Captain's Table, the Captain and a wealthy passenger sing an ironic celebration of culinary extravagance by Adrian Mitchell, based on the actual first-class menu on the night the *Titanic* sank:

> Bring me a bourbon, slosh me a scotch
> Fire off the best champagne
> Pass the bordeaux, let the chablis flow
> Let's have champagne again.
>
> Choicest oysters, fresh on the ice
> Older consommé, not so keen
> Cream of barley, sounds pretty nice
> An entrée serpent with sauce musseline . . .

As they sing the duo pick up the items of food from a sloping table centre-stage and display them for the audience to admire. But we easily see that the 'food' is cleverly made from the detritus of contemporary culture: an old inner-tube has been transformed into an enormous curvy salmon, a wondrous dessert is constructed from bits of cast-off foam rubber. We are being invited to enjoy the decadence, quite literally, on junk-food. Similarly, the profligacy and greed of the Captain and his artistocratic and capitalist guests is signified with crisp humour by using domestic funnels as wine glasses: the champagne simply splashes to the ground as it is poured and poured. The visual joke also has a very practical purpose in solving a technical problem, as the actors have to sing as they 'drink' the wine. This witty transformation of found objects is a major technique of the show. Thus, ironic parallels are drawn between the real materials which make the event and the meanings created by the *Titanic* metaphor. So the container-set suggests that the exploitative social structure which built the ship is still, in reality, with us.

The metaphor of the *Titanic*/society also allows comic comment on the injustices of the class system. Two later inter-cut scenes, for instance show how the hierarchy of the *Titanic* was rendered totally inept and inappropriate when it came to dealing with the disaster. The sinking is represented by the Captain training a cabin-boy in the correct method of pouring water from a teapot over a scale-model of the ship, but because the boy's teapot hasn't got a handle they have to do a silly bow with the pots tucked underneath their arms. Then the intercut scene has a first-class woman passenger locked in her room with the waters gradually rising. As she desperately tries to escape, the Captain and the Purser inform her that the door has been locked to prevent looting (that actually happened), and as she tries to smash her way out they make careful note of the destruction in order to sue her for damages.

Other scenes show characters from the opposite end of the social spectrum. The menials of the crew are represented by a pair of self parodying 'clichéd cleaning ladies', who enter singing a raucous song as they sweep the concrete dock with a couple of anachronistic and obviously knackered vacuum cleaners. The energy of their deliberately predictable lyrics contrasts poignantly with bald statements, addressed directly to the audience, that they can do little but lament the deaths of the poor sailors for whom they speak, who had their wages stopped at the moment the ship sank. In a later scene poverty is depicted in a 'picturesque' picture-tableau of an Asian family 'hung' on the wall of a first class cabin. The cabin's occupants, an American millionaire and his wife, amuse themselves by throwing torn-off chicken limbs and other bits of food into the 'picture'. To their exaggerated amazement the 'picture' comes to life as a native child picks up the scraps and looks pathetically at the people who, to amuse themselves, 'donated' them. So the satiric impulse appears in the show whenever the awful injustice of 'the system' represented by the *Titanic* is re-presented. The satire is harsh and its style is deliberately crude in reflecting the crass lack of care for human life built into the great ship, particularly in the total waste of poor steerage-class people which was the main outcome of the disaster. The brutal statistics of fatalities – reproduced in the programme – obviously demonstrate that the class with most to lose lost least, while the majority with little to lose but their lives lost out most.

The animation of the tableau signals a change of direction in the show, for the blind monster of Western Civilisation bursts into the scene and flails about, destroying everything in its reach. The native child, though, climbs out of the tableau-frame and shoots the monster, finishing it off. Then more signs of pathological optimism emerge as the black-faced stokers attempt to invade the upper decks of the ship, but the rich and decadent fancy-dressers dressed as death beat them down,[4] before also destroying the albatross of hope. As it dies plaintive music drifts across the night air, the container-set is quickly trucked away, so we can see again the glinting dock-waters and the great skeleton hulk of the *Titanic* still suspended from the crane. The wreck is set on fire, and the blazing empty framework of a corrupt society is lowered sizzling into the by-now black waters of the dock, as a giant fire-work ice-berg bursts into glittering silver flame behind. It is a fearsomely beautiful image of nature triumphant.

But it's not over yet. On the dockside, as the blazing white backdrop fades, we see the blue-lit scene of the survivors struggling to clamber onto unstable rafts. The scene develops to combine cod music-hall turn with documentary statement, as the Captain and the Purser banter on about the disaster ('What's the difference between board of trade regulations and sixteen lifeboats on the *Titanic*?' Answer: 'Nothing!') and ask the survivors – three women and two children – what happened to them as the holed monster-liner sank. The three women answer simultaneously, giving a poignant impression of destinies crossing as

Destroying the albatross of hope. *Raising the 'Titanic'*, 1983. (Set/costumes: the company. Photo: Alex von Koettlitz.)

destinies are crossed. Then they and the children sing a truly hauntin
lament:

> When man first flew across the sky
> He looked back into the world's blue eyes
> Man said what makes your eyes so blue
> Earth said the tears in the ocean do
>
> Why is the sea so full of tears
> Because I've wept for so many thousand years.

. . . as a bright and glowing lantern model of the *Titanic* is brought in o
a small truck, and a line of fire-cans stretching in a runway-effect back t
the dock-edge are lit to each side of them. The women/children take th
different parts of the lantern-*Titanic* up in their hands and carry ther
back towards the dock, and as they do this a vision of society gone mad
all wavering skyscrapers, and the grasping claws of capitalism – rises t
horrendous noise from below the dock. The *Titanic* looks for a momer
as if it will be handed back to the monster which made it by the innocer

urvivors, but in an astonishing moment which signifies that the weak
nd the oppressed may well possess the power to cheat the system they
urn away and deny the monster's greed. It is a power born *of* survival
gainst the odds. This is the second way in which, through irony,
athological optimism is stated by the show.

The survivors. *Raising the 'Titanic'*, 1983. (Performers: Hannah Fox,
Celia Gore-Booth, Lois Lambert, Val Levkowitz, Beattie Mitchell.
Photo: Alex von Koettlitz.)

The survivors' refusal is the signal for the final part of the event to
egin, and it is a powerful cue for starting up the dancing. For how better
o celebrate a refusal to accept the demands of ludicrous, exploitative and
ontradictory power? And besides, the late-summer evening has steadily
ot cooler, and limbs are stiff from sitting in the open auditorium. So

once again the real and the surreal, the pragmatic and the poetic ar complementary, and the drinking and the dancing implicitly reinforc the significance of the show. If the evils of developed society – th pollution, the oppression, the technological and ideological hubris – hav at last sunk into the cold deep (at least symbolically) we can assert ou reaction, however inflected, by dancing warm life back into our bodies So written into the dancing, just as dancing (but also as dancing on th metaphorical demise of a corrupt civilisation), is a statement of life agains death, of hope. We are celebrating by recreating for ourselves Welfar State's pathological optimism. Despite all the evidence to the contrary which still surrounds us in the streets and tower-blocks of the rea community context, we are asserting the right to *enjoy* autonomy, t make our own collective definitions of what's good for us, at least in an for the moment. The dance, in this context, if it is done with vigour an enjoyment, represents a profound and paradoxical significance: we ar dancing after witnessing the end of the society that surrounds us still.

And one final statement of hope ends the evening. As the danc finishes a flotilla of flickering lanterns, made by the local community floats gently across the dock. The image stakes a claim: where all th systems of the *Titanic* failed the creativity of the people will, perhaps succeed. For every lantern is reproduced, of course, by the water whic supports it.

(iv) Of contradictions and paradoxes

Welfare State is a risk-taking company of a classic kind: there are ver few, if any, repeat products. It is true, the company entered the terrain o the *Raising the 'Titanic'* with the practice of two previous 'models' unde its belt: *The Tempest on Snake Island*, and *Scarecrow Zoo* (Bracknell 1982). But *The Raising of the 'Titanic'* was a most extraordinary high-risl venture. The only commission of a high-profile international festiva depending for some of its success on untrained young people; a comple: high-tech mission mounted on a derelict dockside; a budget-swallowinﬂ extravaganza that could easily have failed to realise any cultural capital an aesthetic adventure searching the hinterlands between populist com munity carnival and exclusive experimental theatre; an unlikely plan t engineer a meeting between two alien cultural worlds – those of th desperately deprived East End and a privileged international aesthetic élite. The extravagant ambition can be easily read as the product o

rusting opportunism, but that would be to ignore totally the dynamic
teraction between the imaginative and the real in Welfare State's best
reations.

For the company's *Titanic* project *as a whole* was constructed as an
onic mirror of the original historical events that it purported to portray,
s a mega-metaphor of the disaster that was the *Titanic*; the ambition, the
vestment, the commercial risk, the technical audacity, the stylistic
ventiveness, the appeal to a range of social classes, even the claims to
novative structure made by the White Star Line for the great ship, were
ll reproduced and represented by the project within which the show was
ested. For Welfare State, the production of such parallels is the creative
oute that connects the wildest fantasy myths and images of performance
o the bread-and-butter living of the community. It is, then, the dynamic
etween performance text and social context that produces the engage-
nent with current socio-cultural contradictions, and provides the oppor-
unity to turn them into the positive paradoxes that inform all of Welfare
tate's best work.

They are contradictions that often appear in the vicinity of Welfare
tate events (as Tony Coult suggested in Chapter One), so a few of them
re worth briefly stating. For instance: there was a contradiction between
he scale of consumption of materials, of equipment, of people-hours by
he event, and the anti-consumerist ethic it aimed to promote. Ironically,
nuch of the expense was generated by the easily justified decisions to
uild a *conventional* auditorium on the dockside and to use high-tech
nternational-festival-standard lighting and sound equipment. This con-
radiction was the product of a second more fundamental one, between
he demands of the international festival and the desire to make a
pectacular statement with and for the local East End community. The
ormer pushed the aesthetics of the event towards the high-art conven-
ional – good seating, high quality technologies, etc. – while the latter
lemanded a populist breaking of the conventions of 'Culture'. Further,
he need to ensure security for the large amounts of gear on the site was in
erious contradiction to the intention to make the project accessible and
pen to the local community. And finally the scale and complexity of the
vent, more so than in most previous gigs, meant that the project had to
e organised hierarchically, to an extent that sometimes sat uncomfort-
bly with the egalitarian and democratic sympathies that were fun-
lamental to its ambitions.

Many other contradictions flowed from these central ones, and an
nsympathetic analysis would drag out the detail to show that Welfare
tate was having its cake and eating it. But such an analysis would miss
he crucial point to the company's practice, in that these contradictions
vere willingly embraced, and the practical and ideological problems they
osed were the point of undertaking the project in the first place. For the
ompany had quite deliberately chosen to dive in at the cultural deep

end, to encounter the contradictions at the interface between inter
national experimental (i.e., high art) theatre festival and loca
community-based popular get-together. This was part of its deliberat
strategy: to engage with the most rueful cultural problems, and to wres
from their contradictions an encounter with paradox.

It is important to tease out exactly *how* contradictions become para
doxes, as this is a fundamental element in the Welfare State aesthetic
The contradictions that were built into *The Raising of the 'Titanic'* al
relate to a central irony, for the company were using the resources o
western metropolitan civilisation to mount an attack on that civilisatior
in a context where it could clearly be seen to be failing. Had the projec
turned out as disastrous as the original voyage of the *Titanic* then Welfar
State would simply have reproduced and reinforced the values of th
civilisation it was attempting to subvert. However, the risk paid off anc
the project succeeded – this was not another *Titanic* disaster, but i
marvellous recreative and regenerative transformation of its imagery int
a life-enhancing celebration. The project thus became a statement o
hope in a context which promised anything but hope. The ironic mean
by which this was achieved are what turns contradiction into paradox. S
it was necessary to court disaster in order to avoid it. Without security
there would have been nothing to risk. The community had to be kep
out in order to be included. Excess argued for restraint, as extravagan
consumption demonstrated against itself. The hierarchy was essential t
showing that we are all equal. Welfare State are the mistresses anc
masters of such transformations.

But the transformations would simply be the theatrical equivalent of i
philosopher's pastime, or yet another version of post-modernist ideo
logical avoidance, without one further factor that makes the paradoxe
positive in relation to the context in which they are stated. For despite it
paradoxes, and the potential it gave for alternative readings, *The Raising
of the 'Titanic'* was unambiguously on the side of the underdog and th
local community. And as the local community consisted mainly of peopl
who would have been on the steerage decks of the *Titanic*, the shov
constituted a fairly unambiguous attack on the current status quo. S
whilst explicit ironic parallels were drawn in the show between th
Titanic and contemporary society (as represented by the local towe
blocks and Thames-side bolt-holes for the privileged), the dancing, anc
more importantly the *project* implicitly refuted the pessimism of th
parallels by providing grounds for an admittedly tenuous and risk
optimism. It is this sensitivity to the text-context dynamic that aimed t
make all the strategies of the *The Raising of the 'Titanic'* project, and th
overall developing policy and practice of Welfare State in the 1980s
positively paradoxical. The interaction of text and context is thus fun
damental to Welfare State's aim to stimulate social change and generate i
new political will.

(v) Back to home base

Despite the success of *The Raising of the 'Titanic'* and similar 'models' the company has subsequently questioned their validity. In 1988 Welfare State was arguing that:

> The basic flaw . . . of these models was that we were obliged to start from 'art' rather than from 'living', to generate more product than process, and to work to rapid (and to an extent commercial) deadlines in strange lands.[5]

And in the same year John Fox claimed that:

> The work that's going on in Barrow-in-Furness, where we have been since 1979, is much more directly related to responding to people on the ground.[6]

The point of such 'grounded aesthetics', to adopt a term invented by Paul Willis,[7] is that they produce an unalienated art which can invest everyday life with creative meaning. It is not so much that the aesthetics are a means for the community to express itself; rather, they become an essential part of the community's development of its future identity. Thus, Mike White claims that Welfare State has now

> . . . learned to integrate our wayward contemporary arts into the everyday life of communities, producing joyous celebrations and resonating poetic fallacies. These may stir a wish for social change which is conducive both to a new political will and to new original art forms.[8]

The grounded aesthetics of Welfare State's work in the eighties are ascribed with such a new political will. It aims to construct a new ideological balance between the artist and the community, in which new vernacular art forms explore the potential for local and global social change.

It is necessary to make a brief excursion through two such recent forms in order to map out the ideological possibilities in Welfare State's developing practice, before I attempt a final summation of the basic principles underlying the company's work. The two forms illustrate the company's continuing ability to mount a range of innovative events within a short period, for they were both undertaken in the same year as *The Raising of the 'Titanic'* 1983. They also demonstrate the always

eclectic cultural sources that feed even the most modest of the company
projects. The first was probably the first ever domestic lantern pro
cession in Britain, and has now become an annual secular ceremony, t
the point where the *Observer* colour supplement can refer to it as th
'traditional' Ulverston Lantern Procession. However, it derived from
traditional lantern procession seen on the north coast of Japan (where th
company were taking part in an international theatre festival). Th
second event took the form of a community feature film for Barrow-in
Furness. It was based on a script by Adrian Mitchell derived from
Shakespeare's *King Lear*, and called *King Real and the Hoodlums*
Together, these supply especially good examples of Welfare State
negotiation of the text-context dynamic.

Over a hundred people took place in the first Ulverston Lantern
Procession, all carrying glowing lanterns hand-made by themselves i
workshops set up by the company. A band led the long string of warn
lights in the shapes of fish, lobster pots and sails through the autumn
evening, along the traffic-cleared streets. In one sense the event was ju

> . . . a gentle evening stroll on a warm evening – townsfolk wer
> simply taking a walk with their family and friends through their ow
> streets . . . The procession visited residences for the elderly an
> centres for the disabled to receive their handmade lanterns. Fresh
> bathed children in their pyjamas were lifted up to the windows o
> doors of their homes to watch the lanterns pass. Elderly people ha
> been brought to the homes of relatives who lived on the route to se
> the procession. The first Lantern Procession . . . obviously struck
> chord with many people.[10]

In the following year, 1984, more people joined in to make a procession
fish, great head at the front and tail at the rear. In 1985 more 'spurs' wer
added to the route to involve more people, gift lanterns were exchange
between neighbourhoods, and there was a special lantern signifying eac
child born in Ulverston during the year. In 1986 the procession ce
ebrated the links between Ulverston and Bagamoyo in Tanzania (init
ated by the company's Nutcracker project in 1985), with lanterns style
on English and African houses. The procession is now an establishe
annual event involving over 1000 people, which Welfare State artists joi
principally as residents of the town rather than professional animateur
It is now mounted in partnership with the people of Ulverston, who ru
the lantern-making workshops. But why should the town have taken
Japanese-inspired ceremony on board in this way?

It may seem perverse to link this low-key, gentle evening stroll to th
idea of carnival, with all its associations of high-energy and anarchy
Carnival is about release, about a libidinal letting go, about the breakir
of rules and the disruption of the dominant order of the day. Th

Ulverston lantern procession seems to be light years away from, say, the Notting Hill Carnival. Yet whilst the procession obviously lacks the surface wildness and extravagance of traditional carnival, it also shares some of its most fundamental qualities. Foremost of these, perhaps, is grass-roots creativity expressed through an accessible form that is amenable to almost endless elaboration. Virtually anyone can make or contribute to the making of a lantern, and tiny individual efforts, when carried by the people who made them, can be just as impressive as enormous group-made affairs. Then, despite its tone of restraint, the procession is clearly an occasion of collective festivity. The collectivity now comes close to involving the whole town of 12,000 people, with lanterns made by organisations and spur marches and surrogate carriers for those who can't walk. The festivity arises from seasonal connections with long-gone Old-English ceremonies of autumn and with the more recent religious 'walks' that most northern towns once boasted. The subdued quality is really the outcome of this tradition, in which the community turned out to bear witness to its beliefs. But this is a secular ceremony (even pagan, according to the few Ulverston fundamentalist Christians who refuse to join in), so what beliefs are being celebrated? More fundamentally, in what ways might the procession 'stir a wish for social change' or generate a new political will'?

Carrying the seeds of social change. Ulverston Lantern Procession, 1985.
(Photo: John Vogdt.)

Obviously the lantern procession (unlike *Raising the 'Titanic'*) is resoundingly not an occasion for the making of relatively overt political statements. In this respect it perhaps reflects the conservative nature of the town. However, it would be a mistake to dismiss it as simply reinforcing the dominant ideology of the locality and through that the national status quo. For instance, we can read the spread of hand crafting of individual and unique lanterns as an implicit comment on the mass-consumerist ethic and commodity standardisation of so-called developed Western societies. Or we can interpret the collective celebration of Ulverston as a community as an explicit statement against the individualist orientation of 1980s neo-conservatism. The 1986 thematic linking of Ulverston-Bagamoyo suggests ideas of the international unity of small communities, or less whimsically, perhaps, a quiet call for the end of racism. So the procession can be seen to be carrying the seeds of social change, but they are buried deep within its structure rather than displayed overtly in its imagery. Some radical critics might identify this as a weakness, a form of local self-indulgence, having little or no impact on the wider world of politics and power. But such criticism tends to play down the immediate economic and geo-political context of the procession, where the prosperity of Ulverston is dependent on the pharmaceutical and nuclear (or nuclear-related) industries. In this context the implicit meanings of the lantern procession, shared and collectively witnessed by virtually the whole community, may add up to a profoundly radical statement, a reinforcement of positive individual and collective creativity. The beliefs inscribed in the event, in the community's celebration of the identity being formed through the event, may be read as deeply subversive. It is, of course, a paradox that a form as 'conservative' as a quiet evening stroll with warmly glowing lanterns can carry such significance, but in this respect the procession is like any other successful carnival.

Yet as Bakhtin – the principal theorist of carnival[11] – suggests, carnival can all too easily be a surrogate revolution, a placebo used to purge and pacify resistance to oppression, with no real impact on the dominant social order. The 'statement of hope' that is the lantern procession especially in the context of the high-density nuclear zone, may still be no more than a hopeless gesture. On the other hand, the very poignancy in the contrast between the fragile and flimsy luminescence of the lanterns and the black horrors of the zone is surely designed to stir deep resistances which may eventually lead to action. The subdued, contemplative nature of the event – uniting Japanese and English traditions – is aimed to nurture such responses.

But Welfare State also experimented with media of a more high-tech kind on the Barrow peninsula, when the company chose to use a feature film format to achieve a much more overtly subversive impact in Barrow-in-Furness. However, the 'politics' of *King Real and the Hood*

Marching in rowdy procession . . . the Hoodlums. *King Real and the Hoodlums*, 1983.

lums were so radical in context that the company almost came unstuck at the start of what was planned as a very long-term residency. The film was made as a co-production with Sheffield Polytechnic film studies department, as the main part of a three month project with mainly unemployed young people. It was shot in a derelict warehouse and on location in Barrow, about 50 local young people were involved in building sets and making costumes, and all the actors except King Real (who was played by Marcel Steiner) were local non-professionals. In the final product Barrovians could thus easily recognise their daughters and sons in the local landscape, even though they had been transformed into a kind of punk-medieval rabble in a wasted industrial junkyard.

These are the Hoodlums, the citizens of the kingdom of King Real, crazy power-mad denizen of doom. The film opens with the Hoodlums chanting their king's name, marching in rowdy procession to his throne, which is perched on top of a pyramid of bright wrecked cars, just by Walney Sound (where they bring in the nuclear submarines). This is the site for the distribution of the golden keys of power to his three daughters. True to the original Cloudella-Cordelia refuses, while Gonilla-Goneril and Raygal-Regan, together with their consort, the insane Captain Adderman-Cornwall/Albany, of course accept. Cloudella goes off into the wilderness with the fool-figure Lord Thomas, while in a scene of extraordinary goonish domestic brutality Gonilla and Raygal scramble Real's brains and chuck him out into the wasteland. After unsuccessfully searching for Cloudella, he ends up back with the other two sisters and the Captain, who are now ensconced in a nuclear bunker which controls enough weaponry to obliterate the world. Real tries to persuade them not to use the keys of power to shoot off the rocketry, but they scramble his brains again for good measure and fire him out of the bunker through a torpedo tube. Then in a vulgar orgy of mutual- and self-hatred Gonilla, Raygal and Adderman, fight and finally unite to turn the keys of destruction, gorging themselves on an enormous globe of the world constructed from confectionery as the roof of the bunker collapses in on them. In a fire-raised industrial desert we see Real, now blinded from the blasts, still searching for Cloudella. He finds her scorched and dying and begs her forgiveness, which she gives before dying in his arms. The film ends as it began, with a procession, but this time it is marching *away* from King Real's pyramid of power and a blazing bonfire on which the golden keys can be clearly seen ignited.

The film has all the roughness of finish and broad stylistic brush-strokes of Welfare State's work at its best, a combination of startling archetypal imagery and pop-panto performance. It unites the wild visionary world-gone-mad of Shakespeare's Lear with the recognisable socio-political landscape of Barrow-in-Furness, in a poetic vault into a universe of twisted logic and horrifying consequence. The shooting included a huge parade through the streets of the town, centrally featuring 'the Mad King spouting excesses from a crazy junk submarine made by local shipyard welders'[12] and followed by the young Hoodlums their numbers swelled by the street-cred attraction of the event, chanting his praises. The world-première showing was at the Astra, Barrow's only cinema, with all the silly razzmatazz of a feature film opening reproduced in satiric extravagance: with limousines and red carpets. Naturally the ironic significance of these antics and the unmistakable political intent of the film sparked off a local row. To the conservatively-minded the attack on the nuclear powerbase was unjustified aggression towards a community that had no choice about which industry it relied on for its survival. To others it seemed that Welfare State was corrupting their young with enticing but brainwashing subversive fun. Yet even the most critical Barrovian had to admit that it was better that the unemployed young should be creatively engaged rather than roaming the streets, and after all Welfare State had brought a little money into the town with grants from the Arts Council and Marks and Spencer.

The ambivalent reactions were a product of the ironies and paradoxes at the heart of the project, which parallel those of *Raising the 'Titanic'* and the Ulverston Lantern Procession. But with *King Real* the paradoxes move into higher relief, as it were, because of the context. For Welfare State was rooting for sanity, quite deliberately, right on the brink of the cliff-edge it was aiming to destroy. So, King Real's submarine would not

Spouting excesses from a junk submarine.
King Real and the Hoodlums, 1983. (Performer: Marcel Steiner. Photo: Tim Biller.)

exist but for the shipyard that, metaphorically, it aims to sink. So, the Barrow landscape is turned into a post-holocaust wasteland that demonstrates the creativity of the town's youth; the classic Shakespearean excess, condensed brilliantly by Adrian Mitchell's script and galvanised by Peter Moser's poignant music, advocates contemporary caution re-cycled junk represents the necessity to stop producing junk. And to inaugurate a five year community-based creative project it is necessary to demonstrate how the future is jeopardised by the community's economic need to create death. Finally, in order to stop the unthinkable we have to think the unthinkable. And so on and on into the miasma of what Martin Amis calls the 'black dream',[13] the breakdown of logic that is the purpose of nuclear weaponry, the mental contamination that their very existence guarantees.

Now, although the film project and its attendant activities were founded on such ironies and paradoxes, there is, perhaps, one overriding mega-paradox. That is, to be creative in a destructive environment one has to be destructive. In other words, in order to celebrate a community such as Barrow it is necessary in some way to criticise the community's complicity in making the means to deliver armageddon. So in moving into the Barrow project we can say that Welfare State were committing themselves to creating a style of socio-politically critical carnival that might have a lasting effect. In some respects they have already achieved this. According to John Fox, *King Real* encouraged several local people to take up places at art and drama college. On a much larger scale, the initial ambivalent reception was weathered out, and the company has now been working in Barrow for over five years. Their status as Civic Magicians was spectacularly confirmed in 1988, when the Victorian town hall of Barrow was 'sculpturally enhanced' in a celebration that brought out 15,000, and climaxed in the wholesale hooting of all the council transport horns plus fishing boat sirens. Apparently the noise set off the shipyard emergency alarm system!

(vi) Towards a positive beginning

I hope I have shown how Welfare State manages to move beyond the *obvious* contradictions in the company's practice, by using the grounded aesthetics of context-specific projects to explore creative paradoxes. The paradoxes are usually a product of the interaction of performance text and community context. So they are particularly highlighted by the deologically 'difficult' locations that the company regularly chooses to work in – such as Limehouse and Barrow – but they can also be detected in less demanding contexts. As I have already noted, I think that the paradoxes are the source of the 'magical' quality that entrances both spectators and participants, but also they generate an energy that the company hopes will fuel the motor of social change and produce a new political will. This ambition is not simply a matter of ideological generality, for the grounded aesthetics of Welfare State connect high hopes to concrete realities, global visions of the future to local community action.

To characterise the global visions that the company hopes to invoke we need briefly to return to the fundamental paradox created by the company's residence in Ulverston-Barrow. As I have already described it: they have chosen to live where death has its dominion, on the edge of Armageddon. John Fox describes its effect as follows:

> Now it sharpens one's sensibility no end to get on that edge. The fact that we know that inside Windscale the management is incompetent. We know that they are invariably releasing radioactivity and telling lies about it. It sharpens one's sense of life and death, where recently a Vicker's development and marketing manager said that 'We don't care what we sell . . . as long as we get a contract.' I think that's certainly horrific and seems to be mad.[14]

Thus when the local economy is founded on the global military-industrial complex its pathological logic is sitting on your doorstep, living next door, contaminating the community. For the communities of the Barrow peninsula, through no fault of their own, are producing the destructive element. Two central consequences flow from this. First, to be optimistic about the future you may have to be pathological. Second, to effect a 'cure' that will ensure a future you have to out-wit the madness, literally, and that may mean, for a time, you have to follow Brecht's advice:

> Go down in the mire
> Embrace the butcher
> But change the world
> It needs it.

Welfare State's 'embrace' takes two chief forms. First, the company aims to work *with* the whole of the community which is engaged in the production, more or less directly, of the negative agent. And second, the representation of imagery, characters, stories, landscapes drawn from the contaminated zone, the culture of destruction and death, become an essential strategy for defining and dealing with its pathology. For if the

sickness is identified perhaps it can be cured. Or, to draw on a differe
cosmology, the evil has to be named in order to be exorcised. This is wh
John Fox talks of shamanism, and why the company is as muc
concerned with cultural anthropology as with the production of art.[15]
is, of course, a dangerous strategy in cynical times, so the art has to l
especially beguiling to draw in the doubters. But how can the imagery
contamination and the stories of hopeless enmeshment in negativity l
made attractive without reinforcing their horrifically mesmeric fasc
nation? What are the essential features of an art that can encompass tl
paradoxes posed by this context, and more importantly, suggest a wa
beyond them?

In the 1970s Welfare State was most frequently said to be producir
'celebratory theatre', but in the 1980s a more accurate description of tl
company's core practice might be 'carnival performance'. Now carniva
as I have already argued, is a very tricky pursuit. As John Fox notes i
Chapter One, the symbolic revolution of the Feast of Fools may simp
be a safety valve for the release of anti-establishment feelings, a dispers
of resistance to the status quo. Or worse: it may be a cover for tl
assassination of dissidents. It is curious, then, that recently carnival h
become a fashionable concept with leading radical theatre practitioner
John McGrath, for instance, seems attracted to its anarchic possibilitie

> The concept of an unofficial, Rabelaisian merry-making which
> licensed to mock, parody and create obscene versions of the officia
> solemn, censorious world of church and state, is one that . .
> certainly has a meaning in Thatcher's Britain.[16]

This, of course, could be describing one aspect of Welfare State's styl
But in the 1990s it is perhaps pertinent to enquire which authority issu
the licence: is it the status quo or some alternative force? And if it is tl
latter, what might its nature be?

David Edgar has made a fascinating stab at suggesting how contem
porary carnival performance may validate itself.

> What I suppose that most of us are striving for, is a way
> combining the cerebral, unearthly detachment of Brecht's theor

with the all too earthy, sensual, visceral experience of Bakhtin's carnival, so that in alliance these two forces can finally defeat the puppeteers and manipulators of the spectacle [of society]. We are doing so in full knowledge of the dangers of incorporation, of becoming no more than a radical sideshow to divert the masses and dampen their ardour.[17]

o avoid becoming a sideshow a contemporary critical performance ractice must pitch itself at the heart of the fairground, where the most angerous rides hold sway. This is what Welfare State has done in order ▸ discover a means for the making of critical carnival in the 1980s. evitably, it is a dangerous tactic. For the irony that turns contradiction to paradox in order to clarify our common predicaments can imply a ·luctance to make clear commitments. A too vigorous embracing of the ntradictions can produce a mere clash of opposing ideologies that is structive. A paradox can take the form of a vicious circle just as easily it can suggest the possibility of infinity, or eternity.[18] So it may well be at Welfare State, like everyone else perhaps, is a victim, to an extent, of ost-modernist mentality and itself suffers from touches of the ideologi- l paralysis produced by being too close to the heart of darkness, mersed too deep in the horror.

But that very closeness – in reality, on the Barrow peninsula – rescues e company from becoming totally trapped in an ideological vicious rcle. For the *lived* commitment is to the people of the locality, the ommon people' that Brecht so often celebrated. So in its populist ybrid forms, in its context-contaminated carnival performances, the mpany has perhaps come closer than any other to combining Bakhtin's elebratory excesses' with Brecht's radical criticism. But is it criticism at will stick to its object? More importantly, what kind of efficacy ight it have for the future, given the enormity of 'the system' it is tacking?

Perhaps it is too soon to tell, but I think there are signs and portents in Welfare State's recent work that give grounds for guarded hope. For the grass-roots creativity has taken root in the terrain that is most in need of it. Moreover, the company now more openly start on the side of the oppressed, with much less ambivalence about the social ground that they wish to cultivate – though in the encounter with the global network of the military-industrial complex *most* people are underdogs. Still, Welfare State avoids too general a definition of its potential allies by finding them in specific localities through increasingly long-term residencies. So the company proposes and promotes, on the level of mundane community action, a form of creativity that is a basic 'model' for local autonomy and collective endeavour, as a practical foundation for opposition to the status quo (particularly as represented by the nuclear industry). And the company sidesteps the problems of narrow aesthetics in its adoption of critical carnival as the informing creative principle behind most of its work. Thus Welfare State has invented spectacularly ironic forms combining oppositional worlds – that nuclear-bomber looks as if it could almost, just, be a Phoenix – to transform the contradictions generated by the dynamic inter-action between critical texts and hegemonic contexts into positive paradoxes. And it is there, just on the other side of the paradoxes, that the hoped-for shamanistic, curative exorcism has its principal, principled significance.

For the grounded aesthetics of grass-roots creativity counters our cultural pathology with a suggestion of health. This health is partly characterised by a notion of well-being that demotes the work ethic and disdains consumption for its own sake. It is also partly to do with a search for gainful occupation, a way of positive non-exploitative production that occurs locally and has global implications. It is to do with non-standardised productivity as part of a creative collectivity which reclaims and regenerates its own identity, refusing to accept the definitions that the dominant order would force it to swallow. It represents an absolute refusal of the pathological abnormalities generated by over-developed (particularly capitalist) social systems. And on the positive side promises a complementarity between the real and the surreal, the poetic and the pragmatic in a fully democratised society. These are some of the positive principles underlying all of Welfare State's work, though they emerged in higher relief in the 1980s. In this historical context they are fragile ideas. And perhaps this is why the tissue paper and thin withy lantern has become such a feature in the company's practice. They can be consumed by flames in an instant, but when they gather at dusk together to make enormous images of hope it seems like they will last forever.

1 Arthur Koestler, *The Act of Creation* (Picador, 1971).
2 Ivan Illich, *Tools for Conviviality* (Calder and Boyars, 1973).
3 John Fox, 'Between Windscale and Wordsworth,' *Performance Magazine*, No 54, June/July, 1988.
4 John Fox's notes on the working scenario for the *Titanic* point to a particularly prescient contemporary significance for this scene: '"Police" put down strike.' The great miner's strike was just around the corner of history.
5 Mike White, 'Resources for a Journey of Hope: the Work of Welfare State International,' *New Theatre Quarterly*, Vol IV No 15, August, 1988.
6 John Fox, op cit.
7 Paul Willis, *Common Culture* (Open University, 1990).
8 Mike White, op cit.
9 Adrian Mitchell, 'King Real and the Hoodlums,' in *Peace Plays*, ed. Stephen Lowe (Methuen, 1988).
10 John Fox and Sue Gill, 'Welfare State International: Seventeen Years on the S,' *The Drama Review*, Vol 29 No 3, Fall 1985 (T 107).
11 Mikhail Bakhtin, *Rabelais and his World* (Bloomington, 1968).
12 John Fox and Sue Gill, op cit.
13 Martin Amis, *Einstein's Monsters* (Penguin, 1988).
14 John Fox, op cit.
15 Ideas of the nomadic drawn from cultural anthropology are reproduced in the company's processional forms, imitating the nomad's desire to avoid the ties of territoriality, to live in the moment of travel. John Fox suggests that if we possess no land to defend then violence is less likely to occur. See Bruce Chatwin, *What Am I Doing Here* (Picador, 1990).
16 John McGrath, *The Bone Won't Break* (Methuen, 1990).
17 David Edgar, *The Second Time As Farce* (Lawrence and Wishart, 1988).
18 Parick Hughes and George Brecht, *Vicious Circles and Infinity: An Anthology of Paradoxes* (Penguin, 1978).

Appendices

STAGING OUTDOOR EVENTS:
A brief guide to legalities and permissions
HOWARD STEEL *Welfare State's Administrator*

1. Permissions and Insurances

If you are staging a public event on any open space you will obviously need to get the permission of the owners of the land, who for public spaces are most likely to be the Local Authority but could be any institutional body, commercial firm or individual. Most owners will only allow you to use their land if you can demonstrate that you hold an adequate Employers and Public Liability Insurance Policy which will cover (a) their land and property against damage (b) members of your company against accident and (c) members of the public attending the event against accident, so that they can be sure that no damages claim is going to be laid at their door. Many owners will ask you to indemnify them in writing against any claim. You should consult your insurance company or broker before agreeing to any indemnity. They will naturally be most stringent about this where the event involves fire or fireworks.

Even where it is not a condition of the use of the land it is most unwise to stage any public event without public liability insurance. Any personal accident to a member of the public attending it (even as simple as tripping over one of your props and breaking a bone) can be construed as due to your negligence. A major accident can bring a damages claim of hundreds of thousands of pounds for which your company (if it is legally constituted) and you personally (if it is not) will be liable.

It does not solve the problem to announce that people attend at their own risk. If an accident happens and a civil court decides it was due to your negligance the disclaimer can be declared an unfair contract and thus invalid.

Some local Authorities who have outside events regularly on their land have a system of extending their own policy to cover the event and charging you the additional premium, which will certainly be the cheapest way to arrange it.

2. Preparation Period and Residence on Site

If you need to spend a preparation period prior to the day of the event setting up structures etc. in a public space you will need to fence off your orksite from public access and ensure that your insurance covers that eriod too. If any of your structures are designed for public use, i.e. a caffolding seating stand or kids play structure, the Building Inspector om the local Planning Department may want to check it for safety. He as authority over temporary structures as well as permanent ones.

If you are living on the site as the simplest method of maintaining vernight security on your gear, you may live there in tents with the wner's permission, although you may be subjected to a Public Health ispection to check that you have adequate water and toilets. Under the Caravans Act of 1960 you may not live in a caravan other than on a censed caravan site, even with the owner's permission, unless you have n exemption certificate under Schedule 1 of the Act showing that you re a fair or circus with Showmans Guild membership or other group of ona fide professional travelling showmen. Getting these certificates is a ong and difficult process and not worth trying unless you are a ermanent touring caravan-based company.

Fireworks and Bonfires

'ou do not need to get a licence or to conform to any official set of written egulations to stage a public bonfire and/or a display of ready-made reworks and pyrotechnic effects. However it is sensible and useful to ıform the police and the fire brigade well in advance of your event and t them check over your arrangements. This maintains good relations, cts as an additional safety check and avoids the problem of some worried ocal resident dialling 999 and turning out the whole fire brigade during a how. They will want to check that there is adequate fencing and tewarding to keep the audience at an appropriate distance from the onfire and firing site, that there is a proper firework fallout area, that ou have enough firefighting equipment to deal with an emergency ncluding the danger of windblown sparks, whichever way the wind is lowing) and that there is proper access to the site for ambulances and re engines if they're needed. They may offer to have a team of men on and, unless it's November 5th, in which case they'll be too stretched to nanage it. Some fire authorities produce sets of recommended uidelines for public bonfire organisers.

Although there are no controls on the setting off of fireworks there are egulations covering their storage, transport and the use of fuses. To buy lectric detonators, igniter cord and pipematch you need a 'C' licence, which states that you are a 'fit person' to keep the material, and a form 'F' which is a licence to acquire gunpowder and safety fuse. Both these ertificates are issued by the Crime Prevention Officer of your local Police Authority after investigation of both you and the place of storage. In onsidering your application they will be as much concerned with the ecurity of your storage against theft as with your competence to use the naterial safely. To store fireworks for more than 14 days before use you

will need a firework store registered with the local Trading Standard
Authority and meeting their requirements. Transporting fireworks i
also regulated by the law under the Road Traffic (Carriage of Explosive
Regulations) Act 1989, which regulates the type of vehicle you use an
specifies loading arrangements. Copies of these regulations can b
obtained from the HMSO in London.

4. Liaison with Other Authorities
If you're using pyrotechnics or even ordinary theatre lights after dar.
close to a working dock, an airport, a rough coast or on a mountain, te.
the local Harbourmaster, Air Traffic Controller, Coastguard or Rescu
Centre what you're doing. A flare or coloured light in the wrong place ca
launch lifeboats, send out mountain rescue teams, confuse shipping o
landing aircraft, cause unnecessary danger and make you ver
unpopular. If you're planning a big bonfire check with the gas an
electricity boards where their underground mains are and don't site you
fire on top of them. If you're setting off large helium balloons, which ca
rise to several thousand feet before exploding, check that they're nc
rising into the traffic lanes of the local airport. For large public events it'
worth inviting the St. John's Ambulance Brigade to set up a first aid pos
which they will do for a modest donation to their funds.

5. Food and Drink
If you want to serve food or drink to the public you will first need t
check with the owner of the land whether they have already granted
sole catering concession on it, which for a beach area or well used park i
quite likely. If so you will have to ask the concession holder to cater fo
you or come to some special arrangement with him. Secondly, if you ar
selling food or drink to the public – or giving it away as part of the show
it makes no difference – you will be expected to conform to Public Healt.
Authority standards of hygiene. You can be inspected at any tim
without warning and told to close down on the spot if your standards d
not measure up. See Food section for more detail.

6. Licensing
The licensing of outdoor performance is a grey area in the law. Under th
Theatres Act of 1968 all theatre premises giving public performances c
plays need a licence issued to the theatre manager by the relevant loc
authority, which has powers of inspection to ensure that the theatre i
complying with its normally very stringent regulations on width of fir
exits, secondary lighting systems, non-inflammability of scenery an
props etc. Licences can also be granted on applications at 14 days notic
for premises only occasionally used for performance. A 'play' is define
as 'any dramatic piece, whether involving improvisation or not . .
involves the playing of a role' and 'any ballet'. The definition c

'premises' is 'premises include any place'. Thus anything which can be seen as dramatic role-playing on any park, street, riverbank, beach etc. can be theoretically regarded as requiring a licence. On the other hand no licence is required for most traditional forms of outdoor entertainment; fairs, circuses, town carnivals etc.

The authorities are as aware of the anomalies as anyone else. In practice most authorities will be content to treat outdoor theatre events as they treat other outdoor entertainments, rather than stretch the Theatres Act to cover a situation for which it was never really designed and which makes nonsense of most of its detailed regulations. Provided that you are seen to be responsible in treating the safety and comfort of the public in terms of good entrances and exits, stewarding, toilets, lighting etc., the question of a theatre licence is unlikely to arise. It will be used only as a deterrent by unsympathetic authorities who do not want you there in the first place.

The possible exception to this is where you are giving a scripted performance to an audience inside a marquee or other temporary structure, which is a situation much closer to what the Act is designed to deal with. In that case you may well be asked to apply for an occasional licence.

Roughly the same situation exists with the other form of live entertainment licensing, the Music, Singing and Dancing licences issued by local magistrates (clerks of councils in London and the Home Counties) and designed to control Variety Halls, Dance Halls, Concert Halls, pubs offering live entertainment etc. In theory the premises to be licensed can be outdoor spaces and the regulations could be used to control every street parade, carnival or brass band concert in the park. In practice they are very rarely used in this way and you are very unlikely to be asked to apply for an occasional licence for a one-off outdoor event with live music, or to be penalised if you have not got one.

Street Processions

Only some of the above considerations apply to street processions. You do not need anyone's permission to stage an orderly procession along a public right of way provided that you are not seriously impeding pedestrians or vehicles or causing a danger to traffic. The only possible legal problem is where the Home Secretary has used his powers to prohibit street marches in a particular area for a limited period to avoid trouble with political demonstrators. That ban affects all parades and processions.

However it is useful and sensible to tell the police what you're doing and ask for their co-operation and advice, particularly if you're strangers to the area and they can supply local knowledge. Avoid as far as possible the long winded bureaucratic route of writing to the chief constable and keep it on as informal a level as possible. Ideally, once you've planned your route and timings take a map along to the local police station and ask to see the duty inspector. He will inform the local beat bobbies and pandas and may offer you a man to help with traffic control at major junctions.

If you are using the road, as opposed to the pavement, you will need to operate as if you were a motor vehicle, i.e. have stewards at front and back signalling your intention to turn left, turn right, move out to overtake etc., carrying white (front) and red (rear) lights after dark and generally following the rules of the road. You will also need stewards to keep all the kids that a good procession is bound to attract, on the pavement and out of harm's way as they follow you around. You could be construed as liable if one of them goes under a bus.

You may find problems if you want to take a collection as you go. It will help if you can say that you are a registered charity. Otherwise you will probably be subject to whatever the local bye-laws are about street buskers.

Some large modern purpose-built shopping precincts, although they contain what at first sight appear to be public rights of way, are in fact totally owned and controlled by private property companies who employ private security firms to police them. You will need permission to enter them and their attitude towards collections is likely to be particularly strict.

Appendix 2
A Chronology of Welfare State Events

1968

July	THE TIDE IS OK FOR THE 30TH: week-end beach event, with Army DUKW's, an aeroplane full of poems, performance, music.	Instow North Devon
December	HEAVEN & HELL: tribute to William Blake. Day long event around the Ashton Memorial; one hundred performers, real dancing bear, puppets.	Lancaster

1969

Jan. to June	SIGN ON THE DOLE and DR. CALIGHARI: political cabarets with rock group.	Yorkshire

ily	First street theatre show.	Selby Festival
	First naming ceremony for children.	N. Yorks Moors
ugust	Residency, with Interaction, at Rotherfield Hall, for Chalk Farm children.	Sussex
Iovember	EARTHRISE: first multi-media show with Mike Westbrook's band, astronauts, light show, films, images created using 20 gymnasts plus circus acts.	Mermaid Theatre, London

70

ebruary	CIRCUS TIME: city centre carnival celebration with parades, jazz, gymnasts, performance, inflatables and programmed civic bell ringing, public dancing.	Bradford
arch	SPRING EVENT: in huge gymnasium with racing cyclists, mountaineers, jazz, brownies, light shows and dancing. Start of 'Cosmic Circus'.	Exeter
	'Cosmic Circus' was the name of the group constituted for presenting large-scale, once-off high technology shows, founded by John Fox and Mike Westbrook.	
pril	ORIGINAL PETER: first live TV happening, with tattooist, acrobat, live insects, jazz and film.	Arena BBC-TV
ay	A.W.A.K.E. Festival: first tented show around the ghosts of Hepton-stall: coffins, unicyclist and puppets. One of the countrywide 'New Activities' events, organised by Al Beach.	Hebden Bridge
	EARTHRISE: Cosmic Circus.	Univ. of Essex
ily	EARTHRISE: Cosmic Circus.	Exeter
ugust	Street Theatre Tour: SUPERMAN & THE FLEAS; markets, fairs, shows, borstals etc.	N. Yorkshire
	DR. STRANGEBREW'S DIORAMA: indoor grotto with music and performance.	Instow, N. Devon

September	Company moves to Leeds.	
October	Street Theatre plus DIORAMA.	Bath
December	City Station Forecourt: Christmas Grotto with the Fine Art Dept of Leeds Polytechnic.	Leeds
	Alternative Pantomime: NUS Festival.	Southampton
1971		
February	EARTHRISE: Cosmic Circus.	Brighton
March	Blaize Fair Street Theatre	Bradford
	EARTHRISE plus Street Theatre. with Action Space. First of several arrests for breach of the peace.	Swansea
May	EARTHRISE: Cosmic Circus.	Univ. of Liverpool
	EARTHRISE: Cosmic Circus.	Univ. of Southampton
June	Street Theatre.	Serpentine Gallery, Hyde Park
July	EARTHRISE: Cosmic Circus.	Leeds
	Street Theatre tour of summer festivals.	Midland
August	SWEET MISERY OF LIFE tour, own custom-built PVC structure, seating 60 people.	Harrowgate Leith; Edin Festival
	End of the Summer Garden Party.	Serpentine Gallery Hyde Park
October	EARTHRISE: Cosmic Circus.	Lanchester Poly
Nov. to March	SWEET MISERY OF LIFE: winter tour round Students Unions – the work changes here – end of PARODY.	Exeter Lanchester Newcastle Wolverhampton
1972		
January	Second naming ceremony for Children.	Wool Exchange Bradford
February	WINTER RISING: encampment and three day event, which precipitated	

	official UFO investigation in central Coventry.	Lanchester Poly.
pril	Bickershaw Pop Festival: Building a stilt village in a swamp.	Lancs.
ay	MAY RISING: spring event with sword swallowers, drumming bands and a Maypole.	Parliament Hill Fields, London
	TRAVELS OF LANCELOT QUAIL: this show heralded the start of a 7 year cycle.	Surrey Hall, Brixton
ne	URBANE BABOON PROJECT: street events.	Westminster
	URBANE BABOON PROJECT: street events.	Harlow New Town
	LOT SONG: a specially commissioned work with Mike Westbrook to be performed in church. Urban decay as prelude to nuclear holocaust.	Smith Square, London
ly	Last Cosmic Circus production: 'Cosmic Circus' with ravens, high-diver, tightrope, carnival procescions and beggars and Jeff Nuttall as the syphilitic king.	Tower of London
ugust	TRAVELS OF LANCELOT QUAIL: tour, in own circus tent.	Burnley; Leith; Sunderland
ptember	One month's processional theatre from Glastonbury westwards vanishing aboard a submarine off Land's End: THE TRAVELS OF LANCELOT QUAIL.	Somerset, Devon & Cornwall
:tober	Appointed Fellow in theatre to Mid-Pennine Arts Assoc. for one year. Prepare to move to Burnley caravan site and total commitment to the mobile village.	Lancs.
:cember	First New Year's Eve/New Year's Day event.	Barrowford

73

nuary	FANFARE FOR EUROPE: continuous performance piece via	

	North Sea Ferries with performance artists including John Bull Puncture Repair Kit, Jeff Nuttall, Roland Miller, Genesis P. Orridge etc.	Hull Rotterda
	Start of 2 years of DEMON BUSKERS: anarchic, unpredictable street appearances.	Burnl
February	Official status as registered educational charity: GALACTIC SMALLHOLDINGS LTD.	
April	Quarry event on Cow & Calf Rocks, Ilkley Moor, with ice & fire, juke-box, crashed aeroplane, giant blazing scarecrows, unicyclist.	Ilkley Festi
May	Opening ceremony with fire sculptures.	Aberystwy Arts Cen
	BEAUTY & THE BEAST: magic installation piece in landscape, with 3 months preparation. Labyrinth, shanty town built adjacent to living quarters with performances daily.	Burn
June	Special event in the Lake, with surrounding performances and processions.	Durha Museum & A Galle
	Opening of Holland Festival for Dutch TV: BEAUTY & THE BEAST – 6 weeks tour.	Rotterda The Hagu Amsterd
August	DEMON BUSKERS tour.	Lancash
	MAGIC & STRONG MEDICINE: exhibition and canto performances.	Walker Art Ga ery, Liverp
October	Special commission to open the Sherman Studio Theatre.	Card
Oct./Nov.	Hallowe'en & Guy Fawkes – street Processions, events and bonfire.	Burn
November	Mummers Plays, Band, Pub Shows.	North Shie
December	THE RUNWAY IS NEARLY COMPLETE: a rare London appear-ance; 700 fans and a few critics crammed the R.C.A. to see a show designed for 200. All sight lines of cool distant images totally wrecked.	Royal College Art, Lond

Dec./Jan.	Gallery exhibition of Welfare State's work, artefacts, documentation and events.	Burnley
Dec./Jan.	Two day New Year Event: the burning of the Giant of the Old Year, the ride of the Innocent on horseback, plus afternoon family gala, pub shows.	Barrowfield

74

January	Firemen mummers in pub shows.	Burnley
Jan./Feb.	Science Fiction Festival: walk through labyrinth – culthouse – Babel.	Rotterdam
February	Studio Theatre: 4 simultaneous performances in sand craters, repeated as different sections of the audience arrived.	Birmingham Rep.
	Fire sculptures and night on the hillsides with village pub shows to follow.	Yorkshire Dales
	RUNWAY I: special event in the northern fog in a former cemetery, with glass horse-drawn hearse, saxophones, fire sculptures.	Leeds
	MARCH FIRST: a celebration with and for Great George's Project in their temporary home with 20 tons of sand, a heated billiard table, night club comics and Suomi wrestlers.	Liverpool
March	Living site consolidated: water and lavatories installed, still no electricity.	
April/May	Ice and Fire Sculpture with music.	Wolverhampton; Bradford; London
April	Easter Event: Processional Dance.	Skipton Woods
May	May Day Celebration.	Burnley
	Temporary earthwork sculpture with JCB plus theatre foyer performances.	Gulbenkian Theatre, Newcastle

June	First L.P. recorded of own songs & street music with Lol Coxhill.	
	First permanent earth sculpture opened.	Gawthorpe Hall
	Special commission to devise an event for a French Fish Market.	Le Havre
July	HOMAGE TO MEISTER ECKHART: 24 hour vigil in and around the Cathedral, with giant sand knot sculpture, wind sculptures, processions and gargoyle cinema.	Birmingham
	RUNWAY II: special event in cliff-top ruined abbey.	Whitley Bay
August	ISLAND OF THE LOST WORLD: environmental sideshow with processional walks and three legged dog.	Blackburn
	Processional theatre.	Bath Festival
September	Processional theatre tour.	Mid-Pennine
October	Sideshow event with taxidermy.	Univ. of Warwick
	RING MAIN: Arts Lab. A dire show. Incestuous analysis of didactic theatre v. anthropological ceremony.	Birmingham
Oct./Nov.	Hallowe'en and Guy Fawkes events plus Civic bonfire, first of 10.	Burnley
November	Earthwork sculpture.	Chorley
	RING MAIN tour.	Plymouth; Wig
December	First moulded ice giant to appear in fire sculpture and earthworks.	Wath-upon Dearn

1975		
January	DROWNING OF THE BOTTOM HUNDRED: an indoor show with outdoor processions devised for N. Wales tour.	Bango Harlec Aberystwyth
February	DROWNING OF THE BOTTOM HUNDRED.	York Arts Cent
March	Company research month: individual projects.	
April	Company's own nomadic school opens formally with 6 children.	Burnl

May	May Day Celebrations.	Burnley
	MOLE & THE FIRECLOWN: show, incorporating street song, processions and first kiln.	Welwyn Garden City
	CITY OF WINDMILLS: residency in a shabby suburb of Paris.	Aubervilliers
June	Fire sculpture with performance.	Oval House, London
	Continuous build and performance in a summer meadow behind a Museum and Industrial Hamlet.	Sheffield
	Small team with giant puppet in nightly processions around International Sculpture Exhibitions.	Switzerland
July	ALIEN: three weeks residency in downtown Burnley, with community involvement in final spectacular show. Filmed for TV.	Burnley
August	Street Theatre Tour.	Mid-Pennines
September	HARBINGER: car sculpture in city centre, for International Performance Festival.	Birmingham
October	Performance in an old fort outside Antwerp. Week of processions in fishing town. Appearance at Wroclaw Theatre Festival.	Belgium; Holland; Poland
November	Hallowe'en and Guy Fawkes events with giant bonfire and puppets.	Burnley
	Residency, with intimate nightly shows in a booth, straw bales & mulled ale.	Crowborough
December	Return visit with pre-Christmas show.	Wath-upon-Dearne

1976

Jan./Feb.	Construct elaborate mobile sideshow/travelling exhibition: ISLAND OF THE LOST WORLD.	Burnley
March	One month's residency in city centre art gallery, with work in	

	progress and daily performances: ISLAND OF THE LOST WORLD, Lijnbaan Centrum.	Rotterda
April	At this point we have 9 children under 9.	
May	Steve Gumbley, Liz Lockhart, Di Davies and Lou Glandfield left W.S. and co-founded I.O.U. with others.	
June to Sept.	In a specially designed white canvas courtyard, a touring open air show, accompanied by the travelling exhibition, with Pierre Schwartz and Idaho Co. from Holland.	Milton Keyne Leiceste Renne La Rochell Glasgow Barrow-i Furnes Halewoc
November	PARLIAMENT IN FLAMES: community bonfire. Audience 10,000.	Burnl
December	STORIES FOR A WINTER'S NIGHT: in a wooden booth, adapted from an ex-fairground structure, premiered in one of our favourite return visits, with Dogtroep from Holland.	Wath-upo Dear

1977

January	GHOST TRAIN: a highly successful project with a real ghost train running on tracks through a Welfare State environment. With Bob Frith of Horse & Bamboo Theatre.	Burnl
Jan./Feb.	STORIES FOR A WINTER'S NIGHT: tour, with a wooden booth.	Basildon; No wich; Chorl
March	Individual research month.	
May	FOUNTAIN OF CHANGE: a month's work in progress in the courtyard of the former Stock Exchange.	Li
June	Shooting 8mm. film BARRABAS to be shown in September show.	Lancashi

July	Street performances & processions to herald the forthcoming BARRABAS show.	Lancashire
August	Build environment for BARRABAS show and rehearse, with Bob Frith.	Burnley
Sept./Oct.	BARRABAS: six weeks of daily performance. Total theatrical environment to include film, sideshows, performances, processions, and 'ritual', disembowelling of The Dead Man (and his culture).	Burnley
	By this time Welfare State's nomadic school had dissolved, due to changed personnel, changed work programme and different social needs of the children. They enrolled in the local primary school.	
Nov./Dec.	WINTER CHARADES: a performance with a small team designed to tour village halls, in conjunction with N.E. films.	N. Yorks
December	Alternative Christmas Crib for the shopping precinct. Sadly shabby end to Burnley residency of 5 years.	Burnley

1978

January	Naming Ceremony.	Yordas Cave
Feb./March	Dismantling of Burnley base to operate the company on flexible network system. Office established in Liverpool, storage at Howarth's smallholding 'Hilltop'.	
April	Fox family leave for 1 year sabbatical, leaving Boris Howarth as Artistic Director.	
June	UPPENDOWN MOONEY: a tented touring show created from a script commissioned from Adrian Mitchell. Rehearsal Period.	
July	UPPENDOWN MOONEY.	Corby Festival

August	UPPENDOWN MOONEY.	Welwyn and Liverpool
September	UPPENDOWN MOONEY.	Cannon Hill Birmingham
Oct./Nov.	PARLIAMENT IN FLAMES with Idaho Band.	Milton Keynes
November	THE PHANTOM OF A DEVIL MAKETH NO FOOTPRINTS ON THE EARTH: an indoor and outdoor sculpture environment on the life of St. Andrew.	St. Andrews
December	BRIGHT CLOUD: Christmas celebrations based around a village church commissioned by the vicar.	Thorpe Thewles Cleveland

1979

March	PLAGUE AND THE COWMAN: a series of narrative processions for a West Yorkshire village, with students from Bretton Hall.	Ackworth
April	Easter Naming Ceremony.	Helmsley, N. Yorks
	Fox family return from sabbatical.	
May	WHEN THE PIE WAS OPENED: a theatrical feast.	Digswell Arts Trust, Welwyn
June	VOLCANO JUNCTION: a late night water pageant on the canal.	Birmingham
July to Sept.	BLOOD PUDDING: an hour-long touring street show.	Basildon Cumbria S.E. Wales Milton Keynes
September	Fox family move to Ulverston and start establishing a company work base in the town.	
October	Harvest Festival Celebrations. The first use of the Barn Dance format.	Thorpe Thewles
Oct./Nov.	PARLIAMENT IN FLAMES.	Ackworth
November	GARDEN OF EARTHLY DELIGHTS: an animated fantasy garden.	Crawford Arts Centre Liverpool
December	Christmas Celebrations.	Thorpe Thewles

1980

Jan. to April	First Barn Dance tour of village halls with an evening of dances and theatrical interludes.	Lancashire; Cumbria
June	Midsummer Celebrations.	St. Andrews
July	CARNIVAL NIGHT: first participation in our local town carnival.	Ulverston
July to Sept.	EYE OF THE PEACOCK: a second touring street show.	Milton Keynes; Merseyside; Renfrew; Fife; Cumbria; Lancashire
August	STILLPOINT: the opening of a permanent public sculpture garden.	Kentmere, Cumbria
Sept./Oct.	First Summer School: two public week-long residential courses in celebrating theatre.	Lakeside, Cumbria
October	Wedding ceremony, a personal commission from the bride and groom.	Little Easton, Essex
Oct./Nov.	PARLIAMENT IN FLAMES.	Tamworth
December	Workshop week.	Belfast

1981

Jan. to April	Second Barn Dance Tour.	Lancashire; Edinburgh; Cumbria
February	The World Snow Sculpture Championships. We came 10th.	Finland
May	TEMPEST ON SNAKE ISLAND: an island celebration based on themes from Shakespeare's play for the Toronto Theatre Festival.	Toronto
July	Second Carnival Night. A Beach Carnival.	Ulverston Sunderland
August	THE SKELETON, THE PILOT AND THE RAINBOW FISH.	Lyme Park
	RED MOLE WEEK: a celebration of Haematite mining.	Cleator Moor, Cumbria

September	THE CONFERENCE OF THE BIRDS: completion of a second public landscape sculpture piece.	Conishead Priory
Sept./Oct.	Second Summer School.	Lakeside
October	The first D.I.Y. Naming Ceremony with WSI as consultants.	Iken Forest Suffolk
Oct./Nov.	PARLIAMENT IN FLAMES: the end of the line for pure spectacle, audience of 15,000, too successful to be repeated.	Lewisham
December	Workshop Week.	Loftus Cleveland

1982

Jan. to March	STARSHIP VESUVIUS: a third Barn Dance tour with the emphasis on individual storytelling.	Lancashire
Jan. to Apr.	KING REAL AND THE HOODLUMS: Barrow community film involving 150 local people; made for TV with script by Adrian Mitchell.	
April	Howarth family leave for sabbatical. THE DOOMSDAY COLOURING BOOK: an umbrella project uniting all work May–November, a cycle of modern mystery plays performed throughout the season. Rehearsal Period.	
April/May	Mayday Celebrations, the first residency using a community advance team, which worked through the season.	Darlington
June	HOCKLEY PORT TECHNICOLOUR KNEES UP AND MUSICAL SANDWICH.	Birmingham
	THE BIG FLASH, a celebration of salt.	Northwich
July	Third Carnival Night.	Ulverston
	THE WASTELAND AND THE WAGTAIL: a celebration of the themes of King Lear for the First Japanese International Theatre Festival.	Togamura Japan

August	An Illustrated Feast for the Third World Conference on the histocompatibility of the rat.	Babraham, Cambs.
	THE WILD WINDMILL GALA.	Haverhill
September	Town Charter Week Celebrations, including an obstacle raft race on the local canal.	Ulverston
Sept./Oct.	Third Summer School.	Lakeside
October	Office moves to Ulverston, completing gradual evolution of the town as new company base.	
Oct./Nov.	SCARECROW ZOO: the climax of the Colouring Book season, including the Scarecrow Competition and the first mobile bonfire.	
December	WINTER SATELLITE: a Christmas lantern celebration for 3 Lancashire villages.	Trough of Bowland

1983

Jan. to April	KING REAL AND THE HOODLUMS: community film, with script by Adrian Mitchell based on *King Lear*.	Barrow-in-Furness
April 19 to May 1	CAPTAIN WEBB'S MAY DAY, MAY DAY: celebrations, including mummers plays, fancy dress, land rafts, barrel race, and May Day procession.	Telford
June	JUNGLE BULLION: community residency to revive the tradition of Fête Champêtre in the Botanic Gardens. Carnival events with fireworks.	Belfast
July	CARNIVAL NIGHT: open air barn dance for 800 people with street theatre, bands, decorations.	Ulverston
July/August	RAISING THE *TITANIC*: an extended residency in Canal Dock Basin, Limehouse, London. The wreck of the *Titanic* raised from the dock for 12 performances. L.I.F.T. Festival.	London

September	INTERNATIONAL SCULPTURE CONFERENCE: a private banquet for delegates and a public, processional piece with lanterns.	Yorkshir Sculpture Par
September	ULVERSTON CHARTER WEEK: fancy dress raft race, Mariners' Ball and first Lantern Procession.	Ulversto
Oct./November	QUEENS WALK: one month residency in community centre.	Nottinghar
	Percussion Workshops leading to Walney Parade and formation of Redwing carnival band in Ulverston	Barrow-in Furness Ulversto

1984

Feb./March	DOUBLE OR QUIT: a two-man vaudeville pantomime about the revolutionary outlaw, Percy Toplis.	Tourin Northern regio
May	SUMMER SCHOOL on Processional Theatre.	Anglese
	TOLPUDDLE DAY: 2 week residency to animate community carnival.	Darlingto Arts Centr
July	CARNIVAL NIGHT: beginning of the 2 year hand over to local people.	Ulversto
August	TALES FOR ENGLAND: summer street theatre tour.	Edinburgh Cumbri
	ISLAND FOLLIES: summer extravaganza with residents of Ward's Island.	Toront
September	LANTERN PROCESSION: 2nd annual procession, Raft Race and Mariners' Ball.	Ulversto
Nov. to April 85	TEACHING PROJECT: input into first year Creative Arts Degree Course over six months.	Newcastle upon-Tyn Polytechni

1985

February	ON THE PERIMETER: indoor storytelling from a suitcase by John Fox and Sue Gill.	Tourin
March	FLAG AND UMBRELLA PROCESSION: 3 weeks of workshops in fabric dyeing, banner making.	Barrow-in Furnes

ay	MAY DAY PROCESSION: final event in Newcastle Poly Teaching Project.	Newcastle-upon-Tyne
	ROBERT OWEN'S GREAT ESCAPES: theatrical guided tours for a week round a heritage village.	New Lanark
ne	CURSED CROCODILE: sculptural installation inspired by De Quincey, in Dove Cottage for 50,000 visitors.	Grasmere
	5th SUMMER SCHOOL in Celebratory Theatre.	Grange-over-Sands
ly	CARNIVAL NIGHT: completion of hand over.	Ulverston
	TALES FOR ENGLAND: another outing for this touring street show.	York, Liverpool and the Midlands
	FRIENDS' WORLD COLLEGE: domestic celebration of college's twentieth birthday.	New York, USA
eptember	D. H. LAWRENCE CENTENARY: floats and procession.	Eastwood, Notts.
	LANTERN PROCESSION: 3rd annual procession, incorporating more of the town.	Ulverston
ov./December	NUTCRACKER: Joint production with National Performing Arts Company of Tanzania. 10 shows fusing music, dance and visual imagery.	Commonwealth Institute, London

86

nuary	NEW YEAR'S KILN FIRING: community workshops leading to raku kiln firing.	Ulverston
ebruary	WINTER SCHOOL in Domestic Celebration.	Anglesey
arch	DIY THEATRE: 3 months of skills workshops, leading to formation of Electric Ark: community theatre.	Barrow-in-Furness
ly	FALSE CREEK: A VISUAL SYMPHONY: World Expo 86. 6 week residency to create 15 performances in partnership with Canadian artists and musicians.	Vancouver

August	ON THE LOOSE: week-long music residencies, with street band workshops, dances and final Rock'n Roll Ceilidh.	N.E. Coas Stirling, Kilkenny Liverpoo Scunthorp
September	LANTERN PROCESSION: 4th annual procession. Grown to 2 processions, with Third World influences in design and music.	Ulversto
	ICOREC & World Wildlife Fund: animal lanterns made for interdenominational pilgrimage to Assisi, and hung in Winchester Cathedral.	Wincheste
December	LANTERN COACH: *Jack and the Beanstalk*: coach converted to miniature Edwardian theatre touring 20 minute pantomime shows for an audience of 30.	West Cumbri Dumfries Gallowa

1987

April	TRAINING SCHOOL: for 20 Portuguese artists.	Casa Mateus Portug
	A WORLD WASTE: a sculptural work for a national touring exhibition.	
	MUSICIAN IN RESIDENCE – Peter Moser – appointed for 3 years.	Barrow-in Furnes
May	SUMMER SCHOOL: teaching Street Theatre to 25 artists.	Hexhar
	MACHINE MAD: custom cars, punk bands, video project with unemployed young adults.	Workingto
June	THE DENNYSONS OF DISHWATER: an outdoor promenade performance in Carisbrook Castle, Isle of Wight.	
July	THE TOWN HALL TATTOO: a day long outdoor celebration for the 100th birthday of Barrow Town Hall – attended by over 15,000 people and the culmination of 6 months work with the people of the town: choir, writing, school exhibition, kites, posters, banners, floats.	Barrow-ir Furnes

August	ON THE LOOSE: on the road again, running on musical juice, leaving a trail of community street bands.	Cardiff, Trafford, Stirling, Stranraer
September	FIFTH LANTERN PROCESSION: expanded to 3 separate processions, with spectacular Lantern Arch and sculptural illuminated costumes.	Ulverston
October	SHORT FUSE: a mini fireshow in Wigan as part of the town's 'Flash Bang Wallop' celebrations.	
	NORTH AMERICAN LECTURE TOUR to schools of performing arts.	
November	Firework display for the town.	Ulverston
	NUTCRACKER NIGHT: two weeks of workshops towards a November 5th celebration.	Gateshead
	THE LANTERN COACH: *ALADDIN* Victorian body puppets, underground caverns and a 6 foot genie.	Barrow-in-Furness, Warrington, Carlisle
December	THE LANTERN COACH: *ALADDIN* Continuation of tour.	Dumfries, North East, Cumbria

1988

January	GLASGOW: presentation and burying of a time capsule in the precincts of Glasgow Cathedral.	
	CELEBRATORY ARTS AND PRIMARY HEALTH CARE: a week long residency in a doctor's surgery.	Birmingham
February	HURRICANE LAMP: two performances as the culmination of a three week community residency after the hurricane.	Brighton
	ART IN THE RITES OF DEATH AND BEREAVEMENT: workshops and lecture.	Dartington Hall, Devon
March	ROVING RODNEY'S RAMBLES: performances in villages of local stories.	Teesdale

April	Barrow – start of three year arts development programme in Barrow-in-Furness. Numerous workshops.	Barrow-i Furne
	CELEBRATION: ITV half hour programme on Welfare State International/Graeae Workshop for theatre practitioners with disabilities.	
	LANCASTER LITERATURE FESTIVAL: storytelling performances and poster making.	Lancast
May	THE GRAFFITI BAND: processional street music and fireshow and tour.	Bridlingto
	ST. MUNGO: celebration for the Royal Institute of Scottish Architects' Conference and enhancement of the Cathedral.	Glasgo
June	THE BARRACUDAS: 100 strong carnival band with dancers, performed at four local carnivals, and Carlisle Great Fair.	Barrow-i Furne
	ANDOVER: a two week residency building floats and creating a street band for the Carnival.	Andov
	THEATRE CLWYD: decorations, procession and performance for community festival.	Mo
July	LONELY AS A TRUANT CHILD: sculptural residence to accompany Matthew Arnold Exhibition.	Dove Cottag Grasme
July/August	BUFFALO BILL'S RETURN: creation and 12 performances of show in Carew Castle, Pembrokeshire.	
September	6th LANTERN PROCESSION: annual community Lantern Procession.	Ulversto
	SUMMER SCHOOL: 10 day course for theatre practitioners on site specific events.	Sevenoa
October	THE JEWEL TREE: community fireshow with lanterns.	Wig
	WILDFIRE: a large scale community fire show.	Barrow-i Furne

ovember	Bonfire and firework display for the town.	Ulverston
	CHARCOAL AND RAIN: stories, monologues and anecdotes.	Birmingham
ov./December	THE BALLAD OF JIMMI TUNN: creation and shooting of a pilot for Channel 4.	
ecember	LANTERN COACH: *ALADDIN* Tour to Dumfries, Sandwell, Warrington, Blyth and Barrow. Same show, new cast, new venues.	
	CHRISTMAS CAKE: giant exploding cake and music for evening festivities.	St. George's Square, Glasgow

89

nuary	ROBINSON CRUSOE CASTAWAY: 14 performances of a large scale community pantomime in the Civic Hall.	Barrow-in-Furness
bruary	PIRANHA POND: creating and shooting a half hour TV drama for Border TV.	Carlisle
arch	SHADOW'S REVENGE: an opera created with and performed by junior school children.	Barrow-in-Furness
	SPRING ABOARD: a community residency to create a launching ceremony for 'The Little Waster', a passenger boat, with Bank Holiday frolics.	Sunderland
pril	TRAINING COURSES for Birmingham based community artists.	Ulverston
ne	THE BARRACUDAS: five performances at local carnivals by 150 piece costumed carnival band.	Barrow-in-Furness
ly	WORLD STUDIES: Creation of an event for their 10th annual Conference.	Lancaster
ugust	A BRIDGE OF LANTERNS: large scale fireshow on the River Tees.	Riverside Festival, Stockton
	Writer's Workshop launched.	Barrow-in-Furness
	EXPLORATIONS: creation and two performances of street show for the European Festival of Street Theatre.	Aurillac, France

September	SEVENTH LANTERN PROCESSION: annual community Lantern Procession.	Ulversto
	DISCOVERIES: creation and three performances for ACARTE '89. Co-production with Portuguese Artists.	Lisbo
October	Team of Artists starts one year's work towards 'Glasgow All Lit Up' on October 6th, 1990 as part of European City of Culture.	Glasgov
	ROCK THE BOAT: Weekly cabaret club up to Christmas – featuring performances by local people, and local bands and alternative comedians.	Barrow-in Furnes
November	Bonfire and firework display for the town.	Ulversto
	Training Course for Youth Workers, organised in association with Youth Clubs UK.	Ulversto
	STORYTELLING FESTIVAL	Barrow-i Furnes
December	ROBINSON CRUSOE IN SPACE: Lantern Coach tour to Sandwell and Tyneside.	
	STREETLIGHTS: Christmas events around the city and opening of the Lantern Palace.	Glasgov
1990 January	ROBINSON CRUSOE IN SPACE: Lantern Coach tour to North West, Cumbria and Dumfries.	
	WHEELY A BIP BOP: show created by secondary school pupils.	Barrow-in Furnes
February	MUMMERS PLAY: tour of play round schools and community venues.	Glasgov
March	ALIEN FROM SPACE: residency and performance in a special school.	Barrow-in Furnes
	BRITANNIA'S RAGTIME SPLASH: opening ceremony for the Houston International Festival.	US

une	THE BARRACUDAS: five performances at local carnivals and further afield by 150 piece carnival band.	Barrow-in-Furness, Manchester
uly	SHIPYARD TALE: a cycle of twelve shows created for, by and with the people of Barrow-in-Furness. Ranging from a one man show to an opera – performed by the community, as part of the 'Feast of Furness' Festival. The culmination of the company's three year arts development programme.	Barrow-in-Furness
	GOLDEN SUBMARINE: a large scale community fire show – the final 'Shipyard Tale', for an audience of 8,000.	Barrow-in Furness
September	EIGHTH LANTERN PROCESSION: annual community lantern procession.	Ulverston
October	GLASGOW ALL LIT UP: giant lantern procession involving 10,000 people. Finale event in Glasgow Green. Culmination of 12 months' work.	Glasgow

Appendix 3
Six Welfare State statements

1. The Welfare State – Manifesto (1972)

The Welfare State make images, invent rituals, devise ceremonies, objectify the unpredictable, establish and enhance atmospheres for particular places, times, situations and people.

In current terminology we fuse fine art, theatre and life style but we aim to make such categories and role definition in itself obsolete.

We make art using the traditions of popular theatre such as mummers, circus, fairground, puppets, music hall, so that as well as being entertaining and funny and apparently familiar in style to a popular audience our work also has a more profound implication.

We use modern equivalents of Bosch, Brueghel, and Grünewald in the context of 20th-century entertainment and existentialism.

We are artists concerned with the survival and character of the imagination and the individual within a technologically advanced society.

We create openly, freely and publically and never work to make repetitive products. Most of our shows are once off occasions.

We are nomadic and aim to travel more freely, widely and rapidly with a large complex of vehicles, equipment, big top and people to demonstrate the possibilities of a marvellous and rich surreal circus.

We will continue to analyse the relationship between performance and living, acting and identity, theatre and reality, entertainment and product, archetype and need.

We will react to new stimulus and situations spontaneously and dramatically and continue to fake unbelievable art as a necessary way of offsetting cultural and organic death.

2. Pathological Optimists (1979)
Systematically implanting images and ideas

Energy is precious and in short supply. It must be conserved to break through the scab of the old cultural attitudes. Wherever breakthrough is necessary and possible.

Twelve years ago we didn't see it quite like that. We believed an alternative society would grow easily and naturally. Now we know it won't. It will take a hundred years in Britain.

Now old values continue to be reinforced. Creativity is repressed. Gross National Product rules.

It is harder to get public funds for new work than it was five years ago. Fees are lower, expenses are much higher. Meanwhile defence, law and order, nuclear stations etc. flourish. But we are little more than a pea bouncing on an immense military drum. We are a pea under the Queen's mattress.

We can remain a stubborn irritant.

We prefer not to reminisce but to focus ahead.

In the eighties our band will play for dancing. Our trade will be carried out in the street. We will train cultural guerillas (workshops, Lake District, September 1980). Our images will be made of cement (they are harder to destroy). We will extend our scope of Third World connections. We will continue to move into communities to suss out their latent images and reveal their energy with power and celebration. If for a period we have to bury the tablets, at least they will be there to be dug up later.

By 1984 our ship of Fools carrying the holy relics of imagination will voyage joyously. We pathological optimists have no intention of stopping for at least another few decades. Sing and dance with us, we and the culture we find need all the help we can get.

3. Extract from letter to Luk Mishalle – John Fox, Sept., 1980.

As you know Welfare State works entirely pragmatically but within a general philosophy of seeking to liberate the imagination through the catalyst of poetic input. Occasionally we have to work in isolation from the broader social context and then produce a self-contained product which only comes into contact with the 'audience' when it is presented before them. At best it excites and liberates mentally and we have made an initial contact hoping to return. At worst it is merely another vicarious entertainment, a psychedelic elastoplast for playgroups and well-meaning liberals.

We prefer to service a situation, be it a wedding, or the naming of a child, or a necessary situation where we can apply our aesthetic skills in a context. We are happy to teach and spread our knowledge and work in close partnership with positive energy. That energy can come in unlikely places. Communities may be defined vertically or horizontally. They may be middle class or working class, folk groups, families, or gallery or theatre-goers. We prefer to work to a broad cross-section of the population because our images are rough and direct and we tend to get a purer response from an unsophisticated crowd.

We seek however in the end to be un-nostalgic folk artists offering, demonstrating and making manifest what ideally should be a shared iconography. An iconography which if you like draws on the collective unconscious but which in the end is common property. Our problem is that the access to the common poetic dreaming is generally blocked; our job in hand, our current privilege is to unblock the manholes, to clean the channels through which the poetic in all its innocence and directness can flow naturally and easily.

But the times are out of joint. Social problems inhibit communication and creativity. Political and economic manipulation clogs the channels. So as well as creating the painting we have to make the canvas. A microcosm of alternative possibilities, a view finder to the sacred past and future time. We reveal an edge of the eternal cycle, but now in disguise we hide behind our clown's red nose. Others laugh when we laugh at ourselves. The lords of misrule have a sacred duty to rock the boat. Categories and systems beware. Professionals beware. Special publics beware. Actors beware. General Fringe (who is he?) beware. We create (as all can, one day) for ourselves for yourselves and in the end for SELVES.

Welfare State International – Intentions, 1981

1. To fuse boundaries between painting, sculpture, theatre, music and events.
2. To analyse the relationship between aesthetic imput and its social context.
3. To explore non-naturalistic and visual performance styles.
4. To develop theatre of a poetical and mythical nature that is popular and relevant to communities today.

5. To project art into the street and landscapes via carnivals, processions, gardens, elaborate puppet shows and street bands.
6. To extend but not be impaired by existing traditions.
7. To laugh at ourselves to serve others.
8. To explore our own creativity and to objectify it in accessible form.
9. To demonstrate the process of the imagination and the role of the hand-made expendable art work in advanced technological culture.
10. To examine the value of 'non-ordinary reality' in the West.
11. To establish two way links with third world 'minorities'.
12. To redefine primitive and sophisticated.
13. To rediscover the amateur.
14. Not to underestimate the potential healing power of art.

5. Statement for Japan – July, 1982

In common with a number of western nations Britain is moving, albeit unwillingly, into a post industrial phase. We know that creativity has been and is deliberately repressed by political, military and commercial vulgarity. Such materialistic consumption is common in the northern hemisphere and, like lilies on a rubbish tip, we grow innocently to project a microcosm of new primitivism.

We do this by working directly
cheaply
simply
roughly
humorously
relevantly and
collectively.

We demystify high-art by demonstrating the 'home-made' creative process in action, within a community.

Our theatre is celebratory: we liberate the imagination. This task is joyous, essential and sacred and not given to psychedelic elastoplast. Once upon a time the shaman steered the tribe into magical flight. Now jet-set jesters are invited to magnetise the circuits of the global village

WE HAVE NO CULTURAL PRODUCT FOR SALE

We seek to discover for ourselves and our 'audience' and, if the truth we find is as black as night, then the poetry we create is as black as tar. If the vulture is bald we polish its skull till we see our face. Explanation and rationalism are the rats on a sinking ship. If grain silos are disguised missile garages who will bake the bread? If life expectancy in Britain and Japan is more than 70 and in West Africa a mere 40, can we dance round the abyss for 30 years?

'The weight of this sad time we must obey.
Speak what we feel, not what we ought to say.'
King Lear. Act 5, scene III (Edgar)

6. Statements from the eighties, by John Fox

(a) Out of the False Creek (Expo '86, Vancouver)
In the course of our research we discovered, interestingly, that much of the history of the people who lived around False Creek had not been documented. In particular there were immense gaps when it came to the native Indians . . . and hundreds of squatters who lived in shacks until many were burned out by the authorities in the 1950s.

There was however, over the last hundred years, one clear pattern. That of a wave movement which continually rose and fell from boom to depression and back, where amazing occasional affluence and invention was replaced by frequent decline and stagnation. Always a minority suffered, be they native Indians, Chinese, Japanese, poor and elderly whites or women . . . This pattern had kept up to the present day, when sadly three suicides have been attributed this year to the eviction of elderly tenants from downtown hotels (to make way for Expo tourists).

The Creek is a microcosm. The problem is though, that the huge movement of capital with its attendant creative spin-offs and distressing side-effects gets bigger on both a creek and a world scale; so that by now in 1986, it appears to be either entirely out of control, or on such a high self-perpetuating momentum that it could easily kill or anaesthetise us all.

The history of the Creek is repeated on a world scale – but here it is not just the minority who suffer, increasingly it is the majority. First, the total percentage of the extreme poor relative to the affluent, is actually increasing; second, the total physical resources of the whole planet are being so abused that soon little will be left for any of us (rich or poor); and third, the loss of a spiritual centre in the affluent world means that our quality of life will degenerate so that so-called 'civilisation' will disappear.

None of this can we ignore at Expo because Expo is the ultimate shop window demonstration of the values and life-style of the affluent (and that includes W.S.I.). But Art is not the decorative edge of excess; as artists our job is to show the truth. So we tell a story for and of our age. A poetic legend has been re-constituted with fragments dredged from the swamp of History's brackish creek.

(The above was edited out of the official Expo '86 Programme.)

(b) The work is of today. (1987)
We challenge with humour and offer for an instance an image of another world; another world where social purpose and personal creativity are allowed to go hand-in-hand.

The work is of today. It is of a post-industrial and technological economy where leisure has to mean more than negative work. We seek something better; where the architecture, the spirit, the icons, the stories, the plays, the pageants and the clowns and traders are linked with a commonly agreed cosmology. The smallness of the earth herself seems to offer one possible focus; meanwhile the false nose of the clown is a convenient mask of pathological optimism.

(c) Dreams of the future. (1988)
What values are we celebrating, whose heritage is it, and what are we offering to future generations?

If we were truly fulfilled and centred, would any of us need to be tourists at all? Maybe this transient consumerism of the ethnic and the novel is merely a marketable distraction, calculated to inhibit the deeper and necessary development of an indigenous culture?

The poet of the future will certainly make dreams concrete.

But these dreams will not be for sale.

Appendix 4
Scores for music mentioned in Chapter 3

LA DESPEDIDA

A CONTINUATION OF LA DESPEDIDA

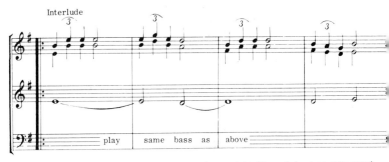

Interlude can be used for solo improvisations (bass only). Keep whole piece quite rough.

Appendix 5
Welfare State International Suppliers List

Many of the materials mentioned in this book are easily obtained from ironmongers, builders' merchants, garden shops . . . or rubbish tips. Some, however, are best obtained from specialist suppliers.

Latex: For making flexible Masks etc.
    Wm. Symington & Sons Ltd.,
    Bath House, 53/60 Holborn Viaduct,
    London EC1A 2ES.
    071 248 0821

Tissue Paper: For Lanterns, essential to use good quality wet strength sulphite tissue or else it breaks up.
    K. Matty Ltd.,
    Thornford Road,
    Headley,
    Nr. Newbury,
    Berkshire RG15 8AG.
    0635 23771

Balloons: All sizes and colours available. It is also possible to hire a balloon sealing machine.
    The Kite and Balloon Co.,
    613 Garrett Lane,
    London SW13 4SU.
    081 946 5962

Processional Torches: Available in boxes of 36 from:
    Standard Fireworks plc.,
    Standard House,
    Half Moon Street,
    Huddersfield HD1 2JH.
    0484 31538

Paper Rope: Used for fire sculptures and also for theatrical making. Available from:
    S.MIC plc.,
    PO Box 8,
    Alliance Works,
    Preston,
    Lancashire.
    0772 794114

Thread: Good quality thread is expensive. Wholesale thread and other haberdashery supplies:
    Maculloch and Wallis,
    Dering Street,
    London W1.
    071 629 0311

    Cheap thread and elastic can be bought from:
    B Courts Ltd.,
    39 Middlesex Street,
    London E1.

Dyes: Dylon provide a reasonable general range, but it is very much cheaper to buy in bulk from:

> Dylon International,
> Worsley Bridge Road,
> Lower Sydenham,
> London SE26 5HD.

Fabric Paint: Pigment dyes for screen printing fabric are very good. Pigments are mixed with binder and fixed by ironing.

> Selectacine Serigraphics Ltd.,
> Screen Printing Supplies,
> 65 Chislehurst Road,
> Chislehurst,
> Kent.
> 081 467 8544

Paints: SPECTRUM COLOURS are liquid pigments which can be mixed with either white emulsion paint or PVA and water to produce strong colours. They are expensive. They can be used on fabric mixed as follows:– 16 parts water: 4 parts PVA: 1 part pigment.

> Spectrum Oil Colours,
> 259 Queens Road,
> South Wimbledon,
> London SW19 8NY.
> 081 542 4729

BOLLOMS manufacture a range of deep coloured emulsion paints that are used frequently in set painting.

KEEPS FLAMBOYANT ENAMELS are translucent, bright coach enamels. Very expensive. Good for painting paper lanterns if diluted with white spirit. Both these and Bolloms emulsions are stocked by:

> J. W. Bollom and Co. Ltd.,
> PO Box 78,
> Croydon Road,
> Beckenham,
> Kent BR3 4BL.
> 081 658 7723

FRENCH ENAMEL VARNISH is also used for painting lanterns and fabric, the colour is vivid, but can fade after prolonged exposure to light. It is stocked by Brodie and Middleton, who also sell a range of theatrical making materials.

> Brodie and Middleton,
> 68 Drury Lane,
> London.
> 071 836 3289

dhesives: PVA – glue and paint medium: can be diluted to required strength and used to stick paper, thin cloth, wood, etc. Slow drying. UNIBOND is probably the best and most easily obtained from ironmongers. Wholesale suppliers are:

> Berol Ltd,
> Old Meadow Road,
> Kings Lynn,
> Norfolk PE30 4JR.
> 0553 761221

LATEX ADHESIVE such as Copidex is faster drying and waterproof. It is used with newspaper, cloth etc. Cheapest source is local Carpet Accessory Wholesalers.

esin Cloth: Trade names Celastic or Celuflex. Theatre prop material especially useful for long lasting masks etc. Used with Acetone as a solvent. Quality 77 (1mm thick) or Quality 88 (1.4mm thick) are the most useful.

> Lee Chemicals Ltd.,
> New Bridge Road,
> Glenhills,
> Leicester LE2 9TD.
> 0533 787565

ring and Rope: BAILER TWINE is very strong and available in various colours. It is obtainable through agricultural suppliers, usually in packages of two.

ire: RYTIE GARDEN WIRE – soft, flexible – useful for binding.
HIGH TENSILE WIRE – useful for hoops, wangy, expensive.
PIANO WIRE – thin and wangy.

bre Glass Rods: In various lengths and widths, available from kite shops and:

> Greens of Burnley,
> 336 Colne Road,
> Burnley,
> Lancashire BB10 1ED.
> 0282 39650

amboos: Long lengths usually sold in bundles of 25 or 50. Lengths available are 10ft, 12ft and 15ft.

> Sim and Coventry Ltd.,
> Sabre House,
> Bridge Street,
> Saltney,
> Chester CH4 8SN
> 0244 678666

Withies: Sold in large bundles by weight – various lengths, but 6ft probably most useful.

J. Burdikinds Ltd.,
Flushdyke,
Nr. Wakefield,
West Yorkshire.
0924 273103

P. H. Coate and Sons,
Mare Green,
North Curry,
Somerset TA3 6HY.
0823 490249

Music Supplies List

Propercussion
205 Kentish Town Road
London NW5
01 485 0822

general
percussion
and marching drums

Ray Mann
Neal Street
Covent Garden

ethnic and
Chinese instruments

Bill Lewington
144 Shaftesbury Avenue
01 240 0584

brass and
reeds

Alodi
72 Mountgrove Road
N6.
01 226 5923

accordions

Clinkscales
The Square
Melrose
089 682 2525

accordions

also – look in your local 2nd hand shops
look in Exchange and Mart.

Appendix 6
Films, TV & Video of WSI's Work

RIGINAL PETER ARENA BBC 2
e first live 'happening' on TV with John Fox & Mike Westbrook
r. Tony Staveacre April 1970

IE JOURNEY OF LANCELOT QUAIL
W. Tour
mm Colour 30 mins National Film School 1972   Hire 'B'

INGALOW
vironmental Construction & Performance, De Lantaren, Rotterdam
mm Colour 30 mins Dir. Ben Mangleschotts 1973   Hire 'B'
so available from the Arts Council of Great Britain (Film Dept.).)

ONEYHOLME AQUARIUS LWT
cumentation of Community Celebration, Burnley, Lancs
mm Colour 30 mins 1975   Hire 'A'

RABBAS GRANADA TV
cumentation of Environmental Build & Performance, Burnley,
ncs
mm Colour 25 mins 1977   Hire 'A'

RLIAMENT IN FLAMES THAMES TV
cumentation of build & Fire Show/Performance Catford, London
v. 5 1981
mm Colour 25 mins 1981   Hire 'A'

RN DANCE
leo Colour 25 mins 1981   Hire 'B'

OOMSDAY FAIR TVS
formance at South Hill Park, Bracknell as part of 'Scarecrow Zoo'
              Celebrations for Hallowe'en & Nov. 5
mm Colour 25 mins Dir. Gerry Harrison 1982   Hire 'A'

E WASTELAND & THE WAGTAIL
formances Togamura International Drama Festival, Japan
eo Colour 40 mins 1982   Hire 'B'

KING REAL & THE HOODLUMS
Film made by WSI, Barrow in Furness
Script Adrian Mitchell
16mm Colour 45 mins Dir. John Fox and Paul Heywood Sheffie
Polytechnic Film Dept. 1983   Hire 'B'

Hire 'A' available from Welfare State International for *non-commerc*
showing only.
Hire 'B' available from Welfare State International for general showir
Write to: Welfare State International, P.O. Box 9, Ulverston, Cumbr

A MIDSUMMER NIGHT'S BELFAST
Documentation of community celebration
Video Colour *Open Space* BBC2 Hire 'A'

Records & Tapes of WSI's Music
TOP GEAR SELECTIONS JOHN PEEL
Track: 'Silence is Requested in the Ultimate Abyss'
BBC Enterprises BBC Rec 525 1969

WELFARE STATE / LOL COXHILL
Virgin Records C1514 1975   Deleted

WELFARE STATE SONGS
WSI LK LP 6347   Available from WSI

MAGIC ISLAND MERINGUE
Songs, dances, processional music
WSI Tape 1981   Available from WSI

KING REAL AND THE HOODLUMS
Songs and Film music from
Barrow Film, 1983   Cassette

JUNGLE BULLION
Songs and music from 1982–84   Cassette

FURIOUS CHICKENS
Songs and music 1985–89   Cassette

Appendix 7
Bibliography

Books featuring WSI's work

Barton, Peter & Lane, John. *New Directions*, McGibbon & Kee, 1970.

Craig, Sandy (ed.). *Dreams and Deconstructions*, Amber Lane Press, 1980.

Grimes, Ronald L. *Beginnings in Ritual Studies*, University Press of America, 1981.

Henri, Adrian. *Environments and Happenings*, Thames and Hudson, 1974.

Itzin, Catherine. *Stages in the Revolution*, Eyre Methuen, 1980.

Liddle, Catherine. *What Shall We Do With the Children?*, Spindlewood, 1981.

Nuttall, Jeff. *Performance Arts Memoirs*, John Calder, 1979.

Shank, Theodore. *Theatre in Real Time* (Materiali per uno Studio sul Nuovo Teatro), Studio Forma, Italy, 1980.

Selected magazines and journals featuring WSI's work

Haynes, G. and A. Tucker. 'Cultural Guerillas', *Another Standard*, Autumn, 1982.

Highart, Catherine & Candy Clark. 'Onstage '81: Toronto Theatre Festival – The Tempest', *The Drama Review*, Vol 24 No 3 (T91), Fall, 1981.

Hunt, Tony. 'Tales for a Winter's Night', *Plays and Players*, March, 1977.

Hunt, Tony. 'The Island of the Lost World', *Plays and Players*, August, 1976.

Dunstan, Graeme. 'In Search of the Sacred', *Simply Living* (Shree Media Productions, NSW, Australia), No 9, 1979.

Ford, John. 'The Welfare State: A Guided Tour', *Plays and Players*, July, 1973.

Fox, John. 'Concerning the Island of the Lost World', *Dartington Theatre Papers*, Series 1 No 2, Dartington, 1977.

Fox, John. 'Pathological Optimists', *Performance Magazine*, Dec./Jan., 1980.

Fox, John. 'Theatre to Liberate Fantasies', *Theatre Quarterly*, Vol 2 No , Oct.–Dec., 1972.

Fox, John. 'Hybrid Products', *Performance Magazine*, No 40, March/April, 1986.

Fox, John and Sue Gill. 'Welfare State International: Seventeen Years on the Streets', *The Drama Review*, Vol 29 No 3, Fall, 1985 (T 107).

Hares, M. 'One-Man's Bursary', *Animations*, No 1, October/November 1986.

Hyde, Phil. 'Profile: On Welfare State', *Performance Magazine*, No 2, April/May, 1983.

Kershaw, Baz. 'Between Windscale and Wordsworth', (An interview with John Fox) *Performance Magazine*, No 54, June/July, 1988.

Powell, Rob. 'Magicians of the State', *New Society*, Jan. 20, 1983.

Rea, Kenneth. 'Welfare State Goes to Africa', *Drama*, No 2, 1986.

Shank, Theodore. 'Artistic Commitment is Social Commitment', *The Drama Review*, Vol 21 No 1, March, 1977.

Shank, Theodore. 'The Welfare State', *Arts in Society*, Vol 12 No Spring/Summer, 1973.

Westlake, Mike. 'Act Locally, Think Globally', *Arts Express*, October 1986.

White, Mike. 'Resources for a Journey of Hope: the Work of Welfare State International', *New Theatre Quarterly*, Vol IV No 15, August 1988.